高职高专经济贸易类专业系列教材

商务英语应用文写作

主　编　吴思乐
副主编　张桂芳　章　超
参　编　杨晓旻　邹宇君

本书以模块化的体例,介绍商务英语应用文写作的相关知识。全书以范例、典型表达和实操训练为主,注重学生商务英语应用文写作能力的提高。本书内容有商务英语写作基础、日常商务礼仪文书、商务办公及行政文书、一般商务文书、对外贸易函电、国际会展文案及商务合同文书6个模块,包含了从日常商务交往中的推荐、介绍、邀请、道歉、慰问、感谢、祝贺、欢迎、申请、辞职等活动所用到的书信,到商务行政管理中常见的电子邮件、传真、便条、电话留言、通知/启事、公告、名片、会议记录、证明信、借据、收条等文本,再到一般商务活动涉及的商业报告、产品描述、使用手册、公司介绍、调查问卷、商业广告以及外贸函电、展会文案、商务合同等内容。

本书内容全面,介绍深入浅出,注重应用性和实践性,既可作为高职高专经济贸易类或商务英语类专业学生的教材,也可供从事外经贸工作的人员阅读和使用。

本书配有电子课件、习题答案、课程教学大纲、课程标准、教案,选用本书作为教材的老师可以从机械工业出版社教育服务网(www.cmpedu.com)免费注册下载或联系编辑(010-88379197)咨询。

图书在版编目(CIP)数据

商务英语应用文写作/吴思乐主编. —北京:机械工业出版社,2021.4(2025.1重印)
高职高专经济贸易类专业系列教材
ISBN 978-7-111-67751-2

Ⅰ.①商… Ⅱ.①吴… Ⅲ.①商务-应用文-写作-高等职业教育-教材 Ⅳ.①F7

中国版本图书馆CIP数据核字(2021)第042997号

机械工业出版社(北京市百万庄大街22号 邮政编码100037)
策划编辑:董宇佳 责任编辑:董宇佳
责任校对:徐梦然 封面设计:马精明
责任印制:刘 媛
涿州市般润文化传播有限公司印刷
2025年1月第1版·第5次印刷
184mm×260mm·15.5印张·372千字
标准书号:ISBN 978-7-111-67751-2
定价:49.50元

电话服务 网络服务
客服电话:010-88361066 机 工 官 网:www.cmpbook.com
　　　　　010-88379833 机 工 官 博:weibo.com/cmp1952
　　　　　010-68326294 金 书 网:www.golden-book.com
封底无防伪标均为盗版 机工教育服务网:www.cmpedu.com

Preface

前　言

《商务英语应用文写作》一书遵循"模块化教学"的要求，体现"简单""实用"的特色，力求切合商务英语、国际商务等专业课程的教学实际。本书通过大量的技能训练，把英语语言和商务知识有机地结合起来，使学生通过学习，具备撰写商务英语应用文的能力。本书内容全面，体例新颖、系统，难易适中，融理论、实践于一体，具有较强的专业性和实用性。

全书根据商务英语应用文写作中常用的信函文本类别，将内容划分为6个模块，每个模块开头都有一个模块介绍、教学目的和教学重难点部分，让学生了解该模块所涉及的知识点、重难点和基本要求。

除第一个"商务英语写作基础"模块以外，其他各模块均由以下几个部分组成：

第一部分：Lead-In Introduction（导入介绍）

介绍相关文种的概念、定义、用途、功能等相关信息。

第二部分：Guidelines for Writing（写作指南）

介绍相关文种的特征和写作方法。

该部分将相关文种的内容、形式、写作步骤和技巧等清晰直观地描述出来，让学生对文种的主要内容一览无遗。这一部分是应用文撰写知识的核心，体现了典型性和实用性。

第三部分：Sample Study（范例学习）

该部分给出相关文种的代表性范文。编写过程中作者尽量选取了真实、时新（有不少是涉外经贸企业近两年的信函和其他相关文本，充分体现涉外经贸业务中的新术语、新理念、新政策和最新的经贸发展动态），并能直观反映该文种写作特点的素材。

第四部分：Useful Phrases and Expressions（常用短语和表达）

第五部分：Typical Sentences（典型例句）

这两部分主要是介绍和总结单元（Section）中出现的最常用、最经典的短语、表达和句型，用以向学生提供一些可供背诵、熟记的素材，从而加深学生对这一部分内容的感性认识，实现知识点的巩固和消化，为下一步的知识运用做好准备。这两部分起总结复习的作用，有较大的归纳性。

第六部分：Training and Practice（操练与实践）

该部分内容的目的是让学生针对不同商务文种的特征进行实操性的练习。这是学生对本单元知识的一个运用，也是考核学生对本单元知识掌握程度的一种方法。本书练习的设计体现了形式新颖、归纳性强、实用性突出、现实指导意义大、适用面广的特点，并能实现运用单元知识的目的，同时也可以适应不同层次的教学要求。

本书主要针对高职高专经济贸易类和商务英语类专业的学生，也可以作为其他层次相关专业的商务英语应用文写作教材。同时，对正在从事或即将从事涉外经贸活动的外经贸工作者来说，本书还可作为自学参考资料。

本书由广东农工商职业技术学院吴思乐统筹、修改定稿并任主编；河北水利电力学院张桂芳、广东农工商职业技术学院章超任副主编；参加编写的还有广东农工商职业技术学院杨晓旻、邹宇君。本书在编写过程中参考了有关书籍和资料，恕不一一详尽说明，仅在参考文献中列出，在此向相关作者致以衷心的感谢。

鉴于编者水平有限，教材中难免有错误和疏漏之处，敬请各位读者不吝赐教！

编者

目 录

Preface（前言）

Module One Fundamentals of Business Writing in English
（商务英语写作基础） ……………………………………………… 1

   Section 1 General Strategies of Business Writing in English
              （商务英语写作通略） ……………………………………… 2

   Section 2 Basic Requirements for Business Letter Writing in English
              （商务英语信函写作的基本要求） ………………………… 7

   Section 3 The Basic Structure of Business Letters in English
              （商务英语信函的基本结构） ……………………………… 9

   Section 4 The Basic Layouts and Styles of Business Letters
              （商务英语信函的基本格式） ……………………………… 13

   Section 5 Training and Practice
              （操练与实践） …………………………………………… 18

Module Two Writings for Everyday Business Communication
（日常商务礼仪文书） ……………………………………………… 19

   Section 1 Letters of Complaint and Apology
              （投诉、道歉信） ………………………………………… 19

   Section 2 Letters of Sympathy and Thanks
              （慰问、感谢函） ………………………………………… 25

   Section 3 Congratulation Letters and Welcoming Speech
              （祝贺信和欢迎词） ……………………………………… 31

   Section 4 Letters of Introduction and Recommendation
              （介绍信和推荐信） ……………………………………… 37

   Section 5 Letters of Application and Invitation
              （申请书、邀请函） ……………………………………… 43

   Section 6 Job Offers and Resignation Letters
              （录用函和辞职信） ……………………………………… 48

Module Three   Writings for Administrative Documents
（商务办公及行政文书）································· 52

Section 1   Notifications / Notices, Announcements and Posters
（通知/启事、公告与海报）························· 52

Section 2   E-mails and Faxes
（电子邮件和传真）································· 60

Section 3   Notes, Telephone Messages and Memos
（便条、电话留言和备忘录）························· 68

Section 4   Name Cards and ID Tags
（名片和个人身份标识牌）··························· 77

Section 5   Meeting Minutes
（会议记录和会议纪要）····························· 81

Section 6   Job Advertisements and Dismissal Letters
（招聘启事和解聘函）······························· 88

Section 7   Job Applications and Resumes
（求职信和求职简历）······························· 96

Section 8   Certificates
（证明信）··· 103

Section 9   IOUs and Receipts
（借据和收据）····································· 108

Module Four   Writings for General Business Activities
（一般商务文书）··································· 112

Section 1   Business Reports
（商业报告或商情调研报告）························· 112

Section 2   Product Description Manuals and Instruction Manuals
（产品描述、说明和使用手册）······················· 120

Section 3   Corporate profiles
（公司介绍）······································· 124

Section 4   Questionnaires
（商务调查问卷）··································· 129

Section 5   Product Brochures and Advertisements
（产品宣传资料、商业广告）························· 134

Module Five Writings for Foreign Trade Correspondence
（对外贸易函电） ·· 140

Section 1 Letters on Establishing Business Relations and Inquiries
（建交、询盘函） ·· 140

Section 2 Letters on Offers and Counter-Offers
（报盘、还盘函） ·· 151

Section 3 Letters on Acceptance/ Confirmation and Orders/ Contracts
（接受、确认函与订单、合同函） ·· 162

Section 4 Letters on Trade Terms Negotiations
（主要交易条款磋商函） ·· 173

Module Six International Event Documents and Business Contracts
（国际会展文案及商务合同文书） ··· 195

Section 1 Invitation Letters to Exhibition and Conference
（展会邀请函） ··· 196

Section 2 Post-Exhibition Reports
（展会报告） ··· 204

Section 3 Conference and Exhibition Agendas
（展会日程表） ··· 211

Section 4 Registration, Application and Booth Reservation Forms
（展会注册、申请与展位预订表） ·· 217

Section 5 Sales Contracts and Sales Confirmation
（销售合同与销售确认书） ··· 229

References （参考文献） ··· 240

Module One 模块一 Fundamentals of Business Writing in English
商务英语写作基础

📢 Module Briefing

Business writing is an important skill especially to those who work in an office. It establishes formality and civility among employees and employers, as well as those who are outside the work places. So business writings can primarily help you succeed in business. For example, applications for jobs, cover letters to resumes, note-taking in a meeting and checklists to keep you from forgetting important steps in a procedure.

In business domain, there are various types of documents required by government that the company must fill out and submit. There are also all sorts of administrative documents and written materials, such as notice, emails, telephone message, business reports, minutes, sales contracts, advertising, marketing surveys, order forms, etc., that go to your colleagues, partners, potential customers, old clients and other companies. With its own outstanding features, English for business document writing focuses on language and skills needed for typical business communication such as presentation, negotiation, meetings, socializing, correspondence, report, and so on.

Statistics show that poor business correspondence can have a detrimental effect on your business as people and companies view poor business letters as a reflection on a company's overall ability. The truth is that writing is a talent and only a few people are privileged with it. But it can also be learned and any one can be almost as creative as a writer with inborn talent if one pays attention to certain rules and thinks it in an organized manner.

Many rules and tactics for certain specific business correspondence and document writing will be introduced in this book and you are going to be trained to write all kinds of business documents for foreign trade and economics business in English. To begin with, you are going to learn some fundamental principles of applied business writing.

📢 Objectives

Upon the accomplishment of this module, you should be able to

1. acquire the primary writing strategies for business writing;

2. understand the basic requirements for business correspondence and document writing;

3. be familiar with all the parts in a standard business letter;
4. know about the different layouts and styles of business letters.

Focuses and Difficult Points

1. To acquire strategies in writing business documents

2. To get familiar with all the 7Cs as basic requirements for business letters and 13 parts of general structure in ordinary business letters

3. To be able to set out all parts of a business letter according to a particular layout or style

Section 1
General Strategies of Business Writing in English
商务英语写作通略

In some ways, all writings in English are similar in that they follow the same basic rules, such as the rules of grammar and syntax. But business writing has its particular purpose, i.e. making money. In ordinary writing, the meaning and significance of what is written are of primary importance, while in business writing, only the result counts. Since business English is designed and used only to make profits and avoid losses, a basic principle in business English writing must be the clear understanding of your purpose.

Jules Renard, a French author, once said: "Writing is the best way to talk without being interrupted". Writing strategies for business writing, simply put, are designs in writing which would help you to talk to your potential customers smoothly and win against your business competitors.

There are many differences between typical business writing and ordinary writing in English. Generally, an effective document usually contains 4 elements, i.e. content, structure and organization, tone and language. But beyond that, you should also pay close attention to planning, editing and the whole process designing.

1.1 About Content: Choosing the Correct Amount of Information

The first step in writing a document is choosing the content. Content is the first element of an effective document. Content depends on your judgment, experience, knowledge, attitude or mood, and choice of readers.

Please remember that you write for a reader. Writing is interactive and how you create a relationship between you and your reader is part of the art of writing. So to do this effectively, ask yourself the following questions before writing.

- Who is my reader? What my reader already knows about the subject?
- How much information does the reader actually need?
- Is my request concise so that the reader knows how to reply? (if you are asking for information)
- Is my message precise and easy to understand? (if you are giving information)

Give the information that your readers need in order to agree to your request, solve a problem, analyze a situation, make a decision, etc.

When writing professional documents, it is easy to include more information than is required. Therefore, it is important to spend time on planning the content of your writing before you start and on editing the content of your documents after you have written the first draft.

1.2 About Structure and Organization: Choosing the Proper Format and Planning the Document

After choosing all the necessary information which is essential for the reader to know, the next step is planning the writing and organizing or sorting the information into a clear and logical format. A sensible way of dealing with this is to write down all the main points and then try to organize them into a logical sequence. To help you organize the content of document well, you may try the four-part document planning as follows.

◆ Purpose (15-second rule)

The "15-second rule" refers to the fact that your readers will take just 15 seconds to decide what your document is about and whether it applies to them. Generally speaking, readers decide very quickly whether a document, such as a report or a multiple-recipient email, is relevant to them. Therefore, it is important to capture their interest, specify the purpose of the document, inform them of what you want them to do, know, or feel within a very short time.

◆ Background or Explanation

To make an impact, your readers may need some additional information to support your key message in part 1. Make sure that you give only the necessary background information and highlight or extend your key message so that it has more impact.

◆ Details

This part of your document should include useful and necessary details to reinforce part 1 and part 2, e.g. schedule, steps in a procedure, technical description, financial information.

Keep this section as short as possible so that readers can follow the development of ideas. Where possible, put supporting information into an appendix. Also remember not to include details just to impress your readers.

◆ What Next?

Repeat the purpose of your document. Make sure your readers clearly know the next steps in terms of who, what and when. Ensure that there are clear channels for future communication if more information is required.

In addition to the organizing and planning of information, the format structure of the document should not be overlooked.

Writing can take the form of a letter, a report, or a memo. Sometimes, it is useful to write a short letter or memo by hand. Your letter, report or memo can be sent by post, by fax or, by e-mail. In particular, the formality (or informality) of the relationship with your reader will help you decide whether you need to follow the classical model of a business letter or whether it is appropriate to use a more informal approach. In short, there are different layouts for different readers.

1.3   About Tone: Choosing the Most Appropriate Tone for Your Readers

Tone in writings refers to the emotional context of your message, the degree of formality or informality you use in your writing, and your attitude towards the reader and the subject. Tone is present in all communication. It affects the relationship and the message as much in writing as it does in speech. It is very important to get the tone right, because using the wrong tone could cause real offence to your reader. So business writers should consider the tone of their message, whether they are writing an e-mail, letter, report or any other type of business document.

Generally speaking, tone comes from:
- your choice of words;
- your sentence structures or sentence length;
- the structure, order, clarity, and precision of the information you present.

Tone is not about right or wrong language, but about choosing the most appropriate way of expressing yourself. So, recognizing the range of tones in written documents and producing the appropriate tone in your documents are two main challenges to the writers of business documents.

1.4   About Language: Choosing the Right Technical Level for Your Documents

A Spanish novelist, Enrique Jardiel Poncela, once said, "When something can be read without effort, great effort has gone into its writing."

Technical level refers both to the information and to the language. Choosing the right technical level for your readers means standing back from both your expertise and your technical language, and putting yourself into your reader's shoes. When you do that, you can start to pitch your writing at an appropriate technical level for your reader.

To be understood without effort, communication usually requires a sensitivity to your readers, an understanding of their technical level, and an awareness of how much information they need. So, please use the vocabularies that your readers understand in your writings. If you are writing to a professional of the same area as yours, then it's likely that he will share common vocabularies with you, including technical terms. You can therefore use these terms with a reasonable expectation that your reader will understand them. If you are writing to someone who doesn't share your professional background, then you may need to simplify your vocabularies because complex vocabularies and abstract ideas often make your language difficult to understand.

Therefore, to avoid the failure of communication in business writing, you'd better NOT
- use jargon from your own technical field;
- use abbreviations unless you know your readers understand them;
- include technical details that are beyond the knowledge of your readers;
- write in complex language (vocabulary, sentence length, sentence structures) that makes the meaning difficult to understand;
- use abstract ideas when concrete facts would be easier to understand.

1.5 About Planning, Editing and the Writing Process: Choosing the Most Efficient Writing

As to the writing processes, the following are the most significant factors that contribute to the most efficient writing:

◆ Write Simply

To write simply is as difficult as to write well. In particular, writings should be clear and simple. In general, clear and simple documents are easier to read and also easier to understand. So, remember to have a mix of shorter and longer sentences in your writings. Where you have a long sentence with several commas, consider splitting it into several sentences. While where you have a series of short sentence, consider combining some of them into a longer sentence.

◆ Write Transparently

In general, visually transparent documents are simpler to skim and therefore easier to understand. To do so, you may use techniques such as headings, bullet points, numbered list, page numbering, font weights, underlining and italics.

◆ Write quickly in order to produce your first draft

One of the biggest challenges when writing in a foreign language is to write quickly. Of course, it would be unrealistic to expect that you can write as quickly in English as in your mother language. However, the amount of time needed should be realistic in relation to the writing task. So, if you feel you are spending too long on writing your e-mails, minutes and reports, then you need to reconsider the efficiency of your writing process. Remember to give yourself a reasonable time limit to write a draft and do not focus too much on accuracy as you will edit your document later.

◆ Review and edit the language in order to produce your final draft

Since most writers have problems with particular types of spelling, grammar, or punctuation errors, you should read through your final drafts carefully, look for those errors which you frequently commit, check and correct the language. Regardless of any style you use when writing, you need to proofread and edit what you have written. Sometimes these can be done together, but it is more effective when they are done sequentially.

1.6 About the Procedure Designing: Choosing a Helpful Procedure and Put All Factors Together

When working with a foreign language, it is especially important to have a procedure for writing. This will help you to write efficiently, too. The following is a helpful brief procedure for your reference.

◆ Step 1: Establish goals and aims.

Think about your readers. What's your purpose in writing to them?

◆ Step 2: Make a start (Collect information).

Consider your readers again. What are their expectations from your documents? Write down the information to support step 1.

◆ Step 3: Select the relevant information (Concentrate on content).

From the information collected in step 2, choose only the information that is relevant for your readers and your purpose; Decide what to write; Plan, organize and sort out information.

◆ Step 4: Write your first draft (Concentrate on structure and style).

How can I present the information in a concise way so that it is easy to understand? We should remember that each paragraph should contain only one main point, and this should be developed with concrete evidence and details. Be specific and concrete, and give examples.

◆ Step 5: Review and edit (Concentrate on structure, style and language).

Is there too many or too few details for my reader? Are there any gaps in the information which will make it difficult for the reader to understand? Is there any redundant information, e.g. repetition? Whether a document contains redundant information will depend on the writer's view of how much information the reader needs and the reader's view of their actual needs in terms of information. Remember to edit your writing to seek for comfortable understanding.

♦ Step 6: Revise and write the final draft (Concentrate on all areas).

Finally, we live in a world with easy access to enormous quantities of data, so make your professional documents accessible and make your readers' lives easier by converting the data into usable and useful information.

Section 2
Basic Requirements for Business Letter Writing in English
商务英语信函写作的基本要求

As Will Shetterly, an American novelist, says: "There are no rules for writing, there are useful principles." As the main channel of choice for written business communication, business letters traditionally have a fixed layout and its own basic requirements for writing. These requirements have also become the essential principles of written business documents. Many business documents writers use this as a starting point for their business writings.

Actually, business letter writing does not differ greatly from any other form of creative writing. Good English is one of the important bases of good English business letters. However, a business letter should serve the purpose for which it is written and achieve the sender's goals. A business message is considered successful when the receiver interprets the message as the sender intends it. Generally speaking, the essential information in the letter should be correct, the language should be polite, the reply should be in time and the expressions should be short and clear with no repetition. Anyway, whatever you are writing, get to the main points, write quickly and simply, and try to avoid any grammatical or spelling mistakes.

In order to meet these objectives, business letter writers are usually supposed to follow Seven C's to meet the basic requirements for business writing, i.e. completeness, concreteness, conciseness, clearness/clarity, courtesy, consideration and correctness. Some scholars combine some of the C's and sum them up into Three or Five C's. The details are as follows.

1. Completeness（完整）

Business letters should avoid incompleteness. A business communication should include all the necessary information. It is essential to check the message carefully before it is sent out to see that all the matters are discussed, and all the questions are answered.

2. Concreteness（具体）

Concreteness means making the message specific, definite and vivid. Business letters should avoid being too general. In some letters, everything seems to be mentioned but actually few are fully expounded. You should use specific facts and figures, vivid and image-building words.

3. Clearness/Clarity（清楚）

Make sure that your letter is so clear that it cannot be misunderstood. An ambiguous point in a letter will cause trouble to both sides, and further exchange of letters for explanation will become inevitable, and thus time will be lost. The writers must try to express themselves clearly. To achieve this, they should keep in mind the purpose of their letters and use appropriate words in correct sentence structures to fully convey their meanings. When you are sure about what you want to say, say it in plain, simple words. Short, familiar, conversational and straight-forward English is what is needed for business letters.

4. Conciseness（简洁，简明）

Conciseness is often considered to be the most important writing principle. It means saying things in the fewest possible words. To achieve this, try to avoid wordiness or redundancy. Clearness and conciseness often go hand-in-hand and the elimination of wordy business jargons can help to make a letter clearer and at the same time more concise. A concise letter is not necessarily a short one. Sometimes a letter dealing perhaps with a multiplicity of matters cannot avoid being long. Generally speaking, you will gain in clearness and conciseness by writing short sentences rather than long ones. A letter can be made clearer, easier to read and more attractive to look at by short sentences and careful paragraphing. One paragraph for one point is a good rule.

5. Courtesy（礼貌）

Courtesy is not mere politeness. It is like a favorable introduction card. The courteous writer should be sincere and tactful, thoughtful and appreciative. You need to prepare every message with the readers in mind and try to put yourself into their place. If conciseness conflicts with courtesy, then make a little sacrifice of conciseness. Punctuality is one of the most important things in being courteous, it will please your customer who dislikes waiting a long time for a reply.

6. Consideration（体谅）

Before we go on to the detailed structure of the business letter, there is one general principle, on which the native English writers lay great emphasis, that is, the "you-attitude". The "you-attitude" is not so simple as only to use "you" instead of "I" or "we". In our letters we should always keep in mind the persons we are writing to, try to see things from their point of view, visualize them in their surroundings, see their problems and difficulties and express our ideas in terms of their experience. The "you-attitude" can help to avoid an awkward situation, and promote cooperation between the trading parties.

7. Correctness（正确）

Business letters must be correct, otherwise they may be misunderstood and run the risk of reaching nowhere or going astray. Correctness means appropriate and grammatically correct language (without spelling or typographical errors) and accurate factual information such as the names of articles, specifications, quantities, prices and units.

All these C's often go hand-in-hand. Anyway, the meaning in the letter should be correct, clear and has no grammatical mistakes; the language should be polite, and the reply should be in time; and the expressions should be short and clear with no repetition.

Section 3
The Basic Structure of Business Letters in English
商务英语信函的基本结构

Generally, there can be 13 parts in an ordinary business letter. Seven parts among them (parts 1-7 in the following) are standard, principal and necessary, while the others (parts 8-13 in the following) are optional, which may be chosen or not as the writer wishes. Some letters may contain one or more optional parts, depending on different situations or writing requirements.

1. Letterhead（信头）

As the first and most obvious part of a business letter, the letterhead usually includes the essential information about the writer — name, address, cable address, zip-code, telephone number, telegram/ telex/ fax number and e-mail address, etc. It is usually designed and printed in the center or on the left margin at the top of the page. The writing of the address is totally different from Chinese letters. The house number and the street name should be put at the beginning while the city and the country at the end. For example, "中国广东省广州市天河区粤垦路198号" should be translated into "No.198

Yueken Road, Tianhe District, Guangzhou City, Guangdong Province, China ".

2. Date（日期）

Every letter should be dated. The position of the date is often one or two lines below the reference number or letterhead (if there is no reference number). It can be put either on the left or the right margin, depending on the style you decide to use.

Always remember to type the date in full. It is inappropriate to abbreviate the name of the month or show the date in figures like 8/9/2020 or 9/8/2020 as this may cause some confusions.

3. Inside Name and Address（封内地址）

Inside Name and Address are always put at the left margin at least two lines below the date. It consists of the name and address of the receiver and appears exactly the same as on the envelope. When the receiver is a company, type the name of the company directly. If the receiver is an individual in the company, the person's name should be preceded by the courtesy title. i. e. "Mr.", "Mrs.", "Miss" or "Ms.". But when the company is named after one or more persons, e. g. James, Smith Co., the "Messrs.", the abbreviation of "Messieurs" and the plural of "Mr.", should be added before the name of the company, e. g.

Messrs. Bob & Michael Trading Co.
32, Duke Street
London N. W. 4, England

If the letter is addressed to the company but directed to the attention of an individual, take the form of "ATTN" (ATTN =Attention = for the attention of), e. g. :

Messrs. Richard Thomas & Baldwins Lt.,
150 Gower Street,
London W. 1, England
Attn: Mr. John Smith, Sales Manager

4. Salutation（称呼）

As in Chinese letters, salutation is a polite greeting with which a letter begins. Being different from that in Chinese letters, the salutation in English letters customarily uses expressions such as "Dear Mr. /Mrs. /Ms. /Miss. …（姓）" or "Dear…（名）" to express respect. "Dear sir (s)" or "Gentleman (men)" is used when the letter is not addressed to a specific person. "Gentleman (men)" is seldom used nowadays, and "Sir (s)" must be used with "Dear". If you are not sure whether or not the woman to whom you are writing is married, use "Ms". This title is now perfectly acceptable, especially in view of the fact that many career women prefer it, e. g. "Ms. Sarah Davis". Since quite often now companies are owned and /or managed by women, it is more and more customary to use the greeting "Dear Madam or Sir" if the writer is not sure whether the letter will be read by a man or a woman. Whatever its form is, the salutation always appears on a line by itself and is followed by a comma or a colon.

This part is one or two lines below the Inside Address. Its form depends upon the relation between the writer and the receiver. To some extent, it settles the form of the complimentary close.

5. The Body of the Letter (正文)

Beginning two lines below the subject line, or two lines below the salutation if there is no subject line, the body of the letter should contain the actual message and be carefully planned and paragraphed. The opening is to give the reason or purpose of writing and often refers to previous correspondence; the actual message is to specify the writer's concrete purposes, requirements and wishes; while the closing is to express thanks, hope or anticipations. Sometimes the closing may be used to sum up the message and to suggest the writer's requirements to the receiver.

6. Complimentary Close (结尾敬语/套语)

Complimentary close is merely a polite way of bringing a letter to a close. It is usually placed two to four lines below the last line of the body in the letter. There are many different types of complimentary close that show respect, but they should match the salutation. The most common sets of salutation and complimentary close are as follows:

Salutation	Complimentary Close	Comment
Dear Sir (s), Dear Madam, Dear Mesdames, Dear Madam or Sir:	1. Yours faithfully, (or: Faithfully yours,)	Formal — It is very commonly used in Britain, but seldom used in the US and Canada
	2. Yours truly, (or: Truly yours,)	Formal — It was once an Ok and common usage in the US and Canada, but not very common in modern business letters
	3. Yours sincerely, (or: Sincerely yours, Sincerely,)	It was once informal — usually used between persons known to each other. But nowadays, it is more and more commonly used in business letters even between persons unknown to each other in modern US and Canada
Dear Mr. ... (姓), Dear Ms. ... (姓), Dear Mary (名),	Yours sincerely, (or: Sincerely yours, Sincerely,)	

7. Signature（落款签字）

Signature is the signed name or mark of the person writing the letter or that of the firm he or she represents. It is usually printed and written under the Complimentary Close with title under it. The place of signature will depend on the layout of the letter. If the writer represents a certain institute, then the name of the institute should be printed above the signature, e. g.:

> The Overseas Co., Ltd
> (Signature)
> John Bell
> General Manager, Sales Department

8. Reference Number（参考号/发文编号）

The Reference Number is generally used as a useful indication for filing and consulting for both sides, so it must be easily seen. It may include a file number, a contract number, a L/C number or the initials of the signer or the typist. If you find a reference number in the incoming letter, you need to take the form "your ref." and "our ref." in your reply. The position of the Reference Number is often one or two lines below the letterhead.

9. Subject Line（事由标题）

Containing the order or contract number or the name of the goods, the Subject Line is put between the salutation and the body of the letter, either beginning at the left margin or the centre depending on which style you are using. You can put "Re:" or "Subject:" in front of it or just underline it. No matter what the style is, it helps to invite attention to the topic and denote the contents in a letter, as it immediately tells what the letter is about. It is also useful as a guide for filing.

10. Reference Notation（经办人代号）

Sometimes, a Reference Notation (also understood as Identification Marks) can be added two lines below the typed signature. The Reference Notation usually shows only the initials of the typist, but it can also be made up of the initials of the letter dictator and those of the secretary or typist. The two sets are separated by a colon or a slant. For examples, for Bill Clinton (manager) and Nancy Brown (secretary), the marking may be as BC: nb or BC/nb.

11. Enclosure Notation（附件）

Sometimes we need to send with a letter some documents such as catalogues, price lists, order, copies of fax, etc. Then, it is necessary to add Enclosure Notation to remind the receiver.

The Enclosure Notation is usually placed two lines below the signature at the left margin. The marking may be in any of the following ways:

> Enclosure: 3 copies of …
> Enc (I). 3 catalogues
> Encls: as stated

12. Carbon Copy Notation（抄送）

This part is placed under the Enclosure Notation on the left. It is used to show that the letter has been sent to someone relevant. The marking may be in any of the following ways: c. c. / cc / bcc—blind carbon copy. For example: c. c. Mr. J. Cooper.

13. Postscript（附言/注）

The postscript takes the short form of "P. S.". It is used to emphasize a point the writer wants to draw the reader's attention to. It is not for a point that the writer forgot to mention in the letter. The P. S. should be at least two lines below any other notations and flushed with the left margin.

Section 4
The Basic Layouts and Styles of Business Letters
商务英语信函的基本格式

Business documents are official pieces of paper with writings on them which can be a piece of text (a letter, for example), a short message, forms, or graphics. The written communication does not always have fixed outlines, and different writers adopt different approaches and layouts. However, as mentioned in Section 2, business letters traditionally have its own basic requirements and a fixed layout since it is the main channel of choice for written business communication.

Basically, there are four main layouts/ styles for business letters illustrated as follows with different parts in place. It is not necessarily the case, however, to cover all parts in a business letter.

4.1 Indented Style / Semi-Block Style（缩格式）

This is a traditional style.

1.   Letter head（信头）
                                  _____
                                  _____

2. Reference Number（参考号/发文编号）

3.   Date（日期）

4. Inside Name and Address（封内地址）
       _____
       _____

5. The Salutation（称呼）

6.   The Subject Line（事由标题）

7. The Body of the Letter（正文）
    _____
_____.
_____
_____.

8.   The Complimentary Close（结尾敬语/套语）

9.   The Signature（落款签字）
                                                         _____

10. Reference Notation（经办人代号）

11. Enclosure Notation（附件）

12. Carbon Copy Notation（抄送）

13. Postscript（附言/注）

4.2 Full-Block Style (完全齐头式)

This is a popular style in recent years.

1. Letter head (信头)

   _____
   _____

2. Reference Number (参考号/发文编号)

3. Date (日期)

4. Inside Name and Address (封内地址)

   _____
   _____

5. The Salutation (称呼)

6. The Subject Line (事由标题)

7. The Body of the Letter (正文)

   _____
   _____.
   _____
   _____.

8. The Complimentary Close (结尾敬语/套语)

9. The Signature (落款签字)

   _____
   _____

10. Reference Notation (经办人代号)

11. Enclosure Notation (附件)

12. Carbon Copy Notation (抄送)

13. Postscript (附言/注)

4.3 Modified-Block Style (改良齐头式)

This style appeals to many readers.

1.   Letter Head (信头)
           _____
           _____

2. Reference Number (参考号/发文编号)

3.   Date (日期)

4. Inside Name and Address (封内地址)
   _____
   _____

5. The Salutation (称呼)

6. <u>The Subject Line (事由标题)</u>

7. The Body of the Letter (正文)
   _____.
   _____
   _____
   _____.

8.   The Complimentary Close (结尾敬语/套语)

9.   The Signature (落款签字)
                _____
                _____

10. Reference Notation (经办人代号)

11. Enclosure Notation (附件)

12. Carbon Copy Notation (抄送)

13. Postscript (附言/注)

4.4 Combined-Form Style（综合式）

This is also known as Modified Block Style with Indented Paragraphs. It is also one of the acceptable styles.

1.　　　　　　　　　　Letter head（信头）
　　　　　　_____
　　　　　　_____

2. Reference Number（参考号/发文编号）

3.　　　　　　　　　　　　　　　　　　　　　　　Date（日期）

4. Inside Name and Address（封内地址）
　　_____
　　_____

5. The Salutation（称呼）

6.　　　　　　The Subject Line（事由标题）

7. The Body of the Letter（正文）
　　_____
　　_____.
　　_____
　　_____.

8.　　　　　　　　　　The Complimentary Close（结尾敬语/套语）

9.　　　　　　　　　　　　　　　　The Signature（落款签字）
　　　　　　　　　　　　　　　　_____
　　　　　　　　　　　　　　　　_____

10. Reference Notation（经办人代号）

11. Enclosure Notation（附件）

12. Carbon Copy Notation（抄送）

13. Postscript（附言/注）

There are two main differences between the Indented form and the Full-block form:

a. the place of Letter Head, Date, Subject Line, Complimentary Close and Signature;

b. the writing set of Letter Head, Inside Name & Address and the Body.

The Modified-block Style and the Combined-form Style mix the two differences above, and it can use the place of the Indented form and the writing of body of the Blocked form, or the place of the Blocked form but the writing of body of the Indented form.

The choice of layout is a matter of individual taste, but it is better to follow established practice, to which the business world has become accustomed. Once you have made up your mind, adopt one form of layout and stick to it.

Section 5
Training and Practice
操练与实践

1. Write down the general rules and strategies about which you know about business writing in English.

2. List all the basic requirements for a modern business letter in English.

3. Arrange the following in proper form as they should be set up in a letter.

1) Sender's name: Guangzhou Import & Export Corporation

2) Sender's address: 351 North Tianhe Road, Tianhe District, Guangzhou 510000, China

3) Sender's Telephone: 0086-20-84593868

4) Sender's Fax: 0086-20-84593866

5) Sender's telex address: 3328 gz CN

6) Date: April 15, 2020

7) Receiver's name: MacDonald & Evans Co. Ltd.

8) Receiver's address: 58 Lawton Street, New York, 52896, U.S.A.

9) Subject: Shoes

10) The message:

We have obtained your name and address from a friend in New York. We are writing you this letter in the hope that you would be willing to establish business relations with us.

We are one of the leading exporters of casual shoes in China. We are sending you our latest catalogue and price list. If you are interested in any items, please let us know.

We look forward to receiving your early reply.

Writings for Everyday Business Communication

Module Briefing

In our day-to-day life, we communicate our feelings, thoughts etc. to our friends and relatives through letters that may be called personal correspondence. A businessman also writes and receives letters in his everyday activities and transactions, which may be called business correspondence. For example, he can express complaint, apology, appreciation, invitation, etc. So business letters may be defined as a medium or means through which views are expressed and ideas or information is communicated. In addition, it plays an important role in maintaining proper relationship among business partners.

In this module, you are going to be trained to accomplish everyday business communication in written English.

Objectives

Upon the accomplishment of this module, you should be able to accomplish everyday business communication in written English.

Focuses and Difficult Points

1. To get familiar with useful expressions and sentences used in everyday business activities

2. To acquire skills in writing or replying to letters relevant to everyday business activities

Section 1
Letters of Complaint and Apology
投诉、道歉信

1.1 Lead-In Introduction（导入介绍）

A: Letters of Complaint

A complaint letter informs a business that an error has been made or that a defect has been discovered concerning a product or service. The objective of a complaint letter is for some practical purpose, for example, requesting compensation for or replacement of defective or damaged merchandise.

B: Letters of Apology

When we get a complaint letter or have said or done something improper, we should take quick actions to remedy the problem and then get on with our bussiness. An effective letter of apology really can improve relationship.

1.2 Guidelines for Writing (写作指南)

A. When writing a complaint letter, the writer shall state the problem clearly and briefly and state what you want in an authoritative tone. Remember to set a specific time for them to respond, and make sure you give your phone number, your address, as well as your name.

An effective letter of complaint should include the following parts:

- Background: to describe the situation.
- Problem: to give the cause and effect.
- Solution: to state out your solution to the problem mentioned above.

B. When writing a letter of apology, the writer is expected to offer his apology at the very beginning of the letter and clearly state the problem, then give some explanations for what happened. The most important thing is to focus on what actions he is taking to solve the problem. Keep the tone sincere and the apology prompt. The last point is to hand-sign the apology letter with a black pen.

An effective letter of apology should include the following parts:

- Emphasize the aim of your letter.
- Explain why you have done the inappropriate thing.
- Give your solution or offer apology to the current situation.

1.3 Sample Study (范例学习)

Sample 1: A Letter of Complaint about Wrong Shipment

MacDonald & Evans Co. Ltd.
58 Lawton Street, New York, USA
Tel: 23456;   Fax: 34567;
Email: smith@mecl.com

Module Two >> Writings for Everyday Business Communication
日常商务礼仪文书

September 20, 2020

Guangdong Textile Import & Export Corporation

52 East Dongfeng Road,

Guangzhou, China

Dear Mr. Wang,

We are writing to complain about the shipment of our order No. BT-6098 for all-cotton, men's golf shirts of various sizes received this morning. These were ordered on May 13 from the Winter Catalogue, page 35, and *confirmed* [1] by telephone and fax on May 15. However, *upon* [2] unpacking the boxes, we found that they contained 350 women's shirts, all size extra large.

Since this shipment does not *conform to* [3] our order and cannot be sold through our golf shops, we cannot accept it as delivered. We do, however, have *firm orders* [4] for the men's shirts requested. Thus, we suggest that you arrange for someone to pick up the wrongly delivered shirts, and reship the correct order within the next week.

Thank you for your prompt attention to this matter.

Sincerely,

John Smith

John Smith

Notes

1. confirm　确认
2. upon　当……时候（后跟表示动作的名词）
3. conform to　符合；遵从
4. firm orders　正式确定的订单；正式签字的订单

Sample 2: A Letter of Apology for Wrong Shipment

Dear Mr. Smith,

Thank you for your letter of september 20, 2020 informing us of the wrong shipment of your order No. 6098 for golf shirts. Your complaint was immediately sent to our *Customer Relations Representative* [1] for investigation.

We have confirmed through our *inventory* [2] and shipping documents that a mistake was indeed made on your May 13 order. The *slip-up* [3] occurred in our new, *automated* [4] inventory control system, which is causing some problems during the data entry stage. Your order number was unfortunately confused with another one (BT-6998), and the error was not discovered before the shirts were sent out.

We are very sorry for this mistake and the inconvenience it has caused you, and we want to do everything possible to help you satisfy your customers promptly. We offer to redeliver the correct shirts under BT-6098 by DHL Express Mail upon receiving your directions. As to the *non-conforming* [5] shirts, we suggest that you send them back to us, *carriage forward* [6].

You are a valued customer and we sincerely regret this mistake. We assure you that every possible action will be taken by our management to prevent a repetition of the same mistake in future orders.

Yours sincerely,
Wang Jie

Notes

1. Customer Relations Representative　客服代表
2. inventory　存货清单
3. slip-up　疏忽
4. automated　自动的
5. non-conforming　不符合要求的
6. carriage forward　运费待付；运费由收件人支付

1.4　Useful Phrases and Expressions（常用短语和表达）

1) complain about　投诉
2) do not conform to our order　与我们的订单不符
3) wrongly delivered shirts　错发的衬衫
4) reship the correct order　重新发货
5) inform sb. of sth.　通知某人某事
6) confirm through sth.　通过……确认
7) take every possible action　采取任何可能的措施
8) prevent a repetition of the same mistake　避免同样的错误发生

1.5　Typical Sentences（典型例句）

1) Upon examining the goods, we discovered to our surprise that they were altogether inferior in quality to the sample on which basis we placed the order.
(检验货物之后，我们惊异地发现货物品质低劣，同我们订货时的样品相差甚远。)

2) The goods we ordered from you on June 6 haven't arrived yet.
(我们6月6日订购的货物至今仍未到达。)

3) The quality of this lot of goods is so far below the standard that we cannot use them for

our purpose.（这批货物的质量远远低于标准，我们无法使用。）

4) We are disappointed to find that the items delivered do not match the samples.（我们遗憾地发现所交付的货物与样品不符。）

5) The goods are not up to the standard.（货物没有达到标准。）

6) We regret that only 20 sets have been received to date whereas our order indicates 25.（我方非常抱歉地通知您，迄今为止我们只收到了20台货物，而我们订购的是25台。）

7) We shall be glad to learn from you that you are preparing to make some allowance for the damage.（希望贵方能对我方造成的损失做出补偿。）

8) We hope that the goods will be sent immediately.（希望货物即刻发运。）

9) In view of our friendly business relations, we are sure that the matter will be settled appropriately.（鉴于我们之间友好的业务关系，我方相信此事定会得到妥善解决。）

10) You'll have to make compensation for all our costs.（你们要赔偿我们的全部损失。）

11) We will do our best to see that such mistakes do not recur.
（今后我们必定尽力，确保这类错误不再发生。）

12) Your order number was unfortunately confused with another one.
（不幸的是，你们的订单号和另外一单弄混了。）

13) We are very sorry for this mistake and the inconvenience it has caused you and we want to do everything possible to help you satisfy your customers promptly.
（为我们的错误和给你方带来的不便深表歉意，我们会竭尽全力及时满足你们顾客的需求。）

1.6 Training and Practice（操练与实践）

1.6.1 Fill in the blanks of the following letters with the words and expressions given. Change the form where necessary.

Letter A: compensation; profit margin; packing; examination; consignment; expense

Dear Sirs,

　　We refer to our order CM1025 for 1,000 dozen towels. The goods were delivered. On ___(1)___, we found the cartons were in a damaged condition. 11 of 100 cartons had burst open due to poor ___(2)___, and all the towels in them were wetted. The rest were in a damaged condition too.

　　We have replaced the whole ___(3)___ in new cartons. The ___(4)___ involved amounted to $130. As you know, the ___(5)___ on this consignment is tight. Therefore, we have no choice but to ask you to make ___(6)___ to us.

　　You will be aware that poor packing will lead to false impression of the quality of goods. We suggest that, in future, you make sure that the goods are properly packed.

　　We look forward to your cooperation.

　　Yours Sincerely,

Letter B: dispatching; delay; computerized; apologize for; enclosed; mislaid; dealing; deter; making up for

Dear Sir,
  Thank you for your letter of November 23. We regret the ___(1)___ in ___(2)___ your order for the five computer programs. Unfortunately, we had programs with our new ___(3)___ system for ___(4)___ with orders and, as a result, your order was ___(5)___. We have ___(6)___ the five programs you ordered together with an extra disk which we hope will go some way to ___(7)___ the delay. Once again we ___(8)___ the inconvenience. We hope that it will not ___(9)___ you from doing business with us in the future.
  Yours sincerely,

1.6.2 Directions: Translate the following English into Chinese or Chinese into English.

1) We checked some of the items and found they were in a damaged condition.
2) It contained articles different from what we have ordered.
3) We hope that the goods will be sent immediately.
4) If you cannot provide qualified goods within 3 days, we'll ask for a refundment.
5) Please accept our apology for any inconvenience this matter has caused you.
6) 3月3日订购的货物的交付时间现已逾期甚久。
7) 请于6月20日之前将替换品送来。
8) 十分抱歉我们不能及时寄出您所要求的目录和价格表。
9) 对于我的问题我希望能尽快获得答复,这样将来我仍然会选择贵公司的产品及服务。
10) 我方期待此事有一个令人满意的结局。

1.6.3 Writing tasks.

Task 1: Write a letter of complaint according to the following information.

Situation: Your company ordered from Delta Company 50 sets of photocopiers. They include 25 sets of Model A and 25 sets of Model B. But when the goods arrived, you found that there were 15 sets of Model A and 35 sets of Model B.

Now you are asked to write to Anderson, sales manager of Delta, and complain about the incorrect delivery of the goods. The letter should cover the message given below.

1) 感谢及时发货
2) 表述货单不符的情况
3) 我们急需那些订单货物
4) 要求6月20日之前发来那些货物并处理错发的货物

Task 2: Write a letter of apology according to the following information.

Situation: Imagine yourself being a manager of Japonica Garments and Exports. A problem with your delivery process delayed the delivery of Alicia Shaw's order for garments. Please write a letter of apology and offer some allowance for the delay.

Now compose a letter of apology covering the message given below.

1）为耽误发货（garments consignment（code number #AS4558））而致歉。
2）已知你特意要求在12月20日之前发货，赶在假期开业之日。
3）我们送货系统出了点问题，正在竭尽全力改善，代表导致错误的员工向你道歉。
4）为弥补错误，我们在订单净价上折扣40%。
5）希望与你们Ruby Fashion Store继续合作。

Section 2
Letters of Sympathy and Thanks
慰问、感谢函

2.1 Lead-In Introduction（导入介绍）

A: Letters of Sympathy

There can be some bad times when your colleague or business partner is suffering from illness, has lost his job or not obtained a job offer, has lost his family member or the one that he loves etc. A letter of sympathy or a consolation letter is necessary to convey your sympathy and affection. It is usually regarded as social courtesy and a means to maintain the relationship between business partners.

B: Letters of Appreciation

Letters of appreciation are used when one party wishes to express appreciation to another party for the receipt of a gift, attendance as a guest, the first-time order of the goods or any of the great varieties of circumstances. As marketing tools, letters of appreciation go beyond simply thanking the receiver for being kind. They can help to maintain your relationship with customers and facilitate your success in the competition.

2.2 Guidelines for writing（写作指南）

A: Letters of Sympathy

Writing a letter of sympathy is one of the most difficult tasks we undertake because it is always hard to know just what to say.

Of course, with the purpose of comforting the recipient and making closer the relationship, a well-written letter of sympathy may follow some rules, such as writing as soon as you learn the bad news, being empathetic, keeping it short and brief, expressing your sympathy in simple words which are warm and convincing, and sending a handwritten letter. The last point indicates that you have taken time with your writing. A letter of sympathy should contain the following parts:

- Start with a statement of sympathy.
- Follow with sentences about mutual experiences, relationship or present situation.
- Close with some expressions of comfort and affection, offering any help if you can.

B: Letters of Appreciation

Saying "thank you" to someone should happen soon after the happening or receiving of the event, gift, favor, or other action for which you're thankful. A well-written appreciation letter should contain the following parts:

- Enter the salutation. Letters to business associates or people you don't know well should include a title in the salutation. If the person doesn't have a more formal title, use the abbreviated "Mr." for men, and "Miss/Mrs./Ms" for women. Letters to someone you already know well can be more personal, such as "Dear Jeff" or "Dear Bridget".
- Begin with a statement of thanks.
- State details about why you're grateful and how their contribution will be put to use.
- End with a positive and genuine statement.

2.3 Sample Study（范例学习）

Sample 1: A Letter of Appreciation for Warmth and Hospitality

Dear Mr. Milton,

I am writing this letter to thank you for your warm *hospitality*[1] *accorded*[2] to me and my *delegation*[3] during our recent visit to your company. I would also like to thank you for your sincere and frank discussion with me about our cooperation on oil exploration.

During the entire visit, my delegation and I *were overwhelmed by*[4] the enthusiasm expressed by your business representatives on cooperation with us. I sincerely hope we could have more exchanges like this one when we would be able to continue our interesting discussion on possible ways to promote our trade relations and bring our business people together.

I am *looking forward to*[5] your early visit to China when I will be able to *pay back*[6] some of the hospitality I received during my memorable stay in your beautiful country.

Faithfully yours,
Li Junfeng

Notes

1. hospitality 款待；好客
2. accord to 给予
3. delegation 代表团
4. be overwhelmed by 被包围
5. look forward to 期待，盼望（后接名词或动名词）
   e. g.：We are looking forward to your prompt reply.
6. pay back 偿还，回报

Sample 2: A Letter of Appreciation for Customer's Suggestion

Dear Mr. Harrison,

Thank you for your suggestion that we build a larger container yard to provide more *dedicated*[1] service to customers. We have carefully looked into your suggestion and concluded that at the present time we are *reluctantly*[2] unable to *put your suggestion into practice*[3]. However, we are going to *keep it on file*[4] for future consideration when we expand our business.

We appreciate the good advice you gave about the *C. Y.*[5], and are grateful that you took the time and effort to encourage us to improve our service. Loyal and helpful customers like you are the reasons we stay in business and prosper.

Thank you so much for writing.

Sincerely yours,

James

Notes

1. dedicated 投入的，专注的
2. reluctantly 勉强地
3. put...into practice 将……付诸实践
4. keep...on file 将……存档
5. C. Y.（贸易词汇）集装箱堆场（container yard 的缩写）

Sample 3: A letter of Sympathy

Dear President Anderson,

We were distressed to read in the *Times* this morning that your Chairman, Mr. Yonga had passed away and I am writing at once to express our deep sympathy *on behalf of*[1] my colleagues.

I *had the privilege of* [2] knowing Mr. Yonga for many years and always regarded him as a personal friend. By his *untimely passing* [3] our industry has lost one of the ablest leaders. We at the representative office in London recall his many kindnesses and the pleasure of doing business together with him. Mr. Yonga will be greatly missed by all of us who have known him and worked with him in building a better community between our two businesses.

Please accept our deepest sympathy and *convey* [4] our best wishes to Lady Yonga and her family.

Sincerely yours,

Kevin Smith

Chief Representative

London Office, L&L Industry Co. Ltd.

Notes

1. on behalf of　代表
2. have the privilege of　相当于"be honored to…",可译为"有幸……"
3. untimely passing (uncommonly early or before the expected time) 过早地离世
4. convey　转达

Sample 4: A Letter of Sympathy

Dear Bill,

When I called at your office yesterday I was very sorry to learn that you had been in a car accident on your way home from work recently. However, I was equally *relieved* [1] to learn that you are making good progress and are likely to *be back at work* [2] again in a few weeks.

I had a long talk with Susan Carson and was glad to learn of your *rising* [3] export orders. I expect to be in Leicester again at the end of next month and shall take the opportunity to *call on* [4] you.

Wish you a speedy recovery.

Yours sincerely,

Peter Jackson

Notes

1. relieved　放松的,宽慰的
2. be back at work　重回工作岗位

3. rising (advancing or becoming higher or greater in degree or value or status) 上升的，增长的
4. call on 拜访

2.4 Useful Phrases and Expressions（常用短语和表达）

1) be shocked to learn/hear that... 惊闻……
2) be sorry to learn that... 遗憾得知……
3) be distressed to read in... that... 很难过地在……上读到……
4) express one's deepest sympathy 深表难过
5) many thanks for 非常感谢
6) Please accept one's profound appreciation for... 请接受对……的诚挚谢意
7) sincerely appreciate one's help 诚挚感谢某人帮助
8) be grateful to sb. for sth. 为某事感谢某人

2.5 Typical Sentences（典型例句）

1) Thank you for considering our company and inviting us to dine with you last night.
（非常感谢你选择我们的公司，并于昨晚邀请我们共进晚餐。）
2) Many thanks for your generous cooperation and support.（谢谢贵方的慷慨合作与支持。）
3) Please accept my sincere thanks for showing me such warm hospitality when I visited your office.（我到贵公司访问时，承蒙您盛情款待，在此请接受我诚挚的谢意。）
4) Please accept my profound appreciation for your help.
（我对你热情的帮助致以诚挚的谢意。）
5) Please allow me to extend my thanks, on behalf of all the attendees, to each of your employees.（请允许我代表全体与会者向你方所有员工表示感谢。）
6) I am grateful to you for the time and effort you put to ensure my trip was a successful and satisfying one.（谢谢你付出了那么多的时间和精力使我的行程如此成功和令人满意。）
7) I am writing to express our deep sympathy on behalf of my colleagues.
（我写信代表同事们表达深深的慰问。）
8) If I can be of any assistance to you, please don't hesitate to let me know at once.
（如果我能提供任何帮助，请即刻告知。）
9) I shall be delighted if I can do anything for you.（很高兴能为你做任何事。）
10) We wish to express deep sympathy and solicitude for the sudden death of your general manager.（对你们总经理的不幸辞世，我们深表难过和慰问。）
11) We wish to express deep sorrow on the news of the death of our president and to convey our condolences to you on this sad occasion.
（在这个悲伤的时刻，对董事长的离世，我们深表痛心和难过，同时表达对你的慰问。）
12) Wish you a speedy recovery.（希望你很快康复。）

2.6 Training and Practice（操练与实践）

2.6.1 Fill in the blanks of the following letter of appreciation with the words and expressions given. Change the form where necessary.

grateful; recommendation; extend; appreciate; for; be pleased; experience; accept

Dear Mr. Zhang,

　　I am writing this letter to ___1___ my sincere thanks to you ___2___ your kind recommendation.

　　I think you will ___3___ to know that I have been hired as an accountant. With your kind ___4___, I have been accepted by Merch Company in New Mexico and will begin to work on May 1st.

　　I am really ___5___ for all the help and instructions you've given me in the past. It was a memorable ___6___ working under you. Please ___7___ my sincere thanks for all you have done for me, especially for your reference. Your guidance and help will forever be ___8___.

　　Yours faithfully,
　　Li Junfeng

2.6.2 Fill in the blanks of the following sympathy letter with the words and expressions given. Change the form where necessary.

patronage; loss; advice; death; distress; grateful; sympathy; convey

Dear Mike,

　　I was deeply ___1___ to hear of the sudden ___2___ of Mr. Thomas Wilson who served on your company for so long. His passing must mean a great ___3___ to your company and his associates.

　　We have been ___4___ to him for the kind ___5___ and ___6___ that he gave us unreservedly. My staffs join me in ___7___ our sincere ___8___ to members of his family.

　　Yours faithfully,
　　David

2.6.3 Writing tasks

Task 1 Write a letter of appreciation according to the following information.

Situation: Suppose you are a hardware wholesaler. On the occasion of 10th anniversary celebration, write a letter of thanks to the manufacturers who have supplied you with the high-quality goods and services for 10 years. It should contain the following points:

Message:
1) 对生产商10年来及时的供货表示衷心的谢意。
2) 生产商一直以公平的价格提供高质量的产品和出色的服务。
3) 生产商一直秉承"顾客总是对的"的理念。
4) 正是生产商一贯的支持以及客户的忠诚才使我们发展壮大。深表感谢。

Task 2 Write a letter of sympathy according to the following information.

Situation: Suppose your friend Alice was not employed by Mobil after an interview, write a letter of sympathy to her. It should contain the following information:

Message:
1. 得知未被美孚公司录用,深表遗憾。
2. 你有很好的专业知识,祝下次顺利。
3. 如我能帮忙,请告知。

Section 3
Congratulation Letters and Welcoming Speech
祝贺信和欢迎词

3.1 Lead-In Introduction (导入介绍)

A: Congratulation Letters

Congratulation letters are written to express the feelings of pleasure and excitement when someone has succeeded in the election, started a business, got promotion or other significant achievements. They are supposed to convey goodwill and best wishes promptly after the event takes place and strengthen the relationship between each other.

B: Welcoming Speech

Welcoming speech is a short and brief speech that is usually used during various business events and occasions, to introduce the event and welcome a specific person. Welcoming with a speech is a great way to establish a close relationship and also give the new person or business a sense of comfort and ease into their new roles.

3.2 Guidelines for Writing (写作指南)

A: Congratulation Letters

Congratulation letters are usually brief and prompt. Be sure to send the letter within a few days after the event; otherwise, all your efforts will be useless. A sincere congratulation letter usually follows these points:

- Begin with the reason for writing. You should present the congratulation at the first part of the letter.

- Tell how you learn about the good news and make the reader feel certain that he/she deserves the praise.

- End the letter by using an encouraging and conversational tone.

B: Welcoming Speech

The aim of a welcoming speech is to welcome and introduce the audience to the event and the reason for the event, so it should be informative, complementary, and positive. Usually a formal welcome speech should contain the following points:

- Begin by welcoming and expressing thanks to special guests and other audience for gracing the occasion with their presence.

- State the reason for the event.

- State the positive experience or comments on past cooperation or good relationship.

- Look forward to the bright future.

- Express blessing and good wishes.

3.3 Sample Study（范例学习）

Sample 1: A Letter of Congratulation for One's Promotion

Dearest Nancy,

I have just heard the wonderful news of your appointment as the new Vice President of ABC Holdings Inc., and I'd like to *extend*[1] my warmest congratulations to you for this accomplishment.

We have always known that one day all your diligence and intelligence would *pay off*[2], and we're so glad that you finally did it! *I hope you are as happy of your promotion as we are proud of it*[3].

I wish you all the best there in New York. And best wishes for your continuing success!

Yours truly,

John

Notes

1. extend 表达

2. pay off 有报偿；得到回报

3. I hope you are as happy of your promotion as we are proud of it 希望你因升职而快乐，正如我们为你的升职而感到骄傲一般

Sample 2: A Letter of Congratulation for One's Excellent Performance

Dear Emma,

Congratulations on your *excellent performance*[1] during the sale.

The displays you created for the coming summer *promotion*[2] are just beautiful. Several of the sales personnel told me they have received *numerous compliments*[3] from the customers.

I sincerely appreciate your effort and please accept my best wishes for your *continuing*[4] success.

Best regards

Yours sincerely,

John

Sales manager

Notes

1. excellent performance 出色表现
2. promotion 促销
3. numerous compliments 很多称赞、赞赏
4. continuing 持续的

Sample 3: A Short Welcome Speech With a Toast[1]

Your Honor Mr. Smith, Our distinguished guests, Ladies and gentlemen,

It's our honor and great pleasure to host this banquet *in honor of*[2] Mr. Smith and other distinguished guests. I would like to take this opportunity to extend our warm welcome to you all. A remark in *The Analects of Confucius*[3] best expresses what I feel now. "It's such a delight that we have friends visiting from *afar*[4]." Evidently, Mr. Smith's current visit has *demonstrated*[5] his determination to *further enhance*[6] the friendly and cooperative relations between our two companies. We greatly cherish this close relationship, and also greatly value the position we enjoy as one of your most important trading partners.

I sincerely wish that we could continue to work closely together to ensure a sustained growth in our cooperation of economy, finance and trade.

On the occasion of[7] this reception, let me propose a toast to the good health of Mr. Smith and all our guests present here tonight!

Thank you.

Notes

1. toast　祝酒。如：Let's propose a toast to our friendship！（让我们为友谊干杯！）
2. in honor of　为纪念；为向……表示敬意
3. The Analects of Confucius《论语》（我国儒家经典之一）
4. afar　在远方，从远方
5. demonstrate　表明
6. further enhance　进一步增强，增进

   eg.：Our goal is to further enhance the communication and understanding that we believe, will build trust and confidence. 我们的目标是为了进一步加强沟通与理解——我们相信这将会建立信任和信心。
7. on the occasion of　值此……之际

Sample 4: A Short Speech Welcoming the Visitors to the Company

Ladies and gentlemen:

We are proud and honored to have such a *distinguished*[1] group of guests *coming all the way from*[2] the United States to visit our company. We have been looking forward to seeing you for a long time. It is a very nice day today. Our staff and employees will do their best to make your visit comfortable and worthwhile.

Today, our sales manager, Mr. Wang Liang will introduce you to our *newly-built plant*[3] and R & D department. Please do not hesitate to ask any questions you may have.

I take great pleasure in expressing a warm welcome to you and sincerely hope that your visit here will be pleasant and meaningful.

Notes

1. distinguished　受人尊敬的
2. come all the way from　从……远道而来
3. newly-built plant　新建的工厂

3.4　Useful Phrases and Expressions（常用短语和表达）

1）I was delighted/pleased/ glad to hear/learn that...　非常高兴获悉……

2）It is delightful news for me to learn that...　得知……让我很高兴

3）delighted to hear of...and wish to offer my very sincere congratulations　很高兴得知……并真心祝贺

4）please accept our heartfelt congratulations on your...　请接受我衷心祝贺你……

5）congratulations on…　祝贺……

　　6）my warmest congratulations to you on being appointed…　衷心祝贺你提升为……

　　7）it is an honor for me to welcome sb.　我非常荣幸地欢迎某人的到来

　　8）on behalf of sb.　代表某人

　　9）express/ extend warm welcome to sb.　对某人的到来表示热烈的欢迎

　　10）thank sb. for one's efforts and support to/towards…　感谢某人为……付出的努力和给予的大力支持

　　11）coming all the way from　从……远道而来

　　12）propose a toast to…　提议为……干杯

　　13）distinguished guests　尊贵的客人

　　14）take this opportunity to express　借此机会表达

3.5　Typical Sentences（典型例句）

1）Congratulations on your promotion!（祝贺您荣升!）

2）I am delighted to hear that you obtained the NO.1 position in sales in your market. Congratulations!（欣闻你的销售额在你们的市场销售中名列第一，祝贺!）

3）I would like to offer my congratulations on your fifty years of business enterprise.（祝贺贵公司开业50年。）

4）Congratulations to you and every good wish for your success in your new position.（祝贺你并祝你在新的岗位取得成功。）

5）My colleagues join me in sending/extending you our warmest congratulations.（我和同事们向你表达由衷的祝贺。）

6）Best wishes for your continuing success.（祝愿继续取得成功。）

7）It is an honor for me to welcome you today to a very special occasion — the celebration of Siemens' 150th anniversary.（今天，值此非常特殊的场合——西门子公司成立150周年之际，我非常荣幸地欢迎大家的到来。）

8）On behalf of all the members of our company, I would like to take this opportunity to express warm welcome to all of you.
（我代表公司全体员工，借此机会对大家的到来表示热烈的欢迎。）

9）Thank you for coming all the way to China.（感谢各位远道来中国进行访问。）

10）"It's such a delight that we have friends visiting from afar."
（"有朋自远方来，不亦乐乎?"）

11）It is an honor and privilege to receive a visit from such a distinguished group.
（能够接待各位贵宾来访，真是我们的荣幸。）（这是非常正式的说法）

12）I take great pleasure to welcome you and thank you for attending tonight's dinner.（我非常高兴地欢迎你们并感谢你们参加今天的晚宴。）

13）May China and Merill Lynch continue to grow strong together.

（愿中国和美林继续共同成长壮大。）

14) Thank you for your efforts and support towards the successful conclusion of this meeting. （感谢你们为本届会议的圆满结束而做出的努力和支持。）

15) Allow me once again to express my sincere thanks to you all for your kindness and hospitality. （让我再一次感谢各位的好意和热情。）

16) To your health! (Good health!) （为健康干杯！）

17) Let's propose a toast to our friendship! （为友谊干杯！）

18) We are very happy to be here tonight when we can have the opportunity to express our thanks and to bid farewell to our Chinese friends.

（很高兴今晚在此聚会，借此机会，我向中国朋友表示感谢并说声再见。）

3.6　Training and Practice（操练与实践）

3.6.1　Translate the following congratulation letter into Chinese.

Dear Mr. Minister,

　　Allow me to convey my congratulations on your promotion to Minister of Trade. I am delighted that the many years of service you have given to your country has been recognized and appreciated.

　　We wish you success in your new post and look forward to closer cooperation with you in the development of trade between our two countries.

　　Sincerely yours,
　　John Smith

3.6.2　Supply the missing words in the blanks of the following letter. The first letters are given.

Dear David,

　　I have just heard of your p___1___ to Reginal Manager for China. Please a___2___ my warmest c___3___!

　　Looking back on your activities so far, I know that your e___4___ and e___5___ are the key q___6___ that are needed for the p___7___. I wish you every s___8___ in managing the affairs of the branch.

　　With kindest regards,
　　John

3.6.3 Put the following welcoming speech into English.

女士们，先生们：

我非常高兴地欢迎你们并感谢你们参加今天的晚宴。举行今天的宴会是为了感谢所有各方为 AB 项目所做出的诸多艰苦努力。在此，我谨代表遍布世界 45 个国家的 55，000 名美林员工，向华能集团和中国技术进出口总公司表示衷心的感谢，正是由于他们的支持和努力，我们才取得 AB 项目最后的胜利。

3.6.4 Writing tasks.

Task 1: Write a letter of congratulation according to the following information.

Message:

1) 喜闻 Mr. Green 建立了自己的广告公司，对其开业表示祝贺。

2) 夸赞对方在广告业多年获赞颇多。基于他的才能和经验，预祝其事业取得成功。

3) 表达自己愿意协助对方并希望将来继续合作。

Task 2: Write a short speech with a toast according to the following message in Chinese.

Situation: You are asked to have a welcoming speech at dinner, on behalf of your general manager, to welcome Mr. Green, president of the Pacific Trade Company. As your company's business partner, he has come to visit your company and negotiate a new contract with you.

Message:

1) 代表总经理王先生，对 Mr. Green 一行的到来表示诚挚的欢迎。

2) Mr. Green 是 Pacific Trade Company 的经理，此行是参观我们公司并商榷签订新合作合同。

3) 我们坚信通过共同努力，新合同可使两公司的关系更加紧密，使双方发展更加欣欣向荣。

4) 你们的到来也一定会增强我们的合作和友谊。我们会竭尽全力使你们此行舒适且有收获。

5) 最后，提议大家一起为我们两个公司的贸易关系发展以及在座所有朋友的健康干杯！

Section 4
Letters of Introduction and Recommendation
介绍信和推荐信

4.1 Lead-In Introduction（导入介绍）

A: Letters of Introduction

A letter of introduction is written to ask the addressee to receive or offer help to the third person who will go to the addressee's place for some business or other purposes. It can be issued by individuals or organizations.

B: Letters of Recommendation

Recommendation letters are written by someone to evaluate an applicant, assessing his capacity to meet the requirements of a program or position he is applying. They are supposed to help the potential employers to get a better picture of the applicant.

4.2 Guidelines for Writing (写作指南)

A: Letters of Introduction

Since a letter of introduction is written to ask help of the addressee, it should be polite, sincere, concise and honest. Usually it contains the following points:

- Whom the person to be introduced is
- What he will do
- What you hope the addressee will do
- Expressing sincere thanks and appreciation for his help

B : Letters of Recommendation

A recommendation letter is intended to put the applicant in a good light for getting a better position, so you can state certain challenges that the employee overcame, or discuss his passion about a certain area of academic study or activity. Some achievements and anecdotes that personify the employee's capabilities and strengths should be included. But make sure that you do not exaggerate. Exaggerating will not do any favors for the subject of the letter when he is later expected to perform up to a level he cannot fulfill. Also, make sure you are not vague when describing the candidate. Therefore, a recommendation letter is always very specific, using examples whenever possible.

Recommendation letters usually have three parts:

- In the opening, express your positive feeling about writing this letter for the applicant's desired position. Then explain your relationship with him (supervisor, teacher, or co-worker etc.)

- In the main part, present the applicant's qualifications for the position, focusing on his personality traits, contributions, skills and potentials, etc. Remember to back them up with details as evidence

- In the conclusion, close with an overall evaluation, or summarize the candidate's best qualities and skills

4.3 Sample Study（范例学习）

Sample 1: A Letter of Introduction

Dear Mike,

    I have the great pleasure to introduce to you by this letter, Miss Green, the sales manager of ABC Trade Company. She is a *personal friend* [1] of mine and is visiting your city to make a *market investigation* [2].

    I shall *be much obliged* [3] if you could give her the benefits of your advice and experiences.

    Sincerely yours,

    Zhang Hua

Notes

1. personal friend 私人朋友，个人朋友
2. market investigation 市场调研
3. be much obliged 非常感谢

    e.g.：We shall be much obliged if you will give us a list of some reliable business houses in Japan. 如果您能提供一些在日本具有可靠信誉的公司名单，我们将感激不尽。

Sample 2: A Letter of Introduction

Dear Mr. Wang,

    This is to introduce [1] Mr. Benjamin, our import manager of Textile Department. Mr. Benjamin will be in Guangzhou from April 5 to mid April to develop our business with *chief manufacturers* [2] and to make purchases of some decorative *fabrics* [3] for the coming season. We shall *be grateful* [4] if you could introduce him to reliable manufacturers and give him any help or advice he may need.

    Sincerely yours,

    Kevin Lee Smith

    General Manager

Notes

1. This is to introduce sb. 兹介绍某人。作为较正式的商务介绍信的经典开头语，这个句式经常用到。

    e.g.：This is to introduce Mr. Frank Jones, our new marketing specialist who will be in London from April 5 to mid April on business. 现向你介绍我们的新任市场专家弗兰克·琼斯，他将因公务于4月5日到4月中旬期间待在伦敦。

2. chief manufacturers 主要生产厂家，主要生产商
3. decorative fabrics 装饰布；装饰织品
4. be grateful 心存感激

Sample 3: A Letter of Recommendation

John Johnson
123 A Street, City center,
NY 12345

January 21, 2020

John Smith
345 B Street, City center
NY 12345

Dear Mr. Smith,

  I'm writing to highly recommend[1] Mr. Andrew Fuller as a *candidate*[2] for the position of sales manager in your organization. Andrew served under my *supervision*[3] as Assistant Manager at Doo Toy Company for the past three years.

  Mr. Fuller was in charge of many sales services programs for our customers and agents. A large part of his job involved *monitoring and improving customers' satisfaction.*[4] Because of his *personable*[5] nature and superior interpersonal skills, he has established an outstanding *rapport*[6] with customers and agents. He also works well with a team, as evidenced by his getting work well done through other co-workers efficiently.

  During his time here, Andrew has consistently demonstrated a strong *work ethic*[7] and a dedication to success. His efforts have produced high quality results time and time again. Last year, based on the customers' requirements, Andrew *developed and successfully implemented*[8] a marketing plan to improve our total sales.

  We are sorry to lose Andrew, but we recognize his desire to advance his career. I am confident that he would be a *tremendous asset*[9] for your company. I *recommend him without reservation*[10]. If you have any questions, please feel free to contact me at the above address.

  Sincerely,

  John Johnson
  General manager

Notes

1. I'm writing to highly recommend sb. 我写信力荐某人。(这是推荐信常用表述方式。)
2. candidate 候选人；应试者
3. supervision 管理；监督
4. monitoring and improving customers' satisfaction 监控和提高客户的满意度
5. personable 英俊的；风度翩翩的
6. rapport 友好关系；融洽
7. work ethic 职业道德
8. developed and successfully implemented 开发并成功实施
9. tremendous asset 巨大的财富
10. recommend him without reservation 毫无保留地推荐他

4.4　Useful Phrases and Expressions（常用短语和表达）

1) have the great pleasure to introduce…　很高兴介绍……
2) this is to introduce…　兹介绍……
3) be much obliged if you could give her some advice　如果能给她些建议，将不胜感激
4) shall be grateful if you could introduce him to reliable manufacturers　如能给他引荐些可靠的生产商，将不胜感激
5) I'm writing to highly recommend sb.　我写信力荐某人
6) be sorry to lose sb.　很遗憾失去某人
7) be a tremendous asset for your company　是你公司的巨大财富
8) will find him satisfactory as a sales manager　发现他作为销售经理来说肯定令人满意
9) recommend sb. without the slightest hesitation/with every confidence　毫不犹豫推荐某人/尽全力推荐某人
10) provide a reference for sb.　为某人提供证明

4.5　Typical Sentences（典型例句）

1) I have the great pleasure to introduce to you by this letter, Miss Green.
   （很荣幸通过这封信向你介绍 Green 女士。）
2) This is to introduce Mr. Ben Benjamin, our import manager of Textile Department.
   （兹写信介绍我们纺织部门进口部经理，Ben Benjamin 先生。）
3) Please allow me to introduce one of my best friends to you.
   （请允许我向您介绍我最好的朋友。）
4) I am writing to introduce Li Ming, one of my colleagues in Beijing.
   （特此致函介绍我在北京时的同事李明。）
5) This is to recommend my student John Smith, who is hardworking as well as brilliant.
   （兹推荐我的学生约翰·史密斯，他才华横溢，勤奋好学。）

6) I am pleased to write on behalf of John Smith who has applied to your company for the position of sales manager.

（约翰·史密斯在您的公司申请了销售部经理职位，我非常高兴为他写推荐信。）

7) In reply to your letter on Sept. 5, 2020 making inquires about Mr. John Smith, I may say that you will find him satisfactory as a sales manager.

（兹复2020年9月5日来函，询问约翰·史密斯先生一事，贵公司将会发现他作为销售经理来说肯定令人满意。）

8) I can recommend John Smith to you without the slightest hesitation. I have always found him to be a totally loyal and honest worker who can be relied upon.

（我毫不犹豫地向您推荐约翰·史密斯，为人诚实可靠，工作尽心尽责。）

9) I can recommend John Smith with every confidence to you. He has proved himself to be a very energetic and enthusiastic worker who is popular with his superiors and subordinates alike. （我谨全力向您推荐约翰·史密斯，他一直是个精力充沛、工作热心的同事，深得上司和下属欢迎。）

10) I am more than pleased to provide a reference for John Smith, who has worked at this company in the capacity of my Personal Assistant since he graduated in 2013.

（约翰·史密斯自2013年毕业后一直在本公司担任我的私人助理。我很乐意为他提供证明。）

4.6　Training and Practice（操练与实践）

4.6.1　Supply the missing words in the blanks of the following letter. The first letters are given.

Dear Mr. Smith,

　　It is my **p 1** to recommend Mr. Wang Gang, my assistant, as a candidate for the **p 2** of sales manager at your company.

　　Wang Gang graduated from Central South University and got a Master degree of Marketing. After his graduation, he worked in our company and has been in my team for 2 years. During these 2 years, he **e 3** himself and doubled the **s 4** of my department. He is a good-natured, even-tempered and well-liked member of our staff, who has shown himself to be a very able **a 5**. According to my knowledge of him, he is also a **h 6** -working, aggressive and responsible person.

　　Mr. Wang Gang wants to move to a position which affords him a better **o 7** for his growth. I gladly **r 8** him for this position. If you need any further **i 9** regarding him, please do not hesitate to **c 10** me.

　　Sincerely yours,

　　Zhang Ming

　　Manger of Marketing Department

4.6.2 Writing tasks.

Task 1: You are required to write a letter of recommendation based on the Chinese listed below. You are not supposed to translate them word for word.

Message:

被推荐人：张亮。商务英语专业学生，勤奋好学，成绩优异，位居全年级前五名，通过了英语六级，获得商务单证员资格，为人自立，勤奋，善于交流，工作负责。

推荐人：王立波，系被推荐人商务英语专业老师。

背景：推荐人应邀为学生写一封推荐信，附在成绩单后面，申请 ABC 贸易公司的国际贸易业务销售职位。

Task 2: You are required to write a letter of introduction based on the Chinese listed below. You are not supposed to translate them word for word.

Message:

写信日期　　2020 年 7 月 19 日
写 信 人　　Peter Lee，生产部经理
收 信 人　　Jones Smith
要　　　点　　被介绍人苏辉是广州国际贸易公司出口部经理，她和介绍人有过多年的业务合作关系。近期苏辉小姐要去纽约开拓海外市场。介绍人希望收信人能为苏小姐提供指点和帮助。

Section 5
Letters of Application and Invitation
申请书、邀请函

5.1 Lead-In Introduction（导入介绍）

A: Letters of Application

A letter of application is written based on the resume to provide information related to the job's requirements and the applicant's qualifications.

In an effective application letter, the applicant explains the reason for his interest in the specific position and identifies his most related skills to impress the prospective employer and get a chance for interview.

B: Letters of Invitation

Invitation letters are very common in business occasions. They are sent to invite people to attend some special business activities, such as annual conference, trade fair, opening ceremony and dinner etc. Business people will meet on these special occasions.

5.2 Guidelines for Writing (写作指南)

A: Application Letters

The purpose of application letters is to persuade the recipient to read your resume and offer you an chance of interview. Therefore, it should be persuasive, brief, concise and straight to the point. To write an effective application letter, you should adhere to the following disciplines:

- Stating the specific position wanted and how you have come to know the vacancy of the position.
- Presenting the information that qualifies you for the position, generally speaking, from three aspects: educational background, experience and personality traits. You should also mention that you know enough about the company and the position.
- Indicating that you would like the opportunity of interview.
- Offering the company the way how to correspond with you.

B: Invitation Letters

Targeted to specific persons or organizations, an invitation letter should be concise, sincere and relatively short. It should include the following three points:

- Inviting the recipient to attend
- Explaining the reason why you invite
- Offering when and where for the gathering

5.3 Sample Study (范例学习)

Sample 1: A Letter of Application for the Position of Market Researcher

Dear Mr. Washington,

    I am a fresh graduate from Chang Jiang University, and I am writing to apply for the position of market researcher, which is posted on our university BBS yesterday. I believe that my education, experience and qualities will *meet your requirements*[1].

    My extensive academic training in marketing has provided me with skills to learn more about customers, and my working experience as an assistant manager of a clothing store has further *polished my abilities*[2]. I am also familiar with MS Office skills, particularly Word, Excel and PowerPoint. Moreover, I have much spare time this semester, which can ensure my time *commitment*[3] for the internship.

    Enclosed is my resume, which more fully *details*[4] my qualifications for the position. I would greatly appreciate it if you could grant me an interview. Please call 0311-123456 or send an email to wangliang@yahoo.com.cn. I could be in your office at your convenience to talk about working for your company.

Thank you for your consideration.

Sincerely,

Wang Liang

Notes

1. meet one's requirements 满足某人的要求
2. polish 使完美，修正，润色（这里"polish one's abilities"相当于"improve one's abilities"可译为"提高某人的能力"）
3. commitment 承诺；承担义务；献身（这里"time commitment for"是"commit one's time for"，可译为"承诺将足够的时间用于……"）
4. detail 详述，阐释细节（这里是动词形式，"detail my qualifications"相当于"give a detailed information about my qualifications"，译为"详述我的资质/资历"）

Sample 2: A Letter of Invitation

Dear Mr. Washington,

We are glad to learn from your letter dated May 13, 2020 that you are considering a personal visit to China to **smooth the way for**[1] our future cooperation. We believe that the meeting will be fruitful and mutually beneficial.

As the next session of the **Chinese Export Commodities Fair**[2] in Guangzhou is to be held from October 6 to 20, we would like to invite you to attend it. The general manager and sales representatives of our company will be there to meet you and conduct **on-the-spot**[3] business talks and discussions with you. You may have a splendid chance to examine **a wide range of**[4] our export commodities as well as new varieties for your selection. After attending the Fair, your may come to visit our factory to learn more details about the production.

We are confident that[5] our meeting at the Fair will be productive to and helpful for our business relationships. So, we sincerely hope that you can come. Once you have **fixed your schedule**[6] for the visit, please inform us so that we will make necessary arrangement to welcome you.

Sincerely yours,

Zhang Qiang

Sales manager

Notes

1. smooth the way for 为……铺平道路，为……做好准备
2. Chinese Export Commodities Fair 中国出口商品展销会
3. on-the-spot 当场，现场，即席
4. a wide range of 种类繁多的；范围广泛的
5. we are confident that 我们确信（相当于 "we ensure"）
6. fix your schedule 安排好行程

5.4 Useful Phrases and Expressions（常用短语和表达）

1) apply for the position of… 申请……职位
2) meet one's requirements 满足/适合某人的要求
3) working experience 工作经历、经验
4) detail my qualifications 详述我的资质/资历
5) at your convenience 在你认为方便之时
6) grant me an interview 给我面试机会
7) enclosed is my resume 随信附上的我的简历
8) invite you to attend 邀请你参加
9) smooth the way for 为……铺平道路，为……做好准备
10) fix one's schedule 安排好某人行程

5.5 Typical Sentences（典型例句）

1) Learning from your Website that you are looking for an experienced accountant/ Learning from your Website that there is an opening for an accountant on the staff of your Company, I would like to apply for the position.
（我从贵公司网站获知你们需要一名会计，我愿申请此职位）

2) As you will see from my enclosed C. V., I have had 4 years' experience with ABC Company as assistant sales manager.
（正如您从本人所附履历表上得知，我在ABC公司作为销售经理助理工作已有4年了）。

3) I believe that I have the training, experience and qualities that you are looking for.
（我相信我所接受的培训以及我的经验和资历，都非常适合贵公司的要求。）

4) I am looking forward to discussing my qualification for the position.
（我期望和您一起谈谈我应聘的资格。）

5) I shall be much obliged if you will accord me an opportunity for an interview.
（如果能给予我面试机会，我将不胜感激。）

6) I would greatly appreciate it if you could grant me an interview at your convenience.
（如果您能在方便时给我面试机会，我将不胜感激）

7) I have enclosed a copy of my resume for your review. （附上简历一份，供您参阅。）

8) Enclosed are a resume and a photo. （随信寄附简历和一张照片。）

9) I would like to take this opportunity to invite you to attend the Chinese Export Commodities Fair in Guangzhou.

（借此机会，我邀请您参加本次在广州举办的中国出口商品展销会。）

10) We would be very happy if you could come to visit our factory to learn more details about our production. （如果您能来工厂了解产品细节，我们将非常高兴。）

11) Please accept our warm welcome and sincere invitation.

（请接受我们的热情欢迎和诚挚邀请。）

12) We sincerely hope you can attend. （我们期待您的光临。）

13) Please let us know as soon as possible if you can come and tell us when you can make the trip. （如果您能来，请尽早与我们联系，并告知具体时间。）

14) Please confirm your participation at your earliest convenience. （请您尽早告知能否参加。）

5.6　Training and Practice（操练与实践）

5.6.1　Translate the following sentences into English.

1. 从贵公司网站获悉招聘地区销售代理，我写信应征这一职位。
2. 我欲申请销售经理助理职位，我相信我的条件能满足你们的现行要求。
3. 我期望很快与您见面讨论我为贵公司服务的可能性。
4. 从随寄的简历你可以了解到我有信心参与竞争销售经理助理这一职位。
5. 请在您认为恰当的时候给予面试机会，我将不胜感激。
6. 随信附上简历一份，供您参阅。

5.6.2　Writing tasks.

Task 1: You are required to write a letter of Application based on the Chinese listed below. You are not supposed to translate them word for word.

申请职位：销售部经理助理

申　请　人：王静，HB技术职业大学商务英语专业毕业生（下月毕业），从ABC贸易公司的网站获悉销售部经理助理空缺。她深信自己所学的知识和工作经验可以胜任这份工作。

资　　历：成绩优秀，有商界兼职经历，较强的沟通交际能力，计算机应用熟练，有较强的英语口语和书面语表达能力。

Task 2: You are required to write a letter of invitation based on the Chinese listed below. You are not supposed to translate them word for word.

写信日期：2020年6月19日

写 信 人：Assistant General Manager of ABC Company, Wang Liang
收 信 人：General Manager, Mr. Washington,
内容要点：王先生欲邀请 Mr. Washington 参加他们公司 7 月 19 日晚 7：00—9：30 在白云大酒店举行的十周年庆典晚会，届时他还安排 Mr. Washington 与本公司总经理刘先生会晤，洽谈未来合作事宜。

Section 6
Job Offers and Resignation Letters
录用函和辞职信

6.1 Lead-In Introduction（导入介绍）

A: Job Offers

Big companies may receive many job applications every day. Some applicants will be accepted while others may be rejected. Job offers are written to those applicants who are luckily recruited and given a job opportunity or work position.

B: Resignation Letters

When an employee is not satisfied with his current job or finds better career opportunities, he will write a resignation letter to express his intent to resign from the company. The letter is usually delivered by the employee to his supervisor or boss.

6.2 Guidelines for Writing（写作指南）

A: Job Offers

As a job offer is written to inform a person that he or she has been selected for a particular position in an organization, it usually adheres to the following rules:

- Being polite and friendly.
- Expressing thanks to the recipient for his interest in the job vacancy.
- Stating the company's decision — to accept his application for the position because of his excellent performance and informing him of the starting date.
- Asking a formal response from the recipient.
- Expressing warm welcome for his coming.

B: Letters of Resignation

The purpose of a resignation letter is to let your boss know that you want to resign from your company without hurting his feeling. A well-written resignation letter can help you maintain a positive relationship with your old employer, while paving the way for you to move on. Therefore, keep any emotion out of the letter; keep it short, concise and direct. Usually, we don't give specific reasons for leaving except for a new career opportunity.

- State that you are resigning and the date of resignation.
- Explain the reason for leaving.
- Express thanks for the enjoyable time in the company or kindness and help from your boss.

6.3　Sample Study（范例学习）

Sample 1: A Job Offer

Dear Mr. David Washington,

Thank you for your application for the position of assistant sales manager.

We are quite satisfied with your *qualifications*[1] and your excellent performance in the interview. We believe you are the most suitable one for the *vacancy*[2].

Please let me know your decision within the next two weeks. The starting date we have in mind is April 18, but of course it depends on your *circumstances*[3].

We are looking forward to your early reply.

Yours sincerely,

Muffy Bulter

Notes

1. qualifications 资历；资格
2. vacancy 空缺；职位
3. circumstance 情况；境况

Sample 2: A Resignation Letter

Dear Mr. Washington,

Please accept my resignation from ABC trading company effective on September 30, 2020. Working for ABC company has been a wonderful experience. I *could not ask for a better group of colleagues*[1]. I do appreciate the management training I've been given here which *prepared me well for*[2] almost any general business career I decide to pursue.

I will be accepting a position as sales manager with Goldline Company. While I *treasure*[3] the friendship and *professional growth*[4] I've gained here, I think it is time for a new challenge and experience for me.

Best wishes,

Peter

Notes

1. could not ask for a better group of colleagues 否定词加比较级表示一个最高级的概念，这里相当于"this group of colleagues are the best"。
2. prepare me well for 相当于"make me well prepared for"，可译为"使我做好……的准备"
3. treasure 珍视，珍惜
4. professional growth 职业成长

6.4　Useful Phrases and Expressions（常用短语和表达）

1) be quite satisfied with your qualifications　对您的资质/资历非常满意
2) a new challenge and experience　新的挑战和历练
3) attend our test for secretary　参加秘书招聘考核
4) offer you the position　为您提供这个职位
5) resign from ... company　辞去……公司的职位
6) tender my resignation　递交我的辞呈

6.5　Typical Sentences（典型例句）

1) Thank you for your application for the position of sales manager.
   （感谢您申请销售经理职位。）
2) Thank you for taking time to attend our test for secretary.
   （感谢您花时间参加我们的秘书招聘考核。）
3) I am pleased to inform you that you have performed quite well in the interview.
   （很高兴通知您，您在面试环节表现很好。）
4) Your experience in business is most impressive.
   （您在商界中的经验给我们印象颇深。）
5) We are quite pleased to offer you the position.（我们很高兴为您提供这个职位。）
6) We hope you can be a member of us.（希望您成为我们的一员。）
7) I hope you can give us a reply before September 9.（期待9月9日前收到您的答复。）
8) I am writing you to tender my resignation from ABC company effective on Friday, August 15th.（我正式向您递交辞呈，我将于8月15日离开ABC公司。）
9) Please accept my resignation as sales manager of ABC company. I plan to leave my job here on September 30th.
   （请允许我辞去ABC公司销售经理一职。我计划9月30日离开公司。）
10) Thank you for the rewarding experience I've enjoyed during my seven-year association with the organization.（非常感谢在公司的七年工作经验。）
11) The decision was a difficult one for me to leave the company.

(对我来说，离开公司是个艰难的决定。)

12) I have decided to accept a post that will give me greater possibilities for promotion and an increase in my salary.

(我决定接受一个能给我更大提升空间且薪级更高的职位。)

13) I think it is time for me to take a new challenge and experience.

(我认为该是尝试新挑战和新体验的时候了。)

6.6 Training and Practice（操练与实践）

6.6.1 Please Translate the Following English into Chinese.

1) tender one's resignation
2) take a new challenge
3) treasure the opportunities
4) accept one's resignation
5) attend our test for Sales Manager
6) be suitable for the vacancy
7) I regret having to leave a situation where I have received so much kindness and made so many friends.
8) However, I find it necessary to seek an appointment which can enable me to earn a higher salary to cope with the growing high cost of living.

6.6.2 Writing tasks

Task 1: Write a job offer according to the following information.

Situation: Mr. David Washington, one of the three applicants, has been an assistant sales manager for 12 years in a foreign trade company and his major in university is marketing. He is qualified for the position of sales manager of ABC trading company. Suppose you are the personnel director, please write a job offer to him.

Task 2: Write a letter of resignation according to the following information.

Situation: Working as a sales manager in ABC company, you want to resign and open your own company. Please write a resignation letter to your general manager, Jones Smith.

Module Three 模块三 Writings for Administrative Documents
商务办公及行政文书

▶ Module Briefing ///

Various types of administrative document writing, including the writing of notices and posters, E-mails and faxes, telephone messages and memos, name cards and ID tags, minutes and meeting summaries, personnel recruiting and dismissal, job applications and resumes, IOUs and receipts, reports and certificates, involve the use of business English. In this module, you are going to be trained to write administrative documents in business English.

▶ Objectives ///

Upon the accomplishment of this module, you should be familiar with the precise method of writing administrative documents.

▶ Focuses and Difficult Points ///

1. To get familiar with useful expressions and sentences used in administrative documents

2. To acquire skills in writing administrative documents

◈ Section 1 ◈
Notifications / Notices, Announcements and Posters
通知/启事、公告与海报

1.1　Lead-In Introduction（导入介绍）

A: Notifications and Notices

A notification is an official written announcement to a particular person or organization, which is usually used by a higher authority to its subordinates or the organization to its members concerning a certain important event. A notice is a formal written announcement issued in public places such as a newspaper or magazine where everyone can read it, and be informed of something that has happened or is going to happen. If you are given notification of something, you are officially informed of it. If you notice something or someone, you become aware of it or him.

A notification/notice can prove useful to companies when they want to acquaint the public with a product, service or event without a great advertising campaign. Even when you want to draw attention to a new opening, a change in policy, a celebration, an appointment, a move, etc., you can consider using notification/notice. A well written notification/notice shows the writer's skill of organization and presentation of matter as well as language accuracy.

B: Announcements

The announcement is one kind of proclamatory (公告的) practical writing. If some organizations, groups or individuals want to illustrate something to the public, or want to ask for help, or have some requirements to tell the masses, they can write what they want to express briefly into an announcement. There are various kinds of announcements, such as Found, Lost, and House for Renting, etc.

C: Posters

A poster is a sign posted in a public place as an advertisement. A poster advertised the coming attractions.

1.2 Guidelines for Writing (写作指南)

A: Notifications/Notices and Announcements

A notification/notice or an announcement can be directed to people outside companies or to employees inside. An effective notification/notice and announcement usually follows the principles stated below:

• State the matter in the first line of the body of the letter or in the first paragraph of the letter.

• Specify the background, details, explanations or qualifications.

• If the event intends to motivate actions, you can provide this information in the last paragraph.

B: Posters

In general, a poster consists of the name of the activity, participants, time, place, sponsor and signature. Posters have no fixed layouts. Their styles are various, but their words should be concise, clear and complete.

1.3 Sample Study（范例学习）

Sample 1: A Notice of Removal

June 16, 2020

Dear Madam or Sir,

Due to the development of new business[1], our company will move to following new premise/building:

New Address: 5th Floor, Block B, Haiyi building, No. 68 Xiahe Road,

Xiamen, Fujian Province, China

Post Code: 361004

Phone No: 86-592-5097889; Fax No: 86-592-5036885

Please update your file accordingly.

We are very sorry for the inconvenience brought to you[2]. We would also like to take this chance to thank you for your continued support over the years and hope that we can keep on working together in the future.

Yours sincerely,

John Smith

John Smith

General Secretary

Notes

1. Due to the development of new business... 由于业务发展的需要……
2. We are very sorry for the inconvenience brought to you. 对由此带来的不便，我们深表歉意。

Sample 2: A Business Merge Notification

September 5, 2020

Dear Client,

ABC is pleased to announce that we have *entered into a definitive merger agreement*[1] with XYZ, a leading provider of computer software.

This merge with XYZ, a company based in LA, USA, *further strengthens our position in*[2] the computer software market. The combination of their product designs with our state-of-the-art technologies and services will provide our clients products and services with highest standards. This partnership is also expected to *result in*⁴ great efficiencies and significantly increase our market share.

As with all important business decisions, we will work closely with our clients, partners and employees to make the integration process as smooth as possible. ABC is now undergoing structural changes. The integration of both companies will take place over the next 3 years. Of course, in the meantime our customers will continue to receive the products and services of the same high quality.

XYZ, which will continue to operate under that name, is now a wholly owned *subsidiary*⁵ of ABC.

Sincerely,

Tim Stinson

Tim Stinson

Managing Director

Notes

1. entered into a definitive merger agreement　进入签订最终合并协议阶段
2. further strengthens our position in...　进一步巩固我们在……的地位
3. state-of-the-art　顶尖的，一流的

   e.g.：Both the light and sound equipments are state-of-the-art.（灯光与音响设备都是最尖端的。）
4. result in　引起；导致；以……为结局

   e.g.：Consensus need not be weak, nor need it result in middle-of-the-road policies.（一致的意见不一定就没有影响力，也不一定就会导致走中间路线的政策。）
5. subsidiary　附属机构，子公司

   e.g.：The company is a wholly-owned subsidiary of a large multinational corporation.（这是一家大型跨国企业的全资子公司。）

Sample 3: An Announcement

April 25, 2020

Dear Sirs,

Because of bad management, we have decided to *discontinue*¹ the part of our business carried on here from next month on.

We are starting to hold a *closing-out sale*² from the day we send this announcement. *Regardless of*³ cost, stock on hand will be cleared. There will be *substantial reductions*⁴ in all departments and, in some cases, prices will be marked down by as much as 60%.

As the sale is likely to be well attended, we hope you *make a point of*[5] visiting the store as early as possible during the opening days.

Yours faithfully,
Xin Hua Department Stores

Notes

1. discontinue 中断，停止
   e.g.: The airline says this route is no longer economic, so they're going to discontinue it. (航空公司说这条航线不再赚钱，因此他们准备关闭。)
2. closing-out sale 抛售，清仓销售
3. regardless of 不管，不计
   e.g.: The fields give high and stable yields regardless of climatic circumstances. (不管天气条件如何，这块地总是保持稳产高产。)
4. substantial reduction 大幅减少
   e.g.: The depreciation of other currencies in Asia has also caused a substantial reduction in tourism. (亚洲其他货币贬值，亦严重打击了旅游业。)
5. make a point of (在文中意为) 拿定主意

Sample 4: A Poster

GOOD NEWS

Summer Clearance Sales

All the goods on show are sold at twenty percent discount. Please examine and choose them carefully before you pay. There will be *no replacement or refunding*[1]. You have been warned *in advance*[2]. You are welcome to make your choice.

Personal Shopping Service
Sep. 30, 2020

Notes

1. no replacement or refunding 不退不换
2. in advance 提前，预先

1.4 Useful Phrases and Expressions（常用短语和表达）

1. state-of-the-art 顶尖的，一流的
2. result in 引起，导致，以……为结局

3. closing-out sale　抛售，清仓销售

4. regardless of　不管，不计

5. substantial reduction　大幅减少

6. make a point of　拿定主意

7. no replacement or refunding　不退不换

8. in advance　提前，预先

1.5　Typical Sentences（典型例句）

1) We are very sorry for the inconvenience brought to you.
（对由此为您带来的不便，我们深表歉意。）

2) We would also like to take this chance to thank you for your continued support over the years and hope that we can keep on working together in the future.
（借此机会感谢您多年以来的支持，希望我们能够长期合作。）

3) This partnership is also expected to result in great efficiencies and significantly increase our market share.
（此次合作将极大提高工作效率并扩大我们的市场份额。）

4) We will work closely with our clients, partners and employees to make the integration process as smooth as possible.（我们将与我们的客户、业务伙伴以及所有员工一起亲密合作，保证这次合并的顺利进行。）

5) In the meantime our customers will continue to receive the same high quality services.
（在此期间，我们的客户将一如既往地受到我们优质的服务。）

6) XYZ, which will continue to operate under that name, is now a wholly owned subsidiary of ABC.
（XYZ 公司仍将使用原先的名字，但现在已正式成为 ABC 下属的全资子公司。）

7) Because of bad management, we have decided to discontinue the part of our business carried on here from next month on.
（因为管理不善，我们将于下个月起停止在该处的业务。）

8) Regardless of cost, stock on hand will be cleared.（不计成本，一律清仓。）

9) There will be substantial reductions on all departments and, in some cases, prices will be marked down by as much as 60%.
（所有部门都将大幅削价，有的商品甚至低至四折。）

10) We hope you make a point of visiting the store as early as possible.
（我们希望您尽早前来购买。）

11) There will be no replacement or refunding. You have been warned in advance.
（商品付款出门后不退不换，特此预先声明。）

1.6　Training and Practice（操练与实践）

1.6.1 Complete the following sentences with one of the given words. Change the forms if necessary.

notify	due to	result in
subsidiary	agreement	regardless of
discontinue	substantial	in advance
refund	as soon as possible	make a point of

1) The club welcomes all new members _____ age.
2) We are pleased to _____ you that our business will be turned into a private corporation on the 21st of August.
3) He is _____ learning English well.
4) Clients normally pay fees _____, monthly, quarterly, or yearly.
5) The company is a wholly-owned _____ of a large multinational corporation.
6) It was decided to _____ the treatment after three months.
7) Dissatisfied customers can return the product for a full _____ .
8) _____ the extreme cold, we were unable to plant the trees.
9) If no _____ was reached, the army would step in.
10) The party has just lost office and with it a _____ number of seats.

1.6.2 Supply the missing words in the blanks of the following letter. The first letters are given.

> **Notice**
>
> With the demolition（拆除）of our premises（经营场所）at the above address under a redevelopment scheme, the part of our **b**____(1)____ carried on there will be **d**____(2)____ after the end of October. On Monday, 1st October, we are holding a **c**____(3)____ sale. Stock on hand will be cleared **r**____(4)____ cost. There will be substantial price **r**____(5)____ in all departments and, in some cases, prices will be marked down by as much as half. Stock to be **c**____(6)____ is unrivaled in both variety and **q**____(7)____ . As the sale is likely to be well attended, we hope you make a point of visiting the store as early as **p**____(8)____ during the opening days.

1.6.3 Put the following English into Chinese or Chinese into English.

1) 大幅减少
2) no replacement or refunding
3) 凭票入场

4) I inform you that I have now moved my factory to the above address.

5) Regardless of cost, stock on hand will be cleared.

6) We are very sorry for the inconvenience brought to you.

7) Having established ourselves in this city, and as merchants and general agents, we take the liberty of acquainting you of it, and solicit the preference of your order.

8) 因为管理不善，我们将于下个月起停止在该处的业务。

9) 借此机会感谢您多年以来的支持，希望我们能够长期合作。

10) 我们将与我们的客户、业务伙伴以及所有员工一起亲密合作，保证这次合并的顺利进行。

1.6.4　Writing tasks.

Task 1: Write an announcement about contributions wanted.

Message:

1) 本报的主要对象为我公司的员工；出版日期（publication date）为每月的 15 日。

2) 欢迎下列各种形式和体裁的稿件（The contents can be as follows）：

① 各部门情况的报道；② 对我公司生产、销售、产品推广的意见和建议；③ 员工的业余生活；④ 其他。

3) 来稿请勿超过 100 字；英文来稿要求打字。

4) 来稿如不采用（adopt），3 个月内退还作者。

5) 联系人：林跃。

6) 联系地址：公司公共关系部（Public Relations Department）。

Task 2: Write a notice according to the following message.

> 尊敬的威廉先生：
>
> 　　我们在此通知您，过去 10 年中，在美国担任我们代表（representative）的莉莉女士已离开我们公司。因此，她不再代表公司接受订单或收款（collect accounts）。以后有什么业务方面的问题，请不要找她。
>
> 　　我们已任命（appoint）史密斯先生代替她的位置。他在我们的销售部门任职多年，完全熟悉您地区顾客的需要。此外，他出生在美国，因此对美国文化非常了解。我们相信您和他能有良好的合作。
>
> 　　谨上。
>
> 　　　　　　　　　　　　　　　　　　　　　　　　　　　凯特
>
> 　　　　　　　　　　　　　　　　　　　　　　　　　2020 年 3 月 15 日

Section 2
E-mails and Faxes
电子邮件和传真

2.1 Lead-In Introduction（导入介绍）

A: E-mails

An E-mail, the short form for electronic mail, is a kind of letter which needs no paper, being sent to others by the Internet. It is one of the modern communication services which can send a brief message quickly and cheaply. E-mail message can be the same as a letter or can include sound and pictures as well. It has more contents and carries more information than a letter does.

B: Faxes

A fax is a kind of letter which is sent through the fax machine. The word of "fax" is the abbreviation of "facsimile". Like the e-mail, it has become one of the main means in modern business communications. It can be communicated as fast as international phone calls. Pictures, charts etc. can be sent by the fax machine easily as well.

2.2 Guidelines for Writing（写作指南）

A: E-mails

This modern channel of written communication does not always have fixed outlines, and different writers adopt different approaches and layouts. As business letters traditionally have a fixed layout, many E-mail writers use this as a starting point for their structure. However, it is important to differentiate between different types of business E-mails. Formal E-mails are written in the style of formal business letters (see Module One for details), and informal E-mails are written in the style of informal letters or even in the style of phone calls.

In general, an E-mail has two main parts: heading and body.

◆ Heading

The heading includes the following contents: From, To, Cc, Bcc, Date, Subject, Attn (Attention) and Attachment.

In the case of multiple receivers, type the E-mail addresses of them in the Cc item. Copies of the document can be sent to them, and this is known by all receivers so they can communicate with each other. Bcc has the same function with Cc item, but it is confidential and every receiver does not know who the other receivers are.

◆ Body

The layout of the body is like that of a private letter, including salutation, body, close and signature. But sometimes it just has the parts of salutation and body, while the parts of close and signature are omitted.

The contents in an E-mail may be set down as follows:

```
From:
To:
Cc:
Bcc:
Date:
Subject:
Attn (attention):
Attachment:

Salutation
Body _____
_____
_____
Close
Signature
```

B: Faxes

A fax is a kind of document which has legal effect. If you make quotation to your customer or convey the content of the contract, you should make sure what you have written is correct. A fax is not an instant operation, and the sender cannot ensure whether the receiver can receive the fax in time or that its content would not be seen by others. Therefore, the sender should carefully handle sensitive and confidential information.

Generally, a fax also consists of two parts.

◆ Heading

The heading includes the following contents: Organization, Address, Tel /Fax No., E-mail; To, From, Date, Attn (Attention), Page (s) and Re (Regarding).

◆ Body

The layout of the body is like that of a private letter, consisting of salutation, body, close and signature.

The contents in a fax may be set down as follows:

```
                        Organization
        Address:                    Fax:
        Tel:                        E-mail:
To:                                 From:
Date:                               Attn (attention):
Fax No.:                            Page (s):
Re (regarding):
Salutation
Body _____
Close
Signature
```

2.3 Sample Study (范例学习)

Sample 1: E-mail

From: shoesco@163.com

To: Smith@go3mop.com

Date: July 25, 2020

Subject: *sales intent*[1]

Dear sir,

  We are the leading dealer of shoes in this city. Our customers are interested in your shoes and want to enquire about their quality.

  If the quality and price are satisfactory, there are *prospects*[2] of good sales here. But before placing a firm order, we should be glad if you would send us, on fifteen days' *approval*[3], ten for men and five for women.

  All of the items unsold at the end of the period, and those which we decide not to keep as stock, would be returned to you at our *expense*[4].

  We look forward to your early reply.

  Yours sincerely,

  Li Ming

Notes

1. sales intent   销售意向
2. prospect 成功的可能性，前景

e.g.: We should have a detailed review of the company's prospects. 我们应该对该公司前景进行详细考查。

3. approval 同意，批准

e.g.: Last November the commission gave its stamp of approval on the deal. 去年11月，委员会核准了这宗交易。

4. expense 费用，开支

e.g.: Owen was against it, on the grounds of expense. 欧文因费用问题对此表示反对。

Sample 2: E-mail

From: Kenneth@yahoo.com
To: Liu Wen@hotmail.com
Date: Tuesday, November 29, 2020, 8:50 A.M.

Subject: New Product Introduction

Dear Ms. Liu,

We are glad to introduce to you our latest[1] development, anti-wrinkle cream "Young Forever". This product has been tested by many volunteers and got only satisfactory and *positive*[2] feedback from all those who have tried the product. We thought your company may be interested in our new product.

One of our *specialists*[3] will contact you shortly in order to describe the product in detail as well as answer your questions in case you have any.

We are also pleased to invite you to the *seminar*[4] *in regard to*[5] this new product next Thursday. Our colleagues will inform you about the details of the event.

Thank you.

Sincerely yours,

Anderson

Anderson
Sales Department

Notes

1. We are glad to introduce to you our latest... 很高兴向您推荐我们最新的……
2. positive 积极的；确实的，肯定的

   e.g.: I'm as positive as I can be about it. 我对它有绝对的把握。
3. specialist 专家；专员；专业人员；专科医生

e.g.: If you are housebound, you can arrange for a home visit from a specialist adviser. 如果你出不了门，可以预约专家顾问上门就诊。

4. seminar 研讨班，讲习会；研讨小组；研讨会；培训会

    e.g.: The seminar aims to provide an overview on new media publishing. 研讨会旨在综览新兴的媒体出版。

5. in regard to 关于

Sample 3: Fax

MacDonald & Evans Co., Ltd.
58 Lawton Street, New York, U.S.A.
Tel: 23456　Fax: 34567　E-mail: abc@mecl.com

TO: Mrs. Fan Fang, General manager　　FROM: Mr. Anderson
DATE: June 25, 2020　　　　　　　　　ATTN: *Pro Forma Invoice*[1] No. 004001
PAGES: 1

Dear Mrs. Fan

　　Have you received the Pro forma Invoice No. 004001 covering the material required under your Order 00653 which we sent to you on the 15th day of this month? Please *proceed*[2] to apply for the *irrevocable*[3] letter of credit as outlined by the *attached*[4] instruction sheet.

　　Thank you once again for your order and support to our business. Please advise if you have additional questions.

　　Best regards,

　　Peter pan
　　Peter Pan
　　Sales Administrator[5] / International

Notes

1. pro forma invoice　形式发票
2. proceed 开始，着手；继续，继续进行

    e.g.: Let's proceed to the next item on the agenda. 让我们进入下个议程吧。

3. irrevocable 不可撤销的
4. attached 隶属，附在……，添加

    attached please find... 随函附上……请查收

    attached instruction sheet 随函所附的说明

5. Sales Administrator　销售管理

Sample 4: Fax

Wills Kenly Toy Ltd.
108 West Street, New York, U. S. A.
Tel: 356731   Fax: 43568   E-mail: dr@wktl.com

TO: Mr. John Smith, General manager   FROM: Mr. Denial Roberts
DATE: Oct. 20, 2020   ATTN: Insurance Issue
PAGES: 1

Dear Mr. Smith,

We are here to refer to the order of 2345[1], which we placed with you last week. We appreciate your cooperation and now we want you to *do us a favor*[2].

As we now desire to have the consignment insured *at your end*[3], we will be thankful if you will kindly arrange to insure *on our behalf*[4] against All Risks.

With all *heartfelt*[5] thanks in advance, we hope you can accept our request after you discuss it.

Best regards,
Danial Roberts

Notes

1. We are here to refer to the order of 2345…我方现在所说的是2345号的订单…对于合作业务比较频繁的交易双方来说，可能订单业务也比较多，所以有时需要运用这种句型来提示对方所指的具体是哪个订单。
2. do sb. a favor 帮助某人
3. at one's end 在某人所在的地方
4. on one's behalf 代表某人
5. heartfelt 衷心的；诚挚的；真诚的；深切
   e. g: We would like to take this opportunity to convey our heartfelt condolences to the families of the victims. 我们谨此向受害人家属表达我们衷心的慰唁。

2.4 Useful Phrases and Expressions（常用短语和表达）

1) sales intent 销售意向
2) on fifteen days' approval 15天的试用期
3) at one's expense 由某人付费
4) in regard to 关于
5) sales administrator 销售管理
6) do sb. a favor 帮助某人

7) at one's end 在某人所在的地方

8) on one's behalf 代表某人

2.5 Typical Sentences（典型例句）

1) We are glad to introduce to you our latest development.
（很高兴向您推荐我们最新研发的产品。）

2) Our specialists will contact you shortly in order to describe the product in detail as well as answer your questions in case you have any.
（我们的专员将很快与您联系，为您详细介绍产品并回答您可能有的任何问题。）

3) Our colleague will inform you about the details of the event.
（我们的同事将告知您关于讨论会的具体情况。）

4) This product has been tested by many volunteers and got only satisfactory and positive feedback from all those who have tried the product.
（该产品已经过测试并得到满意反馈。）

5) This message was undeliverable due to the following reasons.
（该邮件由于以下原因无法发送到收件人。）

6) The user account is disabled.（该用户账户无效。）

7) Please reply to Postmaster@163.com if you feel this message to be in error.
（如果认为该邮件有误，请回邮件给 Postmaster@163.com。）

8) All of the items unsold at the end of the period, and those which we decide not to keep as stock, would be returned to you at our expense.
（到了销售末期那些没卖出的商品和决定不作为库存的商品，我方将付费返还贵方。）

9) We are here to refer to the order of 2345.（我方现在所说的是2345号的订单。）

10) As we now desire to have the consignment insured at your end, we will be thankful if you will kindly arrange to insure on our behalf against All Risks.（我方希望贵方能就托运货物进行投保。如果贵方能代表我方为货物投保一切险，我方将非常感激。）

2.6 Training and Practice（操练与实践）

2.6.1 Complete the following sentences with one of the given words. Change the forms if necessary.

attach	disable	on fifteen days' approval
proceed	positive	do sb. a favor
development	refer to	at one's expense
heartfelt	specialist	on one's behalf

1) We have sent you these goods _____.

2) The new law does not _____ the land used for farming.

3) Peckham, himself a cancer _____, is well aware of the wide variations in medical practice.
4) What are your plans for the _____ of your company?
5) We must never buy easy popularity _____ stockholder's _____.
6) We would like to take this opportunity to convey our _____ condolences to the families of the victims.
7) It is possible to _____ executable program files to E-mails.
8) "What do you mean?" I asked, offended _____ Liddie's _____.
9) The athlete received a two-year suspension following a _____ drug test.
10) The best way to _____ it is by a process of elimination.

2.6.2 Put the following English into Chinese or Chinese into English.

1) 很高兴向您推荐我们的……
2) I am sending an email to ask you to make a homepage for my company.
3) 销售意向
4) I can be reached seven days a week at Howhow@sina.com.
5) Please reply to Postmaster@163.com if you feel this message to be in error.
6) Our colleague will inform you about the details of the event.
7) This message was undeliverable due to the following reasons.
8) 他购买了一台一年包退换的电视机。
9) 如果贵方能代表我方为货物投保一切险，我方将非常感激。
10) 该产品已经过测试并得到测试者的满意反馈。

2.6.3 Writing tasks

Task 1: Write a fax according to the following information.

上海钢铁工业有限公司
地址：淮海路198号　　　　　　　传真：021-49367788
电话：021-49367789　　　　　　　邮箱：csmi@public.pat.net.cn
收件人：孙先生　　　　　　　　　发件人：詹波
公司：双狮公司　　　　　　　　　日期：2020年9月1日
传真号：020-87275432　　　　　　总页数：1页
主题：咨询

亲爱的孙先生：
　　对于您最近几个月销售业绩（sales）大幅度下降一事，我们非常担心。
　　刚开始，我们以为这只是市场不景气（a slack market）而已，但仔细调查此事后，我们发现，市场不景气并非最主要原因。我们想知道能帮上您什么忙。因此，期待收到您关于此情况的详细报告（a detailed report），以帮助您将销售业绩恢复（restore）到从前水平。

您真诚的

詹波

Task 2: Write an E-mail according to the following information.

Situation: *You are William Jones, the director of Syntel Ltd. You are writing an E-mail to John Brown to invite him to the monthly meeting. Now compose an E-mail covering the message below.*

Message:

收信人：johnbrown@syntel.com

1）邀请布朗先生参加6月的会议。

2）会议时间是6月最后一周的周五。

3）希望对方的报告能满足董事会（the board）提出的具体要求，认为对方有时间弄清楚（assimilate）这些要求并做好准备。

4）为防有任何变故或是有需要，向你提前（beforehand）了解细节，建议在你办公室讨论一次。

5）关于具体会面约定（appointment），可与你秘书联系。

Section 3
Notes, Telephone Messages and Memos
便条、电话留言和备忘录

3.1　Lead-In Introduction（导入介绍）

A: Notes

A note is a kind of simple and short letter for various purposes. Its form is quite similar to that of a letter. The content of a note is usually concise and simple, not in a roundabout way. The writer only needs to express clearly his reason, motivation and requirement. Note-writing is very common in daily office work.

B: Telephone Messages

Telephone message is a kind of note taken by other people for the persons who are temporarily off. They are left for people to read, or given to people by the hand. They are often written in informal style, except when they are written for a superior to read, and then the style may become formal.

C: Memos

A memo (memorandum) is an official note, a written communication form from one person to another inside a business or an organization. It is widely used for giving notices or providing information and offering suggestions. It should also be proper in tone and correct in form, and its message should be clear and concise.

3.2 Guidelines for Writing (写作指南)

A: Notes

A note is made up of date, salutation (heading), body, ending and signature.

```
                                                                    Date
Salutation,
Body _____
_____
_____.
                                                                  Close,
                                                              Signature
```

B: Telephone Messages

Telephone messages consist of two kinds: one is formal telephone message card, and the other is informal telephone message note. They may be designed and printed as standard office slips or written in a casual way.

The writing of telephone messages should usually follow the 5W principles as follows:
- Whom is the message for? Whom is the message from?
- What is the message? What is the purpose?
- When is the meeting or appointment scheduled?
  When is the message written?
- Where is the receiver of the message to go or call back?
- Why is the message important?

Layout 1: Telephone message card.

```
                         Telephone Message
Date: _____    Time: _____    A. M. (  )  P. M. (  )
From: _____    Tel No.: _____
To: _____
Of: _____
```

( ) Telephoned   ( ) Please call
( ) Call to see you   ( ) Will call again
( ) Want to see you   ( ) Urgent
Message:
_____
_____

Signed: _____

Layout 2: Telephone message note.

Telephone Message

To: _____
Date: _____
Message: _____
_____
_____
Message taken by: _____

C: Memos

In general, there is a relatively fixed layout in memo writing. It consists of two parts: heading and body, and the heading consists of four or five parts: To, From, Date, Subject and C.C., if necessary. Most companies print their own memo stationery, but the headings are always the same.

Pay attention to the following points:

• C.C. means carbon copies, and indicates that you have sent a copy of the memo to someone else.

• The subject line should summarize what the memo is about.

• No greeting (such as *Dear*...) is needed.

• The text is usually divided into paragraphs. And sometimes you can use bullet points to list items if necessary.

• Put your initials, not your full name, at the end.

Memo

To:
From:
C.C:
Date:

Subject:
Body _____
_____
initials signature

3.3 Sample Study（范例学习）

Sample 1: A Note

NOTE

June 18, 2020

William Salinger,

    I'd like to remind you of an advertisement which I came across while reading Washington Post last night. It's about Tenderby, a fast growing *Hi-tech park*[1] which is *inviting investment*[2]. What interested me is that *favored tax reductions*[3] are offered. Attracted companies are *pouring in*[4], and there are very limited vacancies left. I suppose a visit there is worthwhile.

Sincerely yours,
Eric Giotto

Notes

1. Hi-tech park   高科技园区
2. inviting investment   招商引资
3. favored tax reductions   减税优惠
4. pouring in   蜂拥而至

Sample 2: A Note

June 3, 2020

Dear Manager,

    I very much regret that I am unable to attend office this morning *owing to a severe attack of illness*[1]. I am *enclosing*[2] herewith a certificate from the doctor who is attending me, as he fears it will be several days before I shall be able to *resume*[3] my duties. I trust my *enforced absence*[4] will not give you any serious inconvenience.

Yours respectfully,
Tracy Brown

❋ Notes

1. owing to a severe attack of illness   由于突生急病
2. enclose   随信附上

    e. g.：Please remember to enclose a stamped addressed envelope when writing.
    （请记得写信时在信封里放一个贴好邮票、写明地址的信封。）

3. resume   重新开始；继续

    e. g.：He resumed his former position with the company.（他又恢复了在公司的职位。）

4. enforced absence   被迫缺席；身不由己的缺席；无奈的缺席

Sample 3: A Telephone Message Card

Telephone Message

Date: Nov. 15, 2020   Time: 9:30   A. M. (√) P. M. (   )
From: Bill Jackson   Tel No.: 7859125-223
To: Mr. Green
Of: Import Department
(√) Telephoned   (√) Please call
( ) *Call to see you*[1]   ( ) Will call again
( ) *Want to see you*[2]   ( ) *Urgent*[3]
Message: Call to say your order will be *delivered*[4] next Monday.
Signed: Tom

❋ Notes

1) call to see sb. 来电话约见你
2) want to see sb. 想拜访某人
3) urgent *a.* needing to be dealt with as soon as possible 紧急的
4) deliver *v.* to take sth. to a place 送货，递交

Sample 4: A Telephone Message Note

Telephone Message

To: Miss Lin
Date: 2 p.m. Dec. 12th
Message: Miss Anna called to say that she wanted to discuss some details about the contract with you. Please return call (020 - 87634952) to her.
Message taken by: Mary

Module Three >> Writings for Administrative Documents
商务办公及行政文书

Sample 5: A Memo (without bullet points)

Memo

To: All Managers and Supervisors
From: Donna Kingsley
Date: January 18, 2020
Subject: Merit Ratings

Each of you will receive this week *merit rating forms*[1] for the employees *under your supervision*[2].

I think it is appropriate to point out that these ratings should not be *taken lightly*[3]. They play an important role in employee promotion, salary increases, and opportunities for advancement.

I'm sure you know that you are expected to rate each employee with complete honesty. Yet when some employees are given the *highest rating*[4], I will suspect the rate is *taking the easy way out*[5]. Remember, it is your obligation to discuss with employees the rating you give them.

I intend to *do a random sampling of*[6] the completed merit ratings each of you turns in, and you can expect to hear from me if I think your ratings are unrealistic.

D. K.

Notes

1. merit rating forms 业绩考核表
2. under sb's supervision / under the supervision of sb 在某人的监督/管理之下
3. take lightly 轻视
4. highest rating 满分
5. take the easy way out 马虎过关
6. do a random sampling of 随机抽样

Sample 6: A Memo (With Bullet Points)

Memo

To: All staff   From: Michal McGovern, I. T. Centre
C. C. M. D.   Subject: Computer Access
Date: 18, August 2020

We will be upgrading the software installed on the network over the weekend. It is therefore possible that you may have problems accessing your computer on Monday morning.

If this is the case, please do one of the following:

* Press the restart key when the "access denied" message comes up.
* Phone extension 2291 for help from a technician.

We are doing everything we can to make sure things go smoothly, and would be glad to help if you have any problems or queries.

M. M.

3.4 Useful Phrases and Expressions（常用短语和表达）

1) Hi-tech park 高科技园区
2) inviting investment 招商引资
3) favored tax reductions 减税优惠
4) a severe attack of illness 突生急病
5) call to see sb. 打电话约见某人
6) want to see sb. 想拜访某人
7) In order to…, we will … 为了……，公司决定……
8) I am writing to inform you of … 兹此通知……
9) The purpose of this memo is to announce … 本备忘录是通知……
10) This memo provides information about … 本备忘录是关于……
11) under sb's supervision / under the supervision of sb 在某人的监督/管理之下
12) take the easy way out 马虎过关
13) do a random sampling of 随机抽样
14) The purpose/aim/objective of this memo is to (investigate 调查/evaluate 评估/study 研究/recommend 建议/analyze 分析/give 给予/feedback 反馈/estimate 估算/assess 评估) … 本备忘录是为了……
15) It was (found/discovered/felt/proposed) that… 调查发现/建议如下……

3.5 Typical Sentences（典型例句）

1) I'd like to remind you of an advertisement which I came across while reading Washington Post last night.
（我想就昨晚在《华盛顿邮报》上偶然看到的一则广告提醒你一下。）

8) Attracted companies are pouring in, and there are very limited vacancies left.
（吸引了众多公司的涌入，仅剩非常有限的空位。）

9) I very much regret that I am unable to attend office this morning owing to a severe attack of illness. （非常遗憾，由于突发急病，我今早没能来公司上班。）

Module Three >> Writings for Administrative Documents
商务办公及行政文书

10) I am enclosing herewith a certificate from the doctor who is attending me.
（现附上我主治医生出具的证明一张。）

11) I trust my enforced absence will not give you any serious inconvenience.
（相信我这次身不由己的缺勤不会给您带来很大的麻烦。）

12) Miss Anna has just rung up saying that she wanted to discuss some details about the contract with you.
（安娜小姐刚刚来电话说她要和你商讨一下合同的一些细节问题。）

13) Please call Miss Anna at 020-87634952 about the discussion.
（关于商讨的问题请打电话给安娜小姐，她的电话号码是020-87634952。）

14) Here is a message from Miss Anna for you. （这是安娜小姐给你的电话留言。）

15) He said he would ring later again. （他说他会在打电话过来。）

16) Please ring him as soon as possible. （请尽快给他回电话。）

17) All suggestions are welcome. （欢迎提出建议。）

18) If you have any questions, please call me at (phone number).
（如有疑问，请致电。）

19) This memo responds to the points raised by the general manager in its last memo of Nov. 20th. （本备忘录是对总经理于11月20日发出的上一个备忘录的回复。）

20) The information you asked for are attached. （您需要的信息详见附件。）

21) The key findings are outlined below. （主要结果如下。）

22) The following points summarize our key findings. （主要调查结果如下。）

3.6 Training and Practice （操练与实践）

3.6.1 Complete the following Memo with one of the given words. Change the forms if necessary.

faculty	in respond to	in great need of
detailed	is required to	strongly recommend that…
findings	discuss	to announce
purpose	present	medical conditions

Memo

To: All the ＿＿（1）＿＿

From: Li Ming, Manager's Assistant

Date: May 26, 2020

Subject: Donation of Medicine to Patients in Poor Areas

　　All staff ＿＿（2）＿＿ attend the meeting, which will be held next Monday in the meeting room. The main ____(3)____ of the meeting is to ____(4)____ the medicine donation to the patients in poor areas, where the ____(5)____ are extremely bad and the patients are ____(6)____ our help. Before the meeting, a ____(7)____ donation plan is required for every department.

The meeting will begin at 2 o'clock in the afternoon and everyone should be ____(8)____ on time.

J. W

3.6.2 Put the following English into Chinese or Chinese into English.

1) 非常遗憾无法参加这次会议。

2) 这是王经理给你的电话留言。

3) Please call Edward at 18654600 about your order for 50 computers.

4) 请告诉他给医生办公室打电话,电话是87643216。

5) Please call him back as soon as possible. It's urgent.

6) If you need further information, do not hesitate to contact me at any time.

7) The purpose of this memo is to encourage staff morale.

8) I would like to remind you that we are in want of a telephone for each office.

9) 主要调查结果如下。

10) 相信我这次身不由己的缺勤不会给您带来很大的麻烦。

3.6.3 Writing tasks.

Task 1: Write a telephone message according to the following information.

Situation: Read the information below carefully and use the proper information to fill out the telephone message form.

Message:

The date is October 7th, 2020. While Mr. Green was away, Mr. Peter Schulz called from America. Mr. Schulz asked Mr. Green to call back today before 4:00 pm or any time tomorrow. The telephone number is 001-426-6521477. Mr. Schulz would like to negotiate the discount. The message was taken by Mary Sanders.

Task 2: Write a memo for the situation given below.

Business situation:

Your section moved to a new office on Thursday morning. However, the Maintenance Department (工务处) within your organization has failed to carry out certain work. Computers have not been wired to the laser printer (激光打印机); a metal bookshelf hasn't been built properly; the fire door (防火门) sticks, and the bottom drawer of the filing cabinet (档案橱柜) which holds standard forms was damaged in the move and now doesn't open.

Now, write a memo to complain about the situation and ask for action.

Task 3: Write a note according to the following information.

Situation: You have just had an operation, and received a note of regard from your friend Jenny. Now please write a reply to her to tell her your current situation. You should write 60 words.

Section 4
Name Cards and ID Tags
名片和个人身份标识牌

4.1　Lead-In Introduction（导入介绍）

A: Name Cards

A name card, also called business card, is the most widely-used and economic instrument in interpersonal communication. It is a kind of introductory card for convenient interpersonal contacts. With the holder's name, identification, position etc, it is indispensable to show personal identification in business activities. Name cards stand for professionalism and capability. The goal is to first grab attention, and then provide information.

B: ID Tags

As personal identifying tags, ID Tags are similar to the basic personal information in a resume, and are often clipped or put in business travel bags and suitcases. If the box is accidentally lost, the owner identity can be verified quickly.

4.2　Guidelines for Writing（写作指南）

A: Name Cards

In general, a name card includes the following information:
- Name of the business
- Holder's name
- Holder's position or one's title of technical post
- Contact information (the address of the company, telephone number, fax number, E-mail address etc.)
- More possible information: business covering, business motto/ logo, banking account number, etc.

B: ID Tags

Write clearly about basic personal information or fill in the table correctly, such as the name of the owner, contact, address, telephone number, etc.

4.3　Sample Study（范例学习）

Sample 1: A Name Card

CATARC CHINA AUTOMATIVE TECHNOLOGY & SALES DEPARTMENT

Li Ningyong

General *Vice*[1] Manager

Address: No. 998 Zhongshan Road, Yuexiu District Guangzhou
Office Phone: (020) 31863458　　　Postcode: 6410199
Email: LNY660@pub.catarcchina.net.cn
Mobile: 13899866579　　　Fax: 020-31863460

Notes

1. 表示副职的词有几个: vice; deputy; associate; assistant; sub。

vice 常与 President, Chairman, Chancellor 等职位较高的词连用。

deputy 主要用来表示企业、事业及行政部门的副职。如: Deputy Governor（副省长），Deputy Director in Sales Department（营销部副主任）。

associate 主要用来表示技术职称的副职。如: Associate Professor（副教授），Associate Chief Physician（副主任医生）

assistant 主要用来表示助理。如: Assistant Engineer（助理工程师），Assistant Manager（助理经理）

sub- 一般有"少于、低于"的意思。指级别较低的。如: Sub-Editor（助理编辑），Sub-Lieutenant（陆军中尉）。

Sample 2: A Name Card

Solar *Works*[1], *Inc.*[2]

Lily Johnes
Business Manager

Add: 23/F, Central Tower, 28 Queen's Road Central, Hong Kong, 53277
Tel: (852) 2916 0066　　　Fax: (852) 2523 8981
Website: maslily@netvigator.com

Notes

1. 表达"工厂"含义的词一般有 factory，plant，works，mill，yard 等。在我国，使用频率最高的是 factory，该词适用范围也比较广。但在美国英语中，用得最多的是 works，这个词的用途相当广泛，而 plant 还有"设备"之意。例如：

（1）Works：Solar Works, Inc. 太阳能设备厂；Hudson Boat Works 哈德森船厂；Dog Works, Inc. 狗用具厂；Map Works 地图出版社；Northern Ski Works, Inc. 北方滑雪用品店；Kolb Net Works, Inc. 科伯网络公司

（2）Factory：Pizza Factory, Inc. 比萨制造厂；Mat Factory, Inc. 席垫厂；The Window Factory 门窗厂；Media Factory 媒体工作室

（3）Plant：Small Car Plant, Inc. 小轿车厂；Plastics Plant 塑料厂；Auto Body Plant, Inc. 汽车车身厂；Country View Sewage Plant, Inc. 乡村风光污水处理厂

（4）Mill：Coffee Mill, Inc. 咖啡厂；Alaska Soap Mill, Inc. 阿拉斯加肥皂厂

2. 表达"公司"含义的词一般有 Inc. / Co. / Corp. / PLC. /

（1）Inc. = incorporated *adj*.；Incorporated is used after the name of a company or business to show that it is a legally established enterprise. （公司）合并的；组成法人组织的；股份有限的。如：Air Berlin, Inc.（德国）柏林航空公司；Nike, Inc.（美国）耐克公司

（2）Co. = company *n*.；Company is a business organization that makes money by selling goods or services. 公司。如：New World Trading Company 新世界贸易公司；Japan Telecom Co., Ltd. 日本电信有限公司；Sony (China) Co., Ltd. 索尼（中国）有限公司

（3）Corp. = corporation *n*.；Corporation is a large business or company with special rights and powers. 大公司；企业。如：British Broadcasting Corporation 英国广播公司；Honda Corporation 本田汽车公司

（4）PLC. = public limited company；Public limited company（legally abbreviated to PLC）is a type of public company（publicly held company）in United Kingdom. It is a limited company whose shares are freely sold and traded to the public. 股份有限公司。如：British Petroleum plc. 英国石油公司

Sample 3: An ID Tag

RICHARD ANDERSON

1234, West 67 Street

Carlisle, MA 01741

123-456-7890

4.4 Useful Phrases and Expressions（常用短语和表达）

1) General Manager   总经理
2) Sales Manager   销售经理
3) Marketing Manager   营销经理
4) Personnel Manager/Director   人事主管/总监
5) Director   总监
6) Vice Chairman   副主席
7) Deputy Director   副主任
8) Assistant Manager   助理经理
9) Chief Engineer   总工程师
10) Senior Engineer   高级工程师
11) Secretary-general   秘书长
12) Section Chief   处长
13) Minister   部长
14) Head of the Bureau   局长

4.5 Typical Sentences（典型例句）

1) Room 201, 18 Tianchang Road, Huangyan District, Taizhou City, Zhejiang Province
（浙江省台州市黄岩区天长路18号201室）

2) Room 504, Level 5, Windsor House, Cornwall Road, Harrogate, North Yorkshire, HGI 2PW（北约克郡海诺盖特市康沃尔路温莎大楼5层504室，邮编：HGI 2PW）

3) 23/F, Central Tower, 28 Queen's Road Central, Hong Kong
（香港皇后大道中环28号，中央大楼，23层）

4) 1234, West 67 Street Carlisle, MA 0174
（马萨诸塞州卡莱尔市67号西街1234号，邮编0174）

4.6 Training and Practice（操练与实践）

4.6.1 Put the following English into Chinese or Chinese into English.

1) Personnel Manager/ Director
2) Marketing Dep. Project Manager
3) 人事部经理
4) 助理工程师
5) Machinery & Equipment Import and Export Company
6) Room 1907, Futian Building, Shennan Middle Rd., Futian District, Shenzhen, Guangdong
7) Entrance 29, Bingshui East Lane, Zijinshan West Rd., Hexi District, Tianjin, China

8) 纺织服装有限公司

9) 上海鳞翼机电科技发展有限公司

10) 杭州畅达印染集团股份有限公司

11) 浙江省杭州市高科技园区创业路888号

4.6.2 Writing tasks.

Task 1: Write a name card according to the following information.

Situation: Design a name card for Mr. Wu Bin from China Agricultural Machinery Import and Export Joint Company, according to his personal information given below.

Message:

中国农林机械进出口联合公司

吴斌 总裁

地址：北京市西城区广安门外大街178号

邮编：100055

电话：(010) 62375888　　　传真：(010) 62377788

手机：13908085858　　　　E-mail：Wbin@126.com

Task 2: Write a personal identifying tag according to the following information.

Message:

安妮·布莱梅

纽约市奥利森市1013号，邮编：10000

电话：(212) 555-0264

Section 5
Meeting Minutes
会议记录和会议纪要

5.1 Lead-In Introduction（导入介绍）

Meeting minutes are formal brief notes of the proceedings at meetings. They can keep permanent and formal records of discussions and decisions there. They are written record to be kept for future reference; they may record reviews of past activities, new decisions and policies, and assist the decision-making process. There are two kinds of minutes: detail minutes and summary minutes.

5.2 Guidelines for Writing (写作指南)

Most minutes can be divided into four parts:
- Heading: This part includes the following items:
  the name of the group/ organization holding the meeting;
  meeting title (regular, special, or annual);
  time, date and place of the meeting;
  presiding director;
  list of people attending;
  list of absent member of the group.
- Body: That is a brief summary of the meeting, including:
  minutes of the previous meeting;
  items of new business;
  statements of what actually occurred at the meeting;
  any other business (AOB).
- Adjournment:
  the time the meeting adjourned and when the new meeting is to take place.
- Signature of the minutes recorder

Format

XXX (Co. Name)

MINUTES OF A MEETING OF XXX (Meeting Title)

Date:

Minutes of Meeting Held on _____ (time, date and place)

PRESIDING: _____

PRESENT: _____

APOLOGIES FOR ABSENCE: _____

SUMMARY OF THE MEETING: _____

_____

ANY OTHER BUSINESS: _____

NEXT MEETING: _____ (date and place)

ADJOURNMENT: _____

SIGNATURE: _____

5.3 Sample Study(范例学习)

Sample 1: Detail Minutes

ABC Company Ltd.
MINUTES OF A MEETING OF THE BOARD OF DIRECTORS

October 15, 2020

A meeting of the Board of Directors of ABC Ltd. was held on October 15, 2020, 10:00-12:00 a.m. at the conference room of the Company.

Presiding: Mr. David Brown

Directors Present:
Mr. Tony Montana (Chairman)
Mr. Sheldon Cooper (Sales Manager)
Mr. Matt Mather (Managing Director)
Ms. Rachel Green (Chief Accountant)
And 15 shareholders

Directors Absent:
Ms. Lily Smith
Mr. Jennifer Lively

Call to Order[1]

Mr. Tony Montana, the Chairman called the meeting to order at 10:00 a.m. and Ms. Jane Oliver recorded the minutes. A *quorum*[2] of directors was present, and the meeting, having been duly *convened*[3], was ready to proceed with business.

CEO Report

Mr. Montana reviewed the agenda and welcomed everyone to the meeting. Next, Mr. Montana discussed the current status of the company and its progress. A number of questions were asked and extensive discussion *ensued*[4].

Sales & Business Development Update

Mr. Sheldon Cooper next provided an update on the overall sales progress and *sales pipeline*[5] of the Company. He also presented the status of business development discussions.

Financial Review

Ms. Rachel Green provided a comprehensive update on the company's financial plan and forecast. Ms. Green also reviewed the company's principal financial operating metrics. Discussion ensued.

Financial Planning

The Board next discussed the timing and creation of the 2021 Operating Plan.

Approval of Minutes

Ms. Jane Oliver presented to the Board the minutes of last meeting of the Board for approval, whereupon *motion duly made, seconded and unanimously adopted*[6], the minutes were approved as presented.

There being no further business to come before the meeting, the meeting was adjourned at 12:00.

Respectfully submitted[7]

Jane Oliver, Recording Secretary

Notes

1. call to order 宣布开会
2. quorum *n.* 法定人数
3. convene *v.* 召集；集合

    e.g.: Last August he convened a meeting of his advisers at Camp David.
    （去年 8 月，他召集了他的顾问在戴维营开了一个会议。）

4. ensue *v.* 接踵发生，继而产生

    e.g.: A brief but embarrassing silence ensued.
    （紧接着是短暂却令人难堪的沉默。）

5. sales pipeline 销售渠道
6. motion duly made, seconded and unanimously adopted

    意为：（会议上）做了提议，附议并一致被采纳。

    second *v.* 附议；赞成提案

    e.g.: Your application must be proposed and seconded by current members.
    （你的申请必须由现任成员推荐并得到他们的支持。）

    unanimously *adv.* 全体一致地，无异议地

    e.g.: The Board of Directors has approved the decision unanimously.
    （董事会成员一致批准了该项决定。）

7. respectfully submitted 这里可翻译为：此致敬礼。

Sample 2: Summary Minutes

Minutes of the Meeting of the Capital Improvements Committee

The Foster Lash Company, Inc

October 8, 2020 11:00 a.m. —11:45 a.m. at the conference room of the Company

Presiding: Patricia Stuart

Present: Mike Negron, Sheila Glun, Ellen Franklin

Absent: Fred Hoffman, Gina Marino

The weekly meeting of the Capital Improvement Committee of the Foster Lash Company was called to order at 11 am in the conference room by Mr. Stuart. The minutes of the meeting of October 1 were read by Mr. Negron and approved.

The main discussion of the meeting concerned major equipment that should be purchased by the end of the year.

Among the proposals were these:

Mr. Woo presented information regarding three varieties of office copying machines. On the basis of his cost-benefit analysis and relative performance statistics, it was decided, by *majority vote*[1], to recommend the purchase of a CBM X-12 copier.

Mr. Brown presented a request from the secretarial staff for new typewriters. Several secretaries have complained of the major and frequent breakdowns of their old machine. Mr. Franklin and Mr. Browne are to further investigate the need for new typewriters and prepare a cost comparison of new equipment versus repairs.

The committee will discuss the *advisability*[2] of upgrading account executive's personal computers. The report will be presented by Sheila Glun at the next meeting, to be held on October 15, 2020 at 11 am in the conference room.

The meeting adjourned at 11:45 am

Respectfully submitted

Ellen Franklin, Secretary

Notes

1. majority vote 意为：多数投票

    e.g.: A majority vote of 75% is required from shareholders for the plan to go ahead.

    这项计划若要实施，必须获得股东75%的多数票。

2. advisability *n.* 明智；可行性

    e.g.: I have doubts about the advisability of surgery in this case.

    关于该病例做手术的可行性，我持有疑问。

5.4 Useful Phrases and Expressions（常用短语和表达）

1) call to order　宣布开会
2) topic for discussion　议题
3) put to the vote　进行投票
4) voting results　表决

5) approved unanimously 全体通过

6) majority vote 多数投票

5.5　Typical Sentences（典型例句）

1) A meeting of the Board of Directors of ABC Ltd. was held on October, 15, 2020, 10:00- 12:00 a. m. at the conference room of the Company.（ABC 有限公司董事会于 2020 年 10 月 15 日上午 10:00 至 12:00 在公司会议室召开会议。）

2) The meeting was presided over by Mr. Smith. / Mr. Smith presided over the meeting.（斯密斯先生主持了本次会议。）

3) Absence apologies were received from Ms. Lily Smith.
（莉莉·斯密斯女士缺席了本次会议。）

4) Minutes of last meeting were approved and unanimously adopted.
（上次的会议记录获得赞成并一致通过。）

5) The main discussion of the meeting concerned major equipment that should be purchased by the end of the year.
（会议主要讨论的焦点话题是年底前需要购买的主要设备问题。）

6) The Chairman asked Mr. Smith for a brief report on the accident.
（主席要求史密斯先生就意外事件作一个简短的报告。）

7) Several appointments and dismissals were announced at the meeting.
（会议上宣布了几项人事任免。）

8) The delegates decided to put the issue to the vote.
（代表们决定就这个问题进行投票。）

9) The delegates were not able to vote because they lacked a quorum.
（代表们不能进行投票，因为他们没有达到法定人数。）

10) The members constitute a quorum.（这些成员构成法定最少出席人数。）

11) The next meeting was scheduled for 9 A. M. next Monday.
（下次会议定于下周一上午九点举行。）

12) The report will be presented by Sheila Glun at the next meeting, to be held on October 15, 2020 at 11 a. m. in the conference room.（Sheila Glun 将在下次会议上做报告，会议将于 2020 年 10 月 15 日上午 11 点在会议室举行。）

5.6　Training and Practice（操练与实践）

5.6.1　Complete the following sentences with one of the given words. Change the forms if necessary.

approve	call to order	adjournment
present	second	put to the vote
quorum	unanimously	majority vote

schedule   concern   topic for discussion

1) The meeting was _____ by the Chairman at 10:30 a.m.
2) Bryan Sutton _____ the motion against fox hunting.
3) Mr. Fenster _____ results of survey of office employees.
4) Today its executive committee voted _____ to reject the proposals.
5) A _____ enabled the passage of the resolution.
6) The members constitute a _____.
7) Minutes of last meeting held on 20 August, at 2 p.m., were _____.
8) Before it was fully discussed, the question was _____.
9) The Vice Chairman of the committee introduced a _____.
10) A motion for _____ was made by Mr. Jones.

5.6.2 Put the following English into Chinese or Chinese into English.

1) After calling the May 15 meeting to order at 4 p.m., the president requested the manager's report.

2) 销售经理作了如下报告。

3) The decision was approved unanimously.

4) Absence apologies were received from Ms. Lily Smith.

5) The delegates were not able to vote because they lacked a quorum.

6) Following discussion, the annual report was accepted unanimously.

7) 会议上宣布了几项人事任免。

8) 宣读并通过了上次会议的记录。

9) 晚上9:30休会。

10) 没有其他事项,主席宣布会议结束。

5.6.3 Writing tasks.

Task 1: Write meeting minutes according to the following information.

Message:

董事会议纪要

ABC公司董事会议

2020年11月9日第6号例会纪要

ABC公司例会于2020年11月9日,星期一召开。会议由首席执行官刘冬生召集,时间为上午9:30,地点是公司会议室。

出席人员:刘冬生,保罗·史密斯,查尔斯·琼斯,李琦和王华。
　　　　这些成员构成法定最少出席人数。

缺席人员:尼尔·罗伯特

> 首席执行官报告：董事长就上一季度销售增长情况做了报告。报告提到，以投标的方式与实力强大、人数众多的外国同行争夺主要原材料供应的难度增大。
>
> 一个建立组织负责销售增长的计划被提交董事会讨论：首先，将总公司的行政权（decentralize）放到子公司，使其负责自己的销售和市场推广。其次，重新建立（reinstitute）董事长和总经理的双重（dual）职能，以确保他们专心致力于目前的工作及未来的发展。
>
> 琼斯先生提议休会。会议于上午 11:00 结束。
>
> 秘书：安·布朗

Task 2: Write meeting minutes with the following information.

Situation:

作为 Slate & Johnson 箱包公司（Luggage Company）劳资协调委员会（the Labor Grievances Committee）的秘书，你要为 2020 年 9 月 23 日的每月例会做一份会议记录。请根据下边几个要点用英文写一份完整的会议记录。

1) 开会时间：下午 4:00；开会地点：员工餐厅。

2) 主持人：Mr. Falk。

3) 出席者：Mr. Baum, Ms. Dulugatz, Mr. Fenster, Ms. Liu, Ms. Sun；缺席者：Ms. Penn。

4) 会议内容：秘书宣读前次会议记录（8 月 21 日），主持人就其中的部分内容做了修正（correct a mistake）；应该是 Ms. Dulugatz 而不是 Ms. Penn 对仓库里的员工专用洗手间做调查，修正被通过；Mr. Fenster 对办公室员工所做的调查进行总结，他将就其写一份报告递交董事会。

5) 下次会议：10 月 22 日（时间地点相同）。

6) 会议结束时间：下午 5:50。

Section 6
Job Advertisements and Dismissal Letters
招聘启事和解聘函

6.1 Lead-In Introduction（导入介绍）

A: Job Advertisements

A job advertisement is for hiring employees. To find good employees, you have to write a clear and complete job description listing required skills as well as personality traits and preferred experience. It notes which skills and experience are mandatory and which are preferred.

B: Dismissal Letters

When an employee is dismissed from his/her job, the company would offer him/her a dismissal letter. It is an official notice that an employee has been fired from his/her job.

6.2 Guidelines for Writing (写作指南)

A: Job Advertisement

In general, a job advertisement has four main parts.

1) company description
2) job description
3) requirements/qualifications
4) contact information

New Employees Wanted

ABC Co., Ltd. (公司名称): ABC is _____

Sales Representatives (职位): Number: 4 Persons (人数)

Job Description (职位描述): _____

Key Attributes (职位要求): _____

Contact Information (联系方式):

Tel:　　　　Fax:　　　　Website:　　　　E-mail:

B: Dismissal Letter

Generally, a dismissal letter also consists of four parts.

1) Express regret of dismissal.
2) State the facts of dismissal.
3) Explain the reasons of dismissal. (This part is very important. The reasons should be reasonable and convincing and cannot hurt the other's self-esteem.)
4) Use a few words of encouragement as the ending.

6.3 Sample Study (范例学习)

Sample 1: A Job Advertisement

Sales Manager Wanted

We are a famous producer of new building materials in China. *With the fast growth of the company*[1], we are *recruiting*[2] a sales manager.

Applicants[3] must have the following qualifications for the position:

1. *College diploma or above*[4] in marketing, economics or a related field;

2. At least 3 years of work experience in similar positions;
3. Good knowledge in sales and computer operations;
4. Reliable, *self-motivated*[5] and good analytical skills;
5. Excellent leadership and communication skills;
6. Good command of spoken & written English is preferable.

  The salary for this position is up to RMB 5,000 + benefits

  Please apply in your own handwriting with full English resume and recent photo to xxz@yahoo.com

Notes

1. with the fast growth of the company 可译为"随着公司的快速发展…"。
2. recruit *v.* 招聘，征募；吸收某人为新成员；动员……（提供帮助）；雇用
   e.g.: Firms are now keen to hold on to the people they recruit.
   各公司现在都急切地想要留住招聘来的员工。
3. applicant *n.* 申请人，求职人；请求者
4. college diploma or above 大学或以上学历
5. motivated *adj.* 有动机的，有目的的；有积极性的。self-motivated 可译为"自我激励的"。
   e.g.: The company screened out applicants motivated only by money.
   该公司剔除了那些一心向钱看的申请者。

Sample 2: A Job Advertisement

Personal Assistant/ Secretary

  Required to work for the *Chief Executive*[1] of a new Company *involved*[2] in film and television industry. Requirements include:

◇ Ability as well as *initiative*[3] to work on your own and to develop the position to its full potential;

◇ Good *administrative*[4] and secretarial skills;

◇ Being active, creative and innovative is a plus;

◇ Experience in the film and television industry would be useful, but not essential;

  Good salary, *negotiable*[5] according to age and experience.

  Resume together with a recent photograph and a contact telephone number should be sent to the following address: Mr. Cynthia Kuan, 12 Redstar Square, London EC2 5 BE

Notes

1. chief executive 行政长官；董事长
2. involve in 参与；陷入，牵扯到；涉及
   - e.g.: They expostulated with him about the risk involved in his plan.
     他们指出他的计划有风险，劝他放弃.
3. initiative *n.* 主动权；首创精神；*adj.* 起始的；主动的；自发的
   - e.g.: These workers are able to sort out problems on their own initiative.
     这些工人能主动解决问题。
4. administrative *adj.* 管理的，行政的
   - e.g.: Other industries have had to sack managers to reduce administrative costs.
     其他行业只得精简管理人员以减少行政开支。
5. negotiable *adj.* 可通过谈判解决的；可协商的
   - e.g.: The terms of employment are negotiable. 雇用的条件可以协商。

Sample 3: A Dismissal Letter

June 15, 2020

Dear Allan,

  I am sorry to be the one to tell you this, but your service will no longer be required. However, your pay will continue for two full months. The time is based on your years of service.

  We have repeatedly asked you to put more effort and willingness into your work. We believe you have the *potential*[1] to do a *competent*[2] job; but your last 3 reports were late, incomplete and *inaccurate*[3], and therefore useless to our managers who rely on these reports for making decisions.

  Perhaps you should seek a job that is less demanding and has less *critical*[4] deadlines. I am confident you will soon find a work more suited to your abilities.

  Sincerely

  Tom Madden

Notes

1. potential *n.* 潜力，潜能
   - e.g.: There is enormous, acknowledged and untapped potential in the Indian stock markets.
     印度的股票市场蕴含着巨大的、公认的、尚未挖掘出来的潜力。
2. competent *adj.* 有能力的，能胜任的；能干的，称职的；足够的，充足的；有决定权的

e. g. : Make sure the firm is competent to carry out the work.
要确保这家公司有能力完成这项工作。

3. inaccurate *adj.* 有错误的；不精密的；不正确的；不准确

e. g. : The reports were based on inaccurate information.
这些报告所依据的是不准确的信息。

4. critical *adj.* 批评的，爱挑剔的；关键的；严重的；极重要的

e. g. : Environmentalists say a critical factor in the city's pollution is its population.
环境保护主义者说造成该城市污染问题的一个关键因素是其人口数量。

Sample 4: A Dismissal Letter

To: Francis Qiu, General Office

From: Marc Morgan, Director of Personnel

Date: June 30, 2020

Mr. Qiu,

Subject: **Terminating**[1] Engagement

You may already know that the Directors of the company will soon have finished the reorganization of the business and that this will result in a decrease in staff. I am sorry to inform you that your position is one that will shortly become **redundant**[2], and that your services will not continue after the end of this month.

We have no cause of complaint against you; **on the contrary**[3], we are quite satisfied with your service during the three years. The **reduction**[4] of staff is entirely due to business **doldrums**[5]. You will of course be entitled to a **redundancy payment**[6]. In your case you will be given one month's salary for every year of service with the company. Besides, we shall be pleased to provide any prospective employer with **testimonial**[7] of your character and ability.

Please contact me if you have any questions.

Sincerely

Marc Morgan
Director of Personnel

Notes

1. terminate *v.* 结束；使终结；解雇

e. g. : In the memo, you should also address the chief arguments for terminating the program and rebut them. 在备忘录里面你也必须提到终止该计划的论点，

并加以反驳。

2. redundant *adj.* 多余的，过剩的；被解雇的，失业的；冗长的，累赘的

   e.g.: In the sentence "She lives alone by herself", the word "alone" is redundant.

   "她独自一人生活"，在此句子里，"独自"这个词是多余的。

3. on the contrary   正相反

4. reduction *n.* 减少；下降；缩小

   e.g.: Cost reduction programs are often triggered by a drop in profits.

   降低成本计划的提出，往往是由利润下降引起的。

5. doldrums *n.* 忧郁；无生气，沉闷；赤道无风带；景气停滞；情绪低落

   e.g.: The industry remains in the doldrums, according to official figures published today. 根据今天官方公布的数字，这个行业仍不景气。

6. redundancy payment   解雇费；失业金；解雇津贴；裁员赔偿

7. testimonial *n.* 证明书；推荐书

   e.g.: The boy looking for a job has testimonial from his teacher and his former employer. 那个找工作的小伙子有他的老师和以前的雇主的推荐信。

6.4　Useful Phrases and Expressions（常用短语和表达）

1) proficient in English and Mandarin   能熟练运用英语和普通话
2) good at developing new business relationships   善于发展新的业务关系
3) good communication skills   良好的交际技能
4) ability to work in a team under pressure   能够在压力下进行团队工作
5) person with ability plus flexibility   有能力及适应力强的人
6) enthusiasm and organized working habits are more important than experience   有工作热情和有条不紊的办事习惯，经验不拘
7) ability to communicate in English   会用英语进行沟通
8) able to speak Mandarin and Cantonese   会说普通话和粤语
9) possessing computer operating skill is advantageous   有计算机操作技术者尤佳
10) good at operating the Windows   精通计算机 Windows 系统的操作
11) I regret having to tell you…

    It is with deep regret that I must inform you…

    I am sorry to be the one to tell you …   很抱歉/遗憾地通知您……

6.5　Typical Sentences（典型例句）

1) We are a famous producer of new building materials in China.

   （我们是中国著名的新型建筑材料生产商。）

2) Applicants must have the following qualifications for the position.
（应聘者须拥有以下资格。）

3) Being active, creative and innovative is a plus. （思想活跃，有首创和革新精神尤佳）

4) Good command of spoken & written English is preferable.
（有良好英文说、写能力者优先考虑）

5) Please apply in your own handwriting with full English resume and recent photo to the following address. （请亲自誊写详细的英文简历并附上近照寄至以下地址。）

6) Resume together with a recent photograph and a contact telephone number should be sent to the following address. （个人简历同近照一张及联系电话须寄往以下地址。）

7) I am sorry to be the one to tell you this, but your service will no longer be required. （很抱歉由我来告诉你这个消息：我们将不再需要你的服务。）

8) We shall be pleased to provide any prospective employer with testimonial of your character and ability. （我们愿意为你未来的雇主提供你性格和能力的证明。）

9) I am confident you will soon find work a more suited to your abilities.
（我相信你很快能找到更合适你能力的工作。）

10) We wish you well in your endeavor. （祝你一切顺利。）

6.6　Training and Practice（操练与实践）

6.6.1　Complete the following sentences with one of the given words. Change the forms if necessary.

employment	in one's endeavor	(be) satisfied with
interview	proficient	command of
recruit	qualifications	prospective employer
personality	due to	(be) familiar with

1) Mary is _____ in English and Mandarin.
2) Applicants must have the following _____ for the position.
3) Please call 020-87314839 for an _____.
4) A stable _____ and high sense of responsibility are desirable.
5) I wish you the best in your future _____.
6) We are quite _____ your service during the three years.
7) The reduction of staff is entirely _____ business doldrums.
8) We wish you will _____.
9) With fast growth of the company, we are _____ a sales manager.
10) We shall be pleased to provide any _____ with testimonial of your character and ability.

Module Three >> Writings for Administrative Documents

商务办公及行政文书

6.6.2 Supply the missing words in the blanks of the following letter. The first letters are given.

Market Assistant Wanted

Market Assistant

R ___(1)___ :

◇ Responsible for the local **m** ___(2)___ of marketing and sales activities **a** ___(3)___ to instructions from head office.

◇ Collect **r** ___(4)___ information for the head office.

◇ Develop relationship with local media and customers.

R ___(5)___ :

◇ College **d** ___(6)___ or above with good English skills (speaking and writing).

◇ With basic idea of sales and marketing, related **e** ___(7)___ is preferred.

◇ Working experience in an **i** ___(8)___ organization is a must.

◇ Good **c** ___(9)___ and presentation skills.

Please call 0510-5807123-3629 for an **i** ___(10)___ .

6.6.3 Put the following English into Chinese or Chinese into English.

1) 我很抱歉告诉你我们将不再需要你的服务。

2) 应聘者须拥有以下资格。

3) 有良好的交际技能，善于发展新的业务关系。

4) Computer operating skill is advantageous and working experience in foreign company is preferable.

5) Please apply in your own handwriting in English resume and recent photo to the following address.

6) I am confident that you will soon find a work more suited to your abilities.

7) 思想活跃，有首创和革新精神尤佳。

8) 我们是中国著名的新型建筑材料生产商。

9) We shall be pleased to provide any prospective employer with testimonial of your character and ability.

10) We wish you well in your endeavor.

6.6.4 Writing tasks.

Task 1: You are required to write a Job Advertisement according to the following instructions given in Chinese.

Message:

四季酒店（Four Seasons Hotel）因发展需要，欲招聘一名中国区驻地经理 Station

Managers（China）

  电子邮箱：recruit@fshotel.com

  要求：

  1）大专以上学历，毕业于酒店管理、餐饮管理或相关专业；

  2）在餐饮行业有至少三年以上的管理层工作经验，有国外工作经验者可优先考虑；

  3）有较高的表达沟通能力和人际交往能力；

  4）敏锐的分析能力和优秀的领导技巧；

  5）较强的中英文写作和对话技巧（普通话）；

  6）精通 Microsoft Office。

Task 2: Write a dismissal letter according to the following information.

Message:

中友光学仪器公司（Zhong You Optical Instruments Company）因使用生产过程自动控制系统（the automatic control system of the production process）需要裁减一批员工，其中包括林强。请以董事长 Mr. Carol 的名义写一封解雇信。

Section 7
Job Applications and Resumes
求职信和求职简历

7.1 Lead-In Introduction（导入介绍）

A: Job Applications

A job application letter is a letter written by person who is looking for a job. It aims to make oneself known and accepted by the employer. In the letter, you are marketing your skills, abilities and knowledge. It is mainly used when you are applying for a job and asking for an interview.

B: Resumes

A curriculum vita, also known as a resume in American English, is a kind of written form which includes education, experience, skills, and accomplishments etc., and is used to apply for jobs. A resume is an outline of the highlights of your business and academic careers. It serves as a written inventory of your strengths and qualifications, and provides a window into your professional history. It is one of the most important documents for your job search.

7.2 Guidelines for Writing（写作指南）

A: Job Applications

A job application letter should be concise and to the point of the matter. An effective job application letter should include the three parts stated below:

- In the opening part, tell the addressee where you have heard about his product or company and explain why you write this letter.
- In the following part, introduce yourself, show your identity and personal data, and also show your determination of applying for the job.
- In the closing part, declare that you hope to have a chance to be interviewed and tell the interviewer your available time for the interview. Remember to close your letter with appreciation and a request for an early reply.

B: Resumes

A complete resume consists of the following contents, but some contents can be omitted according to different job requirements.

- Personal Data, such as name, gender, nationality, marital status, height and weight, date of birth, place of birth, etc.
- Contact Information, such as address, telephone, mobile, E-mail, etc.
- Objective, explain what position you are looking for, such as secretary, manager, ECO, etc.
- Specific Information, such as educational background, working experience, professional activities, achievements, hobbies, references, etc.

7.3 Sample Study (范例学习)

Sample 1: A Job Application

Apr. 23, 2020

Dear Sirs,

Your advertisement for a Network Maintenance Engineer on China Daily of May 15 *interested me most*[1], because the position that you described sounds exactly like the kind of job I am seeking.

According to *the job advertisement*[2], your position requires a good university degree, Bachelor or above in Computer Science or the equivalent field and proficiency in Computer. I feel that I am *competent*[3] for this position. I will graduate from Zhongshan University this year with a Master's degree. My studies have included courses in Computer Control and Management and I designed a control simulation system developed with Microsoft Visual studio and SQL Server.

During my education, I have grasped the principles of my major subject area and gained practical skills. Not only have I passed CET-6, but more importantly I can communicate fluently in English. *My ability to write and speak English gets to a high level*[4].

I shall welcome a personal interview at your convenience[5]. *Enclosed is my resume*[6] and if there is any additional information you require, please contact me.

Thank you for your time and I am looking forward to you early reply.

Sincerely yours,

Alice

Alice

Notes

1. interested me most 本人极感兴趣
2. the job advertisement 意为"招聘广告"
3. competent *adj.* 有能力的，能胜任的；能干的，称职的

   e. g.：Make sure the firm is competent to carry out the work.

   （要确保这家公司有能力完成这项工作。）
4. My ability to write and speak English gets to a high level.

   （我的英语口语与写作能力达到了很高的水平。）
5. I shall welcome a personal interview at your convenience. （我希望在您方便的时候能有个个人的面试。）在求职信的末尾，可以用这样的话来表达自己的希望。

   a personal interview 个人的面试

   at your convenience 在方便的时候
6. Enclosed is my resume. （随信附上我的简历。）在信函中附加简历，可以这样说明一下。

Sample 2: A Job Application

Nov. 23, 2020

Dear Sirs,

I'm writing to you to look if you have a vacancy on your staff for an assistant accountant[1].

My education and experience give me the confidence to apply for this position. I graduated from Jinan University of Finance and Economics, majoring in accounting. I have been working in the *costing*[2] department of Star Company for the past five years. The only reason for my seeking another employment is that Star Company is moving to a new location, which is very far away from my home. It would inconvenient for me to go to work every day.

Attached is my *curriculum vita*[3], together with the names of my *referees*[4]. *If there* is some opportunity of a vacancy occurring in the near future, I would greatly appreciate being given an interview[5]. You may call me at 020 – 87614523 or E-mail me at Wanfen00@sina.com.

I look forward to your early reply.

Yours truly,
Wanfen
Wanfen

Notes

1. I'm writing to you to look if you have a vacancy on your staff for an assistant accountant. (我写信给你是想看看你们是否有一个助理会计师的职位空缺。)
   在未知对方公司是否有职位空缺时，可以这样写来表示寻求工作的机会。
   vacancy *n.* 空缺、空位
   accounting *n.* 会计
   assistant accounting 助理会计师
2. costing *n.* 成本核算
3. curriculum vita 个人简历，相当于 resume
4. referees *n.* 推荐人。
5. If there is some opportunity of a vacancy occurring in the near future, I would greatly appreciate being given an interview. (如果在不久的将来有一个职位空缺的机会，我会非常感谢接受面试。)
   在此类信函的末尾，再次申明若有工作机会，请予以告知。

Sample 3: A Resume

Résumé [1]

Personal Data:
Name: Zhang Cheng   Gender: Male
Nationality: Chinese   Marital Status: Married
Date of birth: 15th July, 1979
Place of birth: Heping District, Zhongshan

Contact Information:
Address: Room 350, Block 4, 549 Guangyuan Avenue, Guangzhou
Tel: 020-32145678
Mobile: 13785665986
Objectives: Vice-office manager of Guangzhou Commercial Bureau

Educational Background:

  2003-2004: Zhongshan Finance College, Specialty: marketing

  1996-1998: Zhongshan Vocational School

  1990-1996: Zhongshan NO. 1 Middle School

Work Experience:

  2009-present: Guangzhou Commercial Bureau Assistant to office manager

  2004 — 2009: Qingdao Department Store:

    Shoes & Caps Dept. Salesmen

    Shoes & Caps Dept.

    Head of salesmen,

    supervising 7 sales assistants in all

Achievements: Excellent salesman of Qingdao Department Store;

  Model worker of Heping District

Hobbies: light music, sports and traveling

7.4 Useful Phrases and Expressions（常用短语和表达）

1) apply for… 申请

2) in respond/answer to 作为回复

3) job vacancy 职位空缺

4) job advertisement 招聘广告

5) major in 主修

6) a mastery of… 精通，掌握

7) personal interview 个人的面试

8) curriculum vita 个人简历（同"résumé"）

7.5 Typical Sentences（典型例句）

1) In answer to your advertisement in Guangzhou Daily for an English teacher, I would like to apply for the position.
（拜读《广州日报》上贵公司招聘英语教师的广告，本人特此备函应征该职位。）

2) I have learned from China Daily that your firm is looking for an accountant and I would like to apply for this job.
（我从《中国日报》得知贵公司正在寻找会计，我想要申请这个职位。）

3) I am writing in response to the advertisement you placed on job 51.com for an engineer. I have pleasure in applying for the post.
（拜读昨天51招聘网上贵单位招聘工程师的广告，本人特此备函应征该职位。）

4) Born in Hunan in 1978, I graduated from Peking University majoring in Law.
   (本人于1978生于湖南,毕业于北京大学,专业是法学。)
5) I have been working in CCTV since my graduation.
   (自从毕业后我一直在中央电视台工作。)
6) I believe I have the appropriate qualifications and experience for the post.
   (我相信我有合适的资格和经验去从事这份工作。)
7) I am experienced in operating computers. I have a fair mastery of English, both spoke and written. (我在计算机操作方面很有经验,精通英语口语和写作。)
8) I have passed College English Test Band 4. (我通过了大学英语四级考试。)
9) I would like to work as a programmer for a large insurance company in order to accumulate my programming experience.
   (为了增加我的编程经验,我想在一家大型的保险公司寻找一份编程员的工作。)
10) I would like to work for a large company where my proven ability can be led to full play. (我希望能为更大的一家公司工作,以使我的能力得到更充分的发挥。)
11) I should be glad to have a personal interview.
    (如果能有个个人的面试,我会非常高兴。)
12) I should welcome a personal interview at your convenience.
    (希望能在您方便的时候有个个人的面试。)
13) Enclosed please find a resume, and a photo. (随信附上一份简历和照片。)
14) The enclosed resume will adequately show you my qualifications.
    (随附的个人简历足以向您表明我的资历。)

7.6　Training and Practice（操练与实践）

7.6.1　Complete the following sentences with one of the given words. Change the forms if necessary.

convenient	in person	look forward to
resume	in detail	qualify sb for…
employment	in response to	additional information
application	apply for	be of benefit to

1) I am writing _____ to your advertisement placed on TV for a business interpreter.
2) The enclosed _____ will adequately show you my qualifications.
3) May I have the opportunity of seeing you _____ so that I may discuss this application with you _____?
4) I am confident that my qualifications and experience will _____ your company.
5) I am sure my educational background and working experience will _____ the job you

advertised.

6) I wish to _____ the post of University English Teacher.

7) I would appreciate the opportunity to interview with you at a _____ time.

8) I am desirous of leaving the _____ in order to improve my position and have more responsibility.

9) Enclosed is my resume and if there is any _____ you require, please contact me.

10) I am _____ to hearing from you shortly.

7.6.2　Supply the missing words in the blanks of the following letter. The first letters are given.

> Dear Sirs,
>
> 　　From your **a** ___(1)___ in yesterday's China Daily, I learnt that your company has an **o** ___(2)___ for an experienced consultant in China. Please consider me a **c** ___(3)___ .
>
> 　　I am sending you my CV including career **d** ___(4)___ and personal background knowledge. You will see that I grew up in China and I got an MBA **d** ___(5)___ from Harvard University in 2017, and therefore I have a good knowledge of both Chinese and English. Besides, I have had several years' working **e** ___(6)___ in China, so I am confident I am **q** ___(7)___ for the job.
>
> 　　I would be glad to come to your office to have an **i** ___(8)___ whenever it is **c** ___(9)___ .
>
> 　　If you would give me a phone, you may call me at 023-59873761.
>
> 　　Yours **s** ___(10)___
>
> 　　Xiao Lin

7.6.3　Put the following English into Chinese or Chinese into English.

1) 本人欲应聘在贵公司网站的广告栏中招聘的销售助理一职。

2) In reply to your advertisement for a business secretary in yesterday's China Daily, I respectfully offer my services for the position.

3) 我愿意接受贵方正常的工资标准。

4) I would like to work for a large company where my proven ability can be led to full play.

5) You will find from the attached resume that I am a diligent person.

6) I hope I may have the privilege of meeting you so that I can discuss my qualifications. I can come to your company at your convenience.

7) Because of experience in accounting, I feel I have the qualifications you describe in yesterday's newspaper.

8) 这份工作不仅具有挑战性，而且有更多的机会提高自身能力。

9）如果贵公司现在有职位空缺或者不久会有，请通知我，我将不胜感激。

10）预先感谢贵公司的关照，请早日回复为盼。

7.6.4　Writing tasks.

Task 1: Write a resume according to the following information.

Message:

姓名：约翰·史密斯　国籍：美国

目前所在地址：美国加利福尼亚州洛杉矶市高街506号

电话：101-812-475866

出生日期：1978年5月9号　出生地点：纽约

已婚，生有一女。1991-1994年，在纽约Walshall Elementary School学习，1994-1997年在洛杉矶Lincoln High School学习，1997-2001年在University of California的Law School学习。上大学期间始终学习法语，具有很好的阅读能力，且擅长笔译，并能流利地交谈。从2001-2006年在加利福尼亚大学任助教，2006年至今在该大学任讲师。希望寻求一份律师工作，原因是本人一直渴望做律师，因为这工作不仅有趣，而且有助于提高工作能力，薪金也很诱人。

Task 2: Write a job application letter according to the following information.

Objective：应聘高级文员

Message:

1）在今日报纸看到招聘广告，有意应聘这个职位。

2）个人信息：三年前毕业于天津外国语学院的英语系。在大学里，我最喜欢英语、广告与公关课程。此外，在大学期间，除学习英语，还在ABC外贸有限公司做了三年文秘。跳槽的主要原因是想向这样优秀的跨国公司学习更多的经验。

3）贵公司如对我的申请惠予考虑，本人将竭诚工作。期望你们尽早回复。如果有必要，我可以提供其他相关信息。随函附寄去我的个人简历，毕业证。

Section 8
Certificates
证明信

8.1　Lead-In Introduction（导入介绍）

A certificate is an official document stating that particular facts are true. It can also be an official document that you receive when you have completed a course of study or training. It is usually used to attest to the truth of certain stated facts.

A letter of certification (much like a letter of certificate) is written to verify information, usually in the context of applying for something. For example somebody applying for a visitor visa to a foreign country may obtain a letter of certification from his place of employment verifying his intent.

Somebody in the business world may use a letter to certify a percentage of ownership in a company. A job applicant may use a letter from a friend or former employer as a reference — this is called a "Certification Letter of Knowing a Person".

8.2　Guidelines for Writing（写作指南）

Writing a letter of certification (or a letter of certificate) should follow the principles below:

• Be specific with information, dates, and titles — for a certification has to be accurate.

• Include any relevant supporting documents as evidence that what is being certified is true.

• Write in a formal manner because these letters will invariably be used in a formal setting.

8.3　Sample Study（范例学习）

Sample 1: A Working Certificate

Sep. 19, 2020
To: British Embassy

To Whom It May Concern[1]

Guang Dong Electronic Development Co. Ltd. was founded in 1995 with the registered capital of RMB 20,000,000. We mainly deal with electronic devices.

Mr. Zhao Jian has been working in our company since 2008. Due to his outstanding working behavior, Mr. Zhao was promoted to the post of marketing manager in 2013. Mr. Zhao has worked hard and had opened up market, which has made our company have a stable position despite keen competition. His annual salary is RMB 280,000.

For better development in the future, Mr. Zhao has decided to go to Britain for further study. Our company needs a highly-qualified manager, so we totally agree with his study plan and sincerely hope that Mr. Zhao can come back to our company for further work after finishing his study.

Please do not hesitate to contact us if you require any further information!

Hereby certified[2]!

Wang Liang
General Manager
Guang Dong Electronic Development Co. Ltd.

Notes

1. To Whom It May Concern. 致有关负责人
2. Hereby certified! 特此证明

Sample 2: A Certificate of Employment

Xiong Ying Electrical Equipment Co. Ltd.

Address: No. 63 Guangming Rd., Shijingshan District, Being, 100042

Tel: (010) 69811066　　Fax: (010) 69811065

February 11, 2020

To Whom It May Concern,

　　This is to certify that[1] Mr. Wu Jiang commenced to work with this company in August 2010 after having studied for four years in Beijing University. Mr. Wu Jiang's working experiences are as follows:

　　From 2010 to 2020 his employer has been Mr. Zhang Feng and his position has been the vice president of Xiong Ying Electrical Equipment Limited Company. Mr. Wu Jiang's duty is to be in charge of the production and the research and development of the new products. His income history in our company is as follows:

　　From 2010 to 2020 his salary has been 10,000 Yuan per Month. Year Bonus has been 50,000 Yuan. Year Annual Income: 170,000 Yuan. Personal income taxes have been deducted and the figures listed are net income after tax. *I would be happy to answer further inquiries about*[2] Mr. Wu Jiang's employment with our company.

　　Sincerely yours,

　　HuangTing

　　HuangTing

　　Manager of Personnel Department

Notes

1. This is to certify that... 意为"兹证明……"，经常置于证明信的开头。
2. I would be happy to answer further inquiries about...意思是"我很乐意回答关于……进一步的询问"这是一种客气和客套的表达方法，经常作为证明信的结束语。这句话也可以表达为"For further enquiries, please feel free to contact me."

8.4　Useful Phrases and Expressions（常用短语和表达）

1) in contact with　与…联系
2) To Whom It May Concern　致有关负责人
3) hereby certified　特此证明
4) This is to certify that sb. (has/had/was) _____ as a _____（职务）+ at _____（单位）/doing（时间）　兹证明某人在某单位做某职务多少时间
5) sb. did _____ job (reliable, honest, hard working …)
   某人做_____工作（可靠，诚实，努力……）

8.5　Typical Sentences（典型例句）

1) Due to his outstanding working behavior, Mr. Zhao was promoted to the position of marketing manager in 1996.
   （由于他出色的工作表现，赵先生于1996被提升为市场部经理。）

2) This is to certify that Mr. Wu Jiang commenced to work with this company in August 2010 after having studied for four years in Beijing University.
   （兹证明吴江先生在北京大学学习了四年后，从2010年8月开始在这家公司工作。）

3) Mr. Zhao has worked hard and opened up market, which has made our company have a stable position despite keen competition.
   （赵先生工作努力，开辟了广阔的市场，使公司在激烈竞争中有一个稳定的位置。）

4) Our company needs a highly-qualified manager, so we totally agree with his study plan and sincerely hope that Mr. Zhao can come back to our company for further work after finishing his study.（我们公司需要高素质的经理，所以我们完全同意他的学习计划，并衷心希望赵先生能在完成他的学业后再回到本公司工作。）

5) Please do not hesitate to contact us if you require any further information!
   （如果您需要任何进一步的信息，请务必联系我们！）

6) Mr. Wu Jiang's duty is to be in charge of the production and the research and development of the new products.（吴先生的职责是负责生产和新产品的研发。）

7) Personal income taxes have been deducted and the figures listed are net income after tax.（个人所得税已扣除，所列数字是税后净收入。）

8) I would be happy to answer further inquiries about Mr. Wu Jiang's employment with our company.（我很乐意回答关于吴先生在我们公司工作的问题。）

8.6 Training and Practice（操练与实践）

8.6.1 Filling in the Blanks according to the Chinese.

_____ (1. 身份证明)

June 5, 2020

_____ (2. 兹证明) that Ms Kate Smith, _____ (3. 美国国籍), female, aged 29, is an engineer of our factory. She _____ (4. 持有美国护照) and has registered temporary residence with the police station under _____ (5. 公安局) of the People's Municipal Government of Shanghai.

Yongjiu Bicycle Factory

8.6.2 Put the following English into Chinese or Chinese into English.

1) hereby certified

2) 有关负责人

3) Please do not hesitate to contact us if you require any further information!

4) Our company needs a highly-qualified manager, so we totally agree with his study plan and sincerely hope that Mr. Zhao can come back to our company for further work after finishing his study.

5) 个人所得税已扣除，所列数字是税后净收入。

6) 吴先生的职责是负责生产和新产品的研发。

8.6.3 Writing tasks.

Write a certificate letter according to the following information.

敬启者：

兹证明：张良先生，2011年9月至2020年7月，任我公司销售经理一职。

张良先生是一位精明能干（diligent）、极富创造力（creative）的经理，在他的领导下，我们公司产品畅销（sell well）多个国家，并获得了国际好评。他还有良好的团队意识，懂得分工（delegate）与合作。

张良先生在我们公司的年薪是30万人民币，每月的房屋补贴（house allowance）是4千元。2019年，由于业绩出色，他获得了4万元的奖金（bonus）。

如有其他不明之处，请随时和我联系。

此致

林洋

ABC公司首席执行官

2020年9月20日

Section 9
IOUs and Receipts
借据和收据

9.1 Lead-In Introduction（导入介绍）

IOU is the abbreviation for "I owe you". An IOU is a written promise that you will pay back money or goods that you have borrowed. A receipt is a piece of paper that you get from someone as proof that they have received money or goods from you. In our daily life and business, money or things are often borrowed or lent. In this case, it is necessary for people to write an IOU or a receipt, because they can be important legal evidence.

9.2 Guidelines for Writing（写作指南）

The layouts of IOUs and receipts are like those of notes. There are two kinds of IOUs, informal and formal. Both of these layouts should follow the principles stated below.

• The full names of both the lender and the borrower, the sum of money, or detailed names of things and date should be contained.

• The sum of money should be written both in English words and Arabic numbers or just in English words in order not to be rewritten on purpose.

Layout 1: Formal IOU

```
                                                    Date of borrowing
    Lender's name
    Body _____
    _____.
                                                    Borrower's name
```

Layout 2: Informal IOU

```
                                                    Date of borrowing
        Money or things borrowed,
        Body _____
        _____.
                                                    Borrower's name
```

Layout 3: Receipt

Date of receiving

Body _____

_____.

Lender's name

9.3　Sample Study（范例学习）

Sample 1: A Formal IOU

Feb. 2, 2020

To Mr. Smith[1],

　　IOU three thousand yuan only (RMB), to be paid within three months from this date *with interest at six percent annum*[2].

Lin Qiang

Notes

1. to Mr. Smith: 借款收据一般要写抬头（有时非正式的可省略），而借物借据和收据则可省略抬头。
2. with interest at six percent annum：按年利 6 厘计息

Sample 2: An Informal IOU

Nanjing, July 18, 2020

RMB ￥100,000

　　Two years after this date we promise to pay Mr. Xiao Hua back *the sum*[1] of one hundred thousand yuan (RMB 100,000) *with annual interest at two percent (2%)*[2].

Wang Fang

Li Xiaodong

Notes

1. the sum：总数
2. annual interest at two percent (2%)：按年利 2 厘计息

Sample 3: A Receipt

July 2nd, 2020

Received from Mr. Jerome Kern the sum of EIGHT THOUSAND YUAN only (RMB 8,000), being the rent for the month of June 2017 for the premises occupied by him at the No. 207 Zhongshan Road, Zhuhai.

Wu Ming

9.4　Useful Phrases and Expressions（常用短语和表达）

1) IOU "I owe you.（我欠你）"的缩写，用以表示"欠条""借据"的意思。

2) Borrowed from ＿＿（sb）＿＿（sth）．今借到某人某物

3) Received of/from…　今收到

4) Return on within ＿＿＿＿（date）＿＿＿＿（at the rate/ interest at…%） 某天归还……

（如果是借钱，要写明以百分之多少利息归还）

5) …to be paid back…　归还

9.5　Typical Sentences（典型例句）

1) With interest at six percent per annum.（年息6厘。）

2) Four years after this date we promise to pay Mr. Liu Hua the sum of one hundred thousand yuan (RMB 100,000).

（我们承诺自即日起4年后归还刘华先生人民币10万元整。）

3) With annual interest at two percent (2%).（按年利2厘计息。）

4) To be paid back within two months from this date（自即日起2个月内还清。）

5) Received from Miss Wang Fei the amount of RMB five thousand yuan (RMB 5,000).

（今收到王菲小姐人民币伍仟元（￥5,000）。）

6) Received from Mr. Lin Bo the under mentioned goods: one computer and two books.

（今收到林波先生送来的下列物品：一台计算机和两本书。）

9.6　Training and Practice（操练与实践）

9.6.1 Write a receipt by filling in the following blanks according to the information given in Chinese.

Information: 兹收到 BMW 公司工程部 2020 年 7 月份工资 6,500 元整，此据。陈建国，2020 年 8 月 10 日。

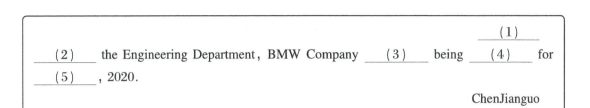

(2)　　 the Engineering Department, BMW Company 　(3)　 being 　(4)　 for 　(5)　, 2020.

ChenJianguo

9.6.2 Put the following English into Chinese or Chinese into English.

1) Three years after this date we promise to pay Mr. Liu Huan the sum of two hundred thousand yuan (RMB 200,000).

2) 今收到章华小姐人民币500元整。

3) with annual interest at three percent (3%)

4) 自即日起6个月内还清。

5) We jointly promise to pay Miss Helen Green back the sum of three thousand US dollars with annual interest at nine percent (9%).

6) Received from Lin Hua $1,000 (one thousand dollars only) in full payment of the loan lent to him on May 1st, 2020 plus interest.

9.6.3 Writing tasks.

Task 1: Read the information below carefully and use the proper information to write an IOU.

Message:

李兵欠格林先生5,000美元，将在立字据起2年内还清，年息为3厘。

Task 2: Write a receipt for the situation given below.

Message:

今收到布鲁斯·华盛顿先生归还2012年7月8日借款本息共计1,096美元（壹千零玖拾陆元整）。

收款人：詹姆斯·约翰逊

Writings for General Business Activities
一般商务文书

Module Briefing

Writing is involved in every part of business, so the ability to write effectively is a valuable business asset. Usually, to inform and persuade is the main function of general business writing.

Messages to inform convey the vast amount of information needed to complete the everyday operations of the business — explaining market potentials, stating business development and business proposals, explaining the functions and instructions of products and introducing corporations, etc. In addition to providing information, some business messages, such as well-designed product brochures, questionnaires, publicity and advertisements, etc., are intended to influence the reader's attitudes and actions and get responses from them.

In this module, you are going to be trained to write for all these general business activities.

Objectives

Upon the accomplishment of this module, you should be able to convey general business messages correctly in written English, make the receiver understand and secure the desired response.

Focus and Difficult Points

1. To get familiar with useful expressions and sentences used in general business writing
2. To acquire skills in writing general business documents

Section 1
Business Reports
商业报告或商情调研报告

1.1 Lead-In Introduction（导入介绍）

A business report is an impartial, objective and planned presentation to serve some business purpose such as giving information, making analysis or providing recommendations about a particular business project. Meanwhile, a business report is also a formal or even official document that investigates, selects and interprets information by using appropriate techniques for a stated purpose. It may be a record of events or it can be a long text discussing in detail a certain project of national importance.

Frequently a report tries to persuade the target reader to agree with a stated message and to make him or her take an action desired by the writer or the sponsor of the report. So the audience of a report shall be those who are interested in the project. In a word, the purpose of a report is to inform someone about a particular subject, and the information should be presented in an ordered way.

There are two kinds of business reports, formal and informal. A formal report is used to document the results of an experiment, a design, or to pass on any type of information. Marketing reports, investigation reports, feasibility reports, etc. are usually written in a formal style. Informal reports are for internal use, particularly within departments and for dealing with routine issues. Memorandum format is often used for these reports.

1.2 Guidelines for Writing（写作指南）

Before we write a business report, we shall define the problem, analyze the reader, collect, arrange and interpret information, and construct the outline. Since a report is written to inform someone about a particular subject, it should be concise, factual, impartial, objective and written from the reader's perspective. Statistics and percentages are often used to express facts.

Generally speaking, a formal business report may contain the following parts:

- Title (or Title Section): may include the report name, author name, and date.
- Terms of Reference (or Executive Summary / Introduction): explain what the report is mainly about.
- Procedure (or Methodology): explains how the information is gathered.
- Findings: present ideas and facts.
- Conclusions: explain and discuss the facts/ideas.
- Recommendations: put forward suggestions for actions to be taken based on the findings.
- Appendix: may include all of your sources and research information in detail.

Some reports may contain one or more of the optional parts, depending on the different situation of each writing requirement.

1.3 Sample Study（范例学习）

Sample 1: A Formal Report

Report on Last Quarter's Computer Sales

(Import and Export Limited Co., Ltd)

◆ Terms of reference

To analyze the sales of computers in *domestic*[1] and international markets in the previous quarter (July, August and September of 2019), draw conclusions about the *prospects*[2] of the computer market and recommend any necessary action.

◆ Procedure

Information of the domestic market was obtained from the Sales Dept., and that of the international market was from the Financial Dep. and from all our overseas agents and representatives. Besides, some major customers were interviewed.

◆ Findings

In general, the *sales volume*[3] of our company in the past quarter was better than expected. *It totaled as*[4] much as USD 7bn. Compared with the same period of last year, it rose by 30 percent. But, compared with the quarter before the previous one, it declined by 10 percent.

1. In the domestic markets

The sales in coastal cities like Shanghai, Xiamen, and Guangzhou etc. sharply increased because of the quick economic development in those areas. But the sales in inland cities, on the other hand, were not as good as we had *anticipated*[5]. People there have not fully realized the importance of computers in business, science, and even in their daily life. Further, their *purchasing power*[6] is also limited. Nevertheless, in the western part of this country, the sales were increasing *dramatically*[7] because those areas have been developing rather fast. The Chinese government focuses on the development of the western part of the country. In addition, our products sold surprisingly well in the three provinces in Northeast China. The sales there reached USD 3m. This is because the central government *attaches*[8] importance to developing the three provinces as well.

2. In the international markets

Sales in the countries of Australia and New Zealand increased mainly due to their good economic situation and excellent purchasing power.

In America, to our great surprise, the sales of *laptops*[9] were declining to some extent. And the desktops sold better than laptops.

In the Russian market, our sales were increasing gradually. This was because the workforce there worked especially hard. What's more, the political situation in Russia is becoming better, and so is the economic situation.

◆ Conclusions

1. There is a good prospect in coastal markets in China.

2. The Russian market is *promising*[10] because of the relatively stable political and economic situations there.

◆ Recommendations

1. Some capable sales representatives must be sent as soon as possible to the inland cities of the country to expand more markets.

2. In the American market, it is suggested that some sales representatives be transferred from the USA to the Canadian market since the purchasing power in the USA has been decreasing slightly.

3. Some managers of the overseas markets should get trained, not only in terms of sales management and sales skills, but also in getting used to foreign cultures and languages.

Notes

1. domestic   of one's own country 国内的
2. prospect   a probability or chance for future success, esp. as based on present work or aptitude 前景
3. sales volume   销售量
4. It totaled as   合计为, total 这里是动词，作 "总数达……，合计" 解
5. anticipate   to foresee and act in advance of 预期
6. purchasing power   the amount of money that a person or group could spend 购买力
7. increase dramatically   戏剧化地增长，指增长很快，相当于：increase sharply
8. attach importance to   重视；着重于……；对……给予重视
9. laptop   a portable computer small enough to use in your lap 笔记本式计算机; desktop 台式计算机。
10. promising: showing promise of favorable development or future success 有前景的

Sample 2: An Informal Report

Report on Reducing Travel and Entertainment Cost

To: Robert Kastens, President
From: Stanley Lindberg, Director of Cost *Accounting*[1] Services
Date: March 3, 2020
Subject: Report on Reducing Travel and Entertainment Cost

　　Here is the report you requested on Feb. 28, 2020 *regarding*[2] the company's travel and entertainment costs.

　　Your suspicion was right. We spent too much on business travel in the past three years. Now they have become the second largest expense.

　　The solutions to the problem are obvious. We need to take some measures as follows to control the *expenses*[3].

　　Put someone in charge of business travel and *entertainment*[4].

　　Make a clear statement of our travel policy.

　　Install[5] an effective business travel control system.

　　Retain *business-oriented*[6] services that can *optimize*[7] our travel arrangements.

　　Change our attitude towards business travel and entertainment.

　　Thank you for giving me the opportunity to work on this assignment. If you have any questions about the report, please call me.

　　Yours sincerely,
　　John

Notes

1. accounting　会计；会计学
2. regarding　关于
3. expense　花费，花销
4. entertainment　娱乐，消遣
5. install　设立，建立
6. business-oriented　以业务为导向的
7. optimize　使最优化，使尽可能有效

Sample 3: An Informal Report

Report on *Suitability*[1] of Ludova Technologies Slovensko (LTS)

◆ Introduction

The aim of this report is to assess whether the Ludova Technologies Slovensko Company would be a suitable supplier of electrical goods for us.

◆ Findings

A recent visit to the company showed that its facilities are quite old, which *results in*[2] a rather limited production capacity. Despite this, LTS produces an extensive range of high-quality electrical products including radios, CD players, cassette and video recorders.

However, the out-of-date machinery means lengthy delivery time of up to three months. This situation may change when the planned modernization takes place next year.

◆ Conclusion

At present LTS would not *be suitable for*[3] large orders requiring quick delivery.

◆ Recommendations

It is recommended that we remain *in contact with*[4] LTS and reconsider a supply contract once the factory modernization is completed.

Notes

1. suitability 合适，适合
   e. g.：We tried to assess his suitability for the job.
   我们想评估一下他是否适合这项工作。
2. result in 引起，导致
   e. g.：The flood resulted in a considerable reduction in production.
   这次水灾造成相当大的减产。
3. be suitable for 合适，适合
   e. g.：I don't think I should *be suitable for* the post. 我认为这个岗位对我不合适。
4. in contact with 与…联系

1.4 Useful Phrases and Expressions（常用短语和表达）

1）to analyze... 分析……
2）draw conclusions about...from... 从……得出关于……的结论
3）information was obtained from... 信息获得于……
4）it is suggested that... 建议……
5）the report concerns（explains）... 报告关于（解释）

6) the purpose of this report is to investigate (study) …
报告目的是调查（研究）……

7) the findings of the investigation indicate that… 调查结果显示……

8) the table (chart / graph / diagram / figure / statistics) shows (describes / illustrates) that… 图表说明……

9) the solutions to the problem are… 问题的解决方法是……

10) it would be advisable to … 是可取的

11) take some measures as follows… 采取以下措施…

12) we strongly recommend that … 我们强烈建议……

13) the main findings were as follows 主要调查结果如下

1.5　Typical Sentences（典型例句）

1) Several changes were put forward. （本报告提出了几处需要改进的地方。）

2) The enquiries/investigations have resulted in the following findings：
（此次调查的结果如下：）

3) The main findings were as follows: （主要调查结果如下：）

4) The table shows that the most significant items are as follows.
（图表显示以下这些是最有意义的数据。）

5) Those conclusions about sales decrease are drawn from the data as follows.
（关于销售下滑的这些结论是从以下数据获得的。）

6) Accordingly, I make the following recommendations. （鉴于此，我建议如下。）

7) On the basis of the research, I would like to make recommendations as follows.
（根据此次研究，我想做如下建议。）

8) A questionnaire was completed by those who were surveyed in this project.
（问卷是由项目中被调查者完成的。）

9) The information was mainly gained from manufacturers.
（这信息主要是从生产商那获悉的。）

10) We need to take some of the following measures to control the expenses.
（我们需要采取以下措施来控制开支。）

1.6　Training and Practice（操练与实践）

1.6.1　Translate the following sentences.

1) On the basis of the research, I would like to recommend that some measures be taken to cut the expenses.

2) The investigation indicates that purchasing power in the USA has been decreasing slightly. The major findings can be summarized as follows.

3) Here is a report about the decisions made by the Board of Directors for the May 2020 meeting.

4) The recommendation is based on the research I've done in the past three years, and I believe it will work well.

5）此报告旨在评估 ABC 科技公司是否可做我们的电器供应商。

6）这些信息主要是从生产商那里获悉的。

7）调查表明这类产品的市场正处于成长期。

8）在问卷调查中，我们主要调查人们喜欢什么类型的音乐和喜欢的原因。

1.6.2 Supply the missing words in the blanks of the following letter. The first letters are given.

Report on: Suitability of Executive Relocation Services (ERS)

I (1)

This **r** (2) aims to assess whether ERS meets Fenway's **n** (3) (see attached document) in relocating employees and their families to Dublin, Ireland.

F (4)

ERS offers a comprehensive house search service including Internet pre-viewing. Although it offers no partner employment service, ERS does place children in local schools. ERS also arranges all necessary documentation and offers full packing, storage and shipping **s** (5). ERS's costs compare favorably with competitors.

C (6)

It was concluded that ERS would fulfill most of our key needs.

R (7)

ERS was felt to offer a high quality service. However, it is **p** (8) that no final decision should be **m** (9) until other companies have also been considered.

◆ *Amanda Ramone*

Human **R** (10) Manager

1.6.3 Writing Tasks.

Situation: The company where Ms. Liu is working plans to launch a new project in the second half of 2020. The Board of Directors asks Mr. Mark Ford, the Marketing Manager of the company, to make an investigation on the staff members' opinions on this plan, and write a report analyzing the plan's possibilities. The report is needed before May 9, 2020, so as to be discussed in the next board meeting. During the past month, more than 200 staff members have been asked to write down some comments on the plan.

Now, write the report on the following findings.

1. "In recent years, our company has lost its advantages over its competitors. So we need to do something." (105 staff)

2. "We are not satisfied with the old pattern of production." (54 staff)
3. "The future is unknown and we'd better be conscious…" (29 staff)
4. "Does that mean we will take great risks on finance?…" (31 staff)

Section 2
Product Description Manuals and Instruction Manuals
产品描述、说明和使用手册

2.1 Lead-In Introduction（导入介绍）

Product description manuals or instruction manuals are written to advertise a specific product — its ingredients, functions, benefits, specifications etc. Meanwhile, they direct the customers how to use the product correctly. These descriptions and instructions may be printed on the package of the product or printed on a pamphlet.

2.2 Guidelines for Writing（写作指南）

In order to save the reader's time and energy, the manuals are usually written based on the following rules:
- Showing clearly what the product is.
- Listing information necessary for customers about the product.
- Being scientific, logical and easy to follow.
- Starting each direction with a verb that instructs the reader to do something.

2.3 Sample Study（范例学习）

Sample 1: Nature Made Fish Oil

Deep sea fish oil is a natural source of *EPA*, *DHA*[1], and biologically active *Omega-3 fatty acid*[2].

Supportive but not conclusive research shows that[3] the consumption of EPA, DHA and Omega-3 fatty acid may reduce the risk of *coronary*[4] heart disease. Omega-3 fatty acid also helps maintain *triglyceride*[5] levels. EPA, DHA and key Omega-3s are important for heart health. Nature Made Fish Oil supply comes from deep ocean waters, not from farm raised fish.

No *Artificial*[6] colors
No Artificial flavors
No *Preservatives*[7]

Contains: Fish and Soy.

Other ingredients: *Gelatin*, *Glycerin*, Water, *Tocopherol*[8]

To use: Take 2 *softgels*[9] daily with a meal.

Caution: If you are pregnant or nursing, or taking medication, facing surgery, having bleeding problems, undergoing any other treatment which may affect the ability of the blood to *clot*[10], consult your physician before taking this product.

To store: Keep the bottle tightly closed. Store in a cool and dry place, out of reach of children.

Notes

1. EPA 二十碳五烯酸, DHA: 二十二碳六烯酸
2. Omega-3 fatty acid ω-3 不饱和脂肪酸
3. Supportive but not conclusive research shows that… 支持但非决定性研究表明……
4. coronary 冠状动脉或静脉的
5. triglyceride 甘油三酯
6. artificial 人工的
7. Preservatives 防腐剂
8. Gelatin 凝胶 Glycerin 甘油 Tocopherol 生育酚
9. softgel 软胶囊
10. clot 凝结；拥塞 the ability of blood to clot 指凝血功能

Sample 2: Setting up Your TV's Cable Network Connection *Manually*[1]

To set up your TV's cable network connection manually, please follow these steps:

1. Follow step 1 through step 2 in the "how to set up *automatically*[2]".
2. Select the IP Setting on network test screen.
3. Set IP Mode to Manual.
4. Press the button on your *remote*[3] to go to the IP Address.
5. Enter the *IP Address*, *Subnet Mask*, *Gateway*, *DNS*[4] server values. Use the number buttons on our remote to enter numbers and arrow buttons to move one entry field to another.
6. When done, select the OK.
7. The network test screen appears, and the network setting is done.

Notes

1. manually 手动地
2. automatically 自动地

3. remote 遥控器
4. IP Address IP 地址，Subnet Mask: 子网掩码，Gateway: 网关，DNS: 域名系统（Domain Name System）

2.4　Useful Phrases and Expressions（常用短语和表达）

1) key ingredients　主要成分
2) to store/storage　保存
3) quality ensured period/expiration　保质期
4) quality standard　产品标准
5) date of manufacture　生产日期
6) shelf life　上架期
7) net contents　净含量
8) administration and dosage　服法与剂量
9) adverse reactions　不良反应
10) No Artificial colors　不含人工色素
11) No Preservatives　不含防腐剂
12) set up　安装
13) follow these steps　执行这些步骤
14) Caution　注意事项

2.5　Typical Sentences（典型例句）

1) Take 2 softgels daily with a meal.（一日两粒软胶囊，随餐服用。）
2) It should be swallowed whole with water.（用水吞服。）
3) For children, the doses should be correspondingly reduced.（儿童剂量酌减。）
4) Avoid high temperatures and direct sunlight.（避免高温及阳光直射。）
5) This guide, showing how the set is operated, will assure you of greater TV enjoyment.
（本使用说明讲述本机的正确操作法，确保您能悦赏电视。）
6) Since the unit contains precision electronic components, never attempt to disassemble it.
（鉴于本机由精密电子元件所组成，切勿拆卸。）
7) Discontinue using if signs of irritation or rash appear.
（如有任何不适，请立即停止使用。）
8) Avoid contact with the eyes. If product gets into eyes, rinse thoroughly with water.（避免进入眼睛，如不慎渗入眼内，用清水彻底清洗。）
9) Use every morning and night, in an upward and outward motion, smooth evenly over face.（每天早晚轻轻以朝上和朝外的方式均匀涂抹于脸部。）
10) Keep battery out of reach of children and in original package until ready to use.
（放置电池于儿童接触不到的地方，用时再拆开包装。）

Module Four >> Writings for General Business Activities
一般商务文书

2.6 Training and Practice（操练与实践）

2.6.1 Match the following English expressions with their Chinese equivalents.

1) Date of manufacture   A) 不含添加剂
2) Adverse reactions   B) 避免高温
3) Expiration date   C) 注意事项
4) No Preservatives   D) 放置电池于儿童接触不到的地方
5) Shelf life   E) 切勿拆卸
6) Caution   F) 上架期
7) Keep battery out of reach of children   G) 保质期
8) Avoid high temperatures   H) 用水吞服
9) Never attempt to disassemble it   I) 不良反应
10) Be swallowed whole with water   J) 生产日期

2.6.2 Complete each sentence based on the information given in the bracket.

1. _____ to sudden changes in temperature.（请勿将相机暴露于温差变化剧烈的环境中）
2. Avoid high temperatures and _____.（阳光直射。）
3. _____（避免进入眼睛）. If product gets into eyes, rinse thoroughly with water.
4. _____（咨询医生）before taking this product.
5. Don't use the chair unless _____（所有部件正确安装和调试）

2.6.3 Writing tasks.

Write a Description Manual for American Ginseng Capsules based on the following messages.

美国洋参胶囊（American Ginseng Capsules）是高科技的健康食品，支持但非决定性研究表明洋参胶囊可以有效去除疲劳。本产品不含兴奋剂（stimulants）、防腐剂和人工色素。

保健作用（health care effects）：　　抗疲劳
适宜人群：易疲劳者
不适宜人群：　　　　　　　　　　　　儿童
净含量：　　　　　　　　　　　　　　0.5 克\1 粒
用法：　　　　　　　　　　　　　　　每日两次，一次一粒
保质期至：　　　　　　　　　　　　　06\12\2020
储存：　　　　　　　　　　　　　　　阴凉干燥处

Section 3
Corporate profiles
公司介绍

3.1 Lead-In Introduction（导入介绍）

A corporate profile is a brief introduction of an organization or a business. It may be used as a marketing tool to attract investors and clients who might be interested in the product or service provided by the company. It can also be used to distribute to the media, the community and any other stakeholders who might be interested in understanding a company's mission and what it does.

3.2 Guidelines for Writing（写作指南）

As a marketing tool, a corporate profile should be concise, creative and attention grabbing by focusing on important information and presenting it in an interesting and engaging way. Meanwhile, the information it conveys should also be accurate and be kept up to date, especially as the business grows and changes over time. A well-written corporate profile should include the following elements.

• Start with brief corporate information, including the company name, location, type of business, corporate structure and a brief history.

• Disclose relevant financial data, such as revenues, profits, assets and scale information.

• State corporate policies and how relationships are maintained with investors, shareholders and other stakeholders.

• State the mission of the company and what products or services it provides to its customers and clients.

• Call attention to important achievements and milestones.

• Talk about the employees who make the business run.

3.3 Sample Study（范例学习）

Sample 1: The Corporate profile of Huawei

Huawei（officially Huawei Technologies Co., Ltd.）is a Chinese multinational networking and telecommunications equipment and services company *headquartered*[1] in Shenzhen, Guangdong, China. It is the largest China-based networking and telecommunications equipment supplier and the second-largest supplier of mobile telecommunications *infrastructure*[2] equipment in the world（after Ericsson）.

Huawei was founded in 1987 by Ren Zhengfei and is a private company owned by its employees. Its core activities are building telecommunications networks; providing *operational*[3] and consulting services and equipment to enterprises; and manufacturing communications devices for the consumer market. Huawei has over 110,000 employees, around 46% of whom are engaged in research and development（R&D）. It has 20 *institutes*[4] in countries including China, Germany, India, Russia, Sweden and the United States, and in 2010 invested CNY 16,556 million in R&D.

In 2010, Huawei *recorded*[5] revenues of USD 28 billion. Its products and services have been *deployed*[6] in more than 140 countries and it currently serves 45 of the world's 50 largest telecoms operators.

Notes

1. headquarter   *v.* 在这里作动词，以……作为总部；总部设在……
2. infrastructure   基础设施
3. operational   pertaining to a process or series of actions for achieving a result 操作的；运作的
4. institute   机构，学院
5. record   记录，记载
6. deploy   施展；有效地利用

Sample 2: The Profile of China International Travel Service Limited（CITS）

China International Travel Service Limited was founded in 1954. It is China's largest and most influential tourist group, honorably placed as the only tourist enterprise on the list of the country's top 500 enterprises by the *National Burean of Statistics Bureau*[1]. CITS has set up 14 *subsidiary*[2] companies in more than 10 countries and regions overseas, and owns 20-*odd*[3] stock-holding subsidiaries and 122

CITS[4] board member agencies nationwide *with a total asset of*[5] 5 billion yuan. It is one of the earliest travel agencies *franchised*[6] by the government to operate *outbound*[7] tours. Its outbound and domestic tour businesses grow rapidly.

Since the 1900s, in order to *effect*[8] a long-term stabilized development, engage in multiple operations and enlarge its scales, CITS began to make investments in other areas. CITS will continue to work hard to achieve gradually its great aspirations to become the most competitive travel agency group among China's central enterprise groups, the strongest transnational tourist operator across the country and one of the most *prestigious*[9] tourist brands in the world.

Notes

1. National Burean of Statistics 国家统计局
2. subsidiary 附带的；附属的
3. 20-odd 二十多；odd 表示"零头的"
4. CITS China International Travel Service 中国国际旅行社
5. with a total asset of 总资产为
6. franchise 赋予经销权；赋予特许权
7. outbound 开往外地的，开往外国的；domestic 国内的
8. effect v. 施行；引起
9. prestigious 受尊敬的，有声望的

3.4 Useful Expressions and Phrases（常用短语和表达）

1) engage in 主要经营，致力于
2) hold the principles of ... 奉行/坚持……原则
3) adhere to the aims of... 以……为宗旨
4) giving costumers priority and serving them with utmost sincerity 用户至上，诚挚服务
5) core activities （公司的）核心活动
6) be awarded the gold prize 获得金奖
7) pass/gain/obtain/be granted the Certificate of ISO9002 International 通过 ISO9002 质量认证
8) be awarded Most Welcome Goods 获最受欢迎产品奖
9) be established/founded/set up (in) 创建于
10) a joint stock company 股份制企业
11) be noted for 以……而著称
12) be listed as the /be ranked 被列入，跻身于

13) be located in, be situated in/by, lie in 位于，坐落于
14) be named one of the world's most recognizable/famous brands
被命名为世界最具影响力/驰名品牌之一
15) have a total asset of …, annual turnover…, annual trading value…
拥有资产总额……年销量……年贸易额……
16) have advanced facilities and well-experienced staff
有先进的设备和经验丰富的员工
17) be enlisted in the Top Ten Enterprises of… 列为……领域十强企业
18) premiere product 主打产品

3.5　Typical Sentences（典型例句）

1) It is situated in the heart of the city's business and financial district.
（它位于本市商业及金融中心。）
2) In recent years, the region has had one of the fastest growing economies and has attracted large concentration of foreign investment.
（近年来，该地区经济发展迅速，吸引了大量的国外投资。）
3) Our company boasts of the range of advanced facilities and well-experienced staff.
（我们公司拥有成套先进设施，员工经验丰富。）
4) Our company is staffed with personnel qualified in finance, law, information, management etc.
（我们拥有金融、法律、信息、管理等方面的优秀专业人才。）
5) Our company is noted for its strong capacity in processing.
（我们公司以雄厚的加工实力著称。）
6) Our company has a competent technical team and strong capability to develop new products. （我们公司技术实力雄厚，新产品开发能力强。）
7) After many years of hard work, our company has steadily evolved into a modern enterprise with standardized corporate management system and operation procedures.
（经过多年的努力，我公司现已逐步发展为具有统一规范化管理机制与操作程序的现代化企业。）
8) The company won the international ISO9002 certificate in 2012.
（公司于2012年取得ISO9002国际标准认证。）
9) Our company has a general asset of 60 billion RMB, over 10,000 employees at home and abroad and the annual trading value is 60 million RMB.
（我公司固定资产600亿元，海内外员工10,000多人，年贸易额达6,000万元。）
10) The enterprise has grown to be one of the largest textile and garment production and export bases in China.
（本企业已经发展成为中国最大的纺织服装生产和出口基地之一。）
11) Our company holds the principle of giving consumers priority and serving them with

utmost sincerity.（我们公司遵循"用户至上，诚挚服务"的宗旨。）

12) Youngor has never ceased their step in the way "to create an international brand and to create a century enterprise".

（雅戈尔公司奉"创国际品牌，铸百年企业"为目标，前行不止）

3.6　Training and Practice（操练与实践）

3.6.1　You are required to complete the sentence according to the Chinese information.

1. The corporation is a _____ top-quality illuminating products.
   该公司是致力于研发高端优质照明产品的股份制企业。

2. Since 1995, it _____ by National Bureau of Statistics of China for consecutive years.
   自1995年以来，该公司连年被国家统计局确定为纺织行业十强企业。

3. Our company has steadily evolved into _____.
   我公司现已逐步发展为具有统一规范化管理机制与操作程序的现代化企业。

4. With the ethic of "_____", our company will continue to provide prompt service at the lowest cost but with highest efficiency.
   本着"用户至上、热诚服务"的理念，我公司将继续为广大客户提供经济快捷和高效的服务。

5. The company has _____ of 50 billion Yuan, more than 100,000 _____ and more than 560 outlets.
   该公司拥有资产500亿元，海内外员工100,000多人，经销店560余家。

6. Our company _____ qualified in finance, law, information, management etc. 我们拥有金融、法律、信息、管理等方面的优秀专业人才。

3.6.2　Translate the following English expressions into Chinese.

1) subsidiary companies
2) global fast-food service retailer
3) won the international ISO9002 certificate
4) annual turnover
5) be awarded the gold prize
6) the world's most recognizable/famous brands
7) most prestigious tourist brands
8) headquartered in Shenzhen
9) the second-largest supplier of …
10) premiere product

3.6.3　Writing tasks.

Situation: Write a brief profile for Youngor Group Co., Ltd., according to the following

Chinese information:

1. 创建于1979年，中国服装行业的龙头企业，拥有雅戈尔集团股份有限公司以及各类子公司近四十家。

2. 20多年来的发展，本企业已经发展成为中国最大的纺织服装生产和出口基地之一。

3. 我公司固定资产60亿元，海内外员工10,000多人，年贸易额达101亿元。综合实力 (overall strength) 列全国500强第49位。

4. 主打产品雅戈尔衬衫连续九年获市场综合占有率第一位，西服也连续三年保持市场综合占有率第一位。

5. 奉"创国际品牌，铸百年企业"为目标，前行不止。

Section 4
Questionnaires
商务调查问卷

4.1 Lead-In Introduction（导入介绍）

Questionnaires are common tools used by companies which intend to gather more information on customer's needs, preferences, evaluation of the products or services, company's image, etc. They always consist of a series of questions on a topic designed to be answered by a number of people. The results can lead to re-branding, decision-making, and policy changes if the feedback is sound.

4.2 Guidelines for Writing（写作指南）

Questionnaires are made to gather information. Making a questionnaire can seem very straightforward, but the results can be skewed and unreliable unless it is designed properly. So the questions involved should be brief, clear, easy to answer, and avoid difficult terms or technical words. Besides, when you make a questionnaire, make sure all questions are closely related to the aim of the questionnaires and your answers include all the possible alternatives.

A questionnaire usually consists of the following parts:

• Instructions on how to complete the questionnaire and how to return it

• A series of questions related to the topic including some optional questions such as the age, gender and profession of the person who fills it

• Expression of appreciation to people who have spent time and effort in filling the questionnaire

4.3 Sample Study（范例学习）

Sample 1: A Service Quality Questionnaire

Thank you for answering the following questions. After you finish it, please return this paper to the person who gives you this questionnaire. Thank you!

1. Have you purchased a Pizza hut's pizza in the last week?
   ☐ yes   ☐ no   ☐ unsure

2. The last time you bought a Pizza hut's pizza, did you: (check only one)
   ☐ Have it delivered to your house?
   ☐ Have it delivered to your place of work?
   ☐ Pick it up yourself?
   ☐ Eat it at the Pizza *parlor*[1]?
   ☐ Purchase it some other way?

3. In your opinion, the taste of a Pizza hut's pizza is: (check only one)
   ☐ poor   ☐ fair   ☐ good   ☐ excellent

4. Which of the following *toppings*[2] do you typically have on your pizza? (multiple check)
   ☐ pepper   ☐ onion   ☐ sausage   ☐ mushroom
   ☐ *hot pepper*[3]

5. How do you *rate*[4] the speediness of Pizza hut's in-restaurant service once you have ordered? (check only one)
   ☐ very slow   ☐ slow   ☐ average   ☐ fast
   ☐ very fast

♦ **Optional**[5]:
   Gender: _____
   Age: _____
   Occupation: _____

Thank you for taking time to answer these questions.

❋ Notes

1. parlor   店家，厅
2. toppings   浇头，这里指比萨饼最上层撒的香肠、辣椒、洋葱等。
3. hot pepper   小辣椒；腌辣椒
4. rate v.   作动词时，指"评价"，"测算"。这里指对比萨店服务的速度进行评价。
5. optional   非强制的，任选的

Module Four >> Writings for General Business Activities
一般商务文书

Sample 2: A Customer feedback Questionnaire

Thank you so much for your support during our cooperation! We would like to take this opportunity of Customer Satisfaction Survey to continuously improve our products and service. Please take some time to fill out this form, and E-mail the filled form back to us.

Your advice and suggestions will be highly appreciated!

Thank you!

◆ **About Products**

How often do you purchase products?	☐ weekly ☐ monthly ☐ quarterly ☐ yearly
Range of your purchased products, such as BNC, CC4 or any others?	
Quality of our products	☐ excellent ☐ very good ☐ good ☐ fair ☐ poor ☐ very poor ☐ disappointing
Pricing of our products	☐ very expensive ☐ expensive ☐ somewhat expensive ☐ fair ☐ inexpensive ☐ somewhat inexpensive ☐ very inexpensive
Based on your last experience of our products, would you purchase products again from us?	☐ yes ☐ no ☐ maybe

◆ **About our Service**

The *accuracy*[1] and honesty of the information we supply you with	☐ excellent ☐ very good ☐ good ☐ fair ☐ poor ☐ very poor ☐ disappointing
Our ability to meet your orders/requirements	☐ excellent ☐ very good ☐ good ☐ fair ☐ poor ☐very poor ☐ disappointing
Timeliness[2] of our deliveries	☐ excellent ☐ very good ☐ good ☐ fair ☐ poor ☐very poor ☐ disappointing
Our *complaint handling system*[3]	☐ excellent ☐ very good ☐ good ☐ fair ☐ poor ☐very poor ☐ disappointing

131

| Based on your last experience of our products, would you purchase products again from us? | ☐yes ☐no ☐maybe |

Please share us any other information you would like to help us serve you better.

Comments[4]/suggestions	
complaint	
Compliment[5]	

Your company name: _____
Signature: _____

Notes

1. accuracy   准确，精确
2. timeliness   及时性；合时
3. complaint handling system   投诉处理系统
4. comment   评价，评论
5. compliment   赞赏；表扬的话

4.4 Useful Phrases and Expressions（常用短语和表达）

1) quality of our products   产品质量
2) pricing of our products   产品定价
3) improve our products and service   提高产品和服务
4) take some time to fill out this form   花费时间填表
5) E-mail back   电子邮件寄回来
6) thank you for your cooperation   感谢你的合作
7) return this questionnaire to sb.   交回问卷给某人
8) check only one   只选一项

4.5 Typical Sentences（典型例句）

Questions on the questionnaire may be yes-or-no questions, true-or-false questions, or questions that ask the respondent to agree or disagree with a statement. These are known as open-ended questions. Closed-ended questions may have only a few options respondents can use to answer. The following questions 1–7 are closed-ended questions.

1) Have you shopped here before?（以前在这购过物吗？）

2) If so, how often do you shop here?（如果是，多久购物一次?）

3) How satisfied are you with your experience today?（今天购物感受如何?）

4) Would you recommend this store to a friend?（你会向朋友推荐这家店吗?）

5) Who referred you to this store?（谁介绍你来这家店的?）

6) Where else do you normally shop?（你还在其他什么店购物?）

7) Thank you for taking time to answer the following questions.（感谢你回答下列问题。）

8) Please take some time to fill out this form.（请花些时间填写这张表。）

9) Please E-mail the filled form back to us.（请把填好的表电子邮件发给我们。）

10) Please return this paper to the person who gives you this questionnaire.
（请把问卷还给原交给你的人。）

11) We would like to take this opportunity to improve our products and service.
（我们想借此机会提升我们的产品和服务。）

12) Your advice and suggestions will be highly appreciated.
（非常感谢您的意见和建议。）

13) Please select the options below to order.（请按顺序选择下列选项。）

14) The first one will be the option you concern most.
（第一个选项应是你最关注的。）

4.6　Training and Practice（操练与实践）

Writing task: Write a questionnaire (A Survey on Shampoo' Potential Market) according to the situation given below, applying the principles discussed in this section.

Message:

问卷中包括：

1. 顾客常用的洗发露的品牌

2. 选择这个品牌的原因

3. 愿意接受的这个品牌产品的价位

4. 这个品牌产品的哪一项对你最重要（功能，包装，便捷，价格，实用性等）

5. 对这个品牌产品的满意度

6. 是否会推荐给朋友、同事或者家人

7. 是否会经常换品牌用

可选回答项：年龄　性别　职业

Section 5

Product Brochures and Advertisements
产品宣传资料、商业广告

5.1 Lead-In Introduction（导入介绍）

A: Product Brochures

A brochure is a thin magazine or a leaflet advertisement with or without pictures that gives you information about a product or service. It may advertise discount activity, hotel, product and service, etc. Brochures are usually succinct in language and eye-catching in design. At trade fairs, samples and product brochures are offered to the prospective customers together. An effective product brochure may help to sell the product well in the market.

B: Advertisements

Commercial advertising is a form of communication that typically attempts to persuade potential customers to purchase or to consume more of a particular brand of product or service. Therefore, many advertisements are designed to generate increased consumption of those products or services through the creation and reinforcement of brand image and brand loyalty.

Usually, advertising conveys information in three ways: audio, visual, and the language, among which the language in a way provides more exact, detailed and dependable information, and thus plays a crucial role in making a successful advertisement.

5.2 Guidelines for Writing（写作指导）

A: Product Brochures

Brochures are written to sell the products well. So a well-written and designed product brochure can be an effective tool to win the customers. When designing a brochure, we should follow these guidelines:

- State product benefits as well as its selling points.
- Build a consistent image of the company where the product comes from.
- Be succinct in language and eye-catching in design.
- Grab customers' attention and stimulate their interest.

B: Advertisements

Advertisements try to give the readers immediate impact and rapid persuasion, so the

advertising language should be accurate, definite, recognizable and moderate in length. Avoid using vague words and try some words that could arouse readers' interest. It is important to stress the benefits of the product or service and to keep AIDA in mind:
- attract Attention
- hold Interest
- arouse Desire
- motivate Action

5.3　Sample Study（范例学习）

Sample 1: An Advertisement for a Hotel

JinJiang Hotel

In the Heart of Shanghai

Location: right in the center of *vibrant*[1] Shanghai

Facilities: 728 beautiful and well *appointed*[2] guest rooms and suites

Food: wide range of fine restaurants including the ***Blue Heaven Revolving Restaurant***[3], the Bund Restaurant, French Grill room and Bamboo Garden Restaurant for delicious ***cuisine***[4]

Recreation: extensive *recreational*[5] facilities for your leisure and relaxation. Grand Ballroom for international conventions, meetings and *banquets*[6]

Traffic: only 20 minutes to HongQiao Airport by car, 8 minutes to the Railway Station

For Reservation and more information, please contact:

　　161 Jingmen Road, Shanghai, China

　　Tel & Fax: 86-21-64151188

　　Zip Code: 200020

　　www.Jinjiangtowerhotel-shanghai.com for fast & easy online booking

Notes

1. vibrant　充满生命力的；令人鼓舞的；生机勃勃的
2. appointed　provided with furnishing and accessories (especially of a tasteful kind) 装饰精良的
3. Blue Heaven Revolving Restaurant　蓝天旋转餐厅
4. cuisine　菜肴，饭菜
5. recreational　消遣的，娱乐的
6. banquet　宴会

Sample 2: An Advertisement for American Express

Around the corner, around the world
(We're around to help)

The **time zone**[1] may change. The **currency**[2] may change. The language may change. But one thing remains constant as you travel: the help of American Express at more than 1,200 Travel Service Offices in over 130 countries. Even if you never need us, it's nice to know we're there to help.

(Don't leave home without us.)

Travel Service Offices of **American Express**[3] Travel Related Services Company, Inc., its **subsidiaries**[4] and representatives.

Notes

1. time zone   时区
2. currency   货币
3. American Express   美国运通公司
4. subsidiaries 子公司   下属公司

Sample 3: Panasonic Battery Brochure

PANASONIC LITHIUM BATTERY provides:
Extra long life
Expected storage life up to 10 years. (when not in use)

♦ Extreme temperature range (−200℃ to 600℃)

The **color coding system**[1] on PANASONIC LITHIUM BATTERY makes it easy to select the right PANASONIC battery whenever you need one. Just match the color or model number.

♦ CAUTION

Fire and burn **hazard**[2]. Do not **recharge**[3], **dissemble**[4], heat above 100℃ or **incinerate**[5]. Keep battery out of the reach of children and in original package until ready to use. **Dispose**[6] of used batteries promptly.

Notes

1. color coding system　色标检查系统
2. hazard　危险
3. recharge　重装
4. dissemble　拆卸
5. incinerate　焚化
6. dispose　处理掉，丢掉

5.4　Useful Expressions and Phrases（常用短语和表达）

1）selling well all over the world　畅销全球
2）elegant and graceful　典雅大方
3）making things convenient for customers　方便顾客
4）a wide selection of colors and designs　花样繁多
5）attractive designs; fashionable (in) style　款式新颖
6）attractive and durable　美观耐用
7）ideal gift for all occasions　节日送礼之佳品
8）Water-proof and shock-resistant　防水且防震
9）door to door service　上门服务
10）latest technology　最新工艺
11）with a longstanding reputation　久享盛名
12）selected materials (high quality materials)　原料精选
13）perfect in workmanship (exquisite workmanship)　加工精细
14）first-rate facilities　一流设备
15）professional design　设计合理
16）rational construction　结构合理
17）elegant shape　式样优雅

5.5　Typical Sentences (Advertising Slogans)

1）Good to the last drop. 滴滴香浓，意犹未尽。(麦斯威尔咖啡)
2）Obey your thirst. 服从你的渴望。(雪碧)
3）The new digital era. 数码新时代。(索尼影碟机)
4）We lead, others copy. 我们领先，他人仿效。(理光复印机)
5）Impossible made possible. 使不可能变为可能。(佳能打印机)
6）Take time to indulge. 尽情享受吧！(雀巢冰激凌)
7）The relentless pursuit of perfection. 不懈追求完美。(凌志轿车)
8）Poetry in motion, dancing close to me. 动态的诗，向我舞近。(丰田汽车)

9) Come to where the flavor is Marlboro Country. 光临风韵之境——万宝路世界。（万宝路香烟）

10) To me, the past is black and white, but the future is always color.
对我而言，过去平淡无奇；而未来，却是绚烂缤纷。（轩尼诗酒）

5.6　Training and Practice（操练与实践）

5.6.1　Match the following English and Chinese advertising slogans.

1) Just do it.　　　　　　　　　　A. 没有不做的小生意，没有解决不了的大问题。（IBM 公司）

2) Ask for more.　　　　　　　　　B. 只管去做。（耐克运动鞋）

3) The taste is great.　　　　　　　C. 让我们做得更好。（飞利浦电子）

4) Feel the new space.　　　　　　D. 拥有东芝，拥有世界。（东芝电子）

5) Intelligence everywhere.　　　　E. 味道好极了。（雀巢咖啡）

6) The choice of a new generation.　F. 我们集大成，您超越自我。（三菱电工）

7) We integrate, you communicate.　G. 渴望无限。（百事流行鞋）

8) Take TOSHIBA, take the world.　H. 感受新境界。（三星电子）

9) Let's make things better.　　　　I. 智慧演绎，无处不在。（摩托罗拉手机）

10) No business too small, no problem too big.　　J. 新一代的选择。（百事可乐）

5.6.2　Match the following English and Chinese expressions.

1) superior materials　　　　　　　　　　　　　A. 样式入时

2) to make best use of materials　　　　　　　　B. 技艺精湛

3) exquisite craftsmanship (excellent craftsmanship)　C. 巧用原料

4) latest technology　　　　　　　　　　　　　D. 款式齐全

5) professional design　　　　　　　　　　　　E. 设计合理

6) water-proof and shock-resistant　　　　　　　F. 节日送礼之佳品

7) ideal gift for all occasions　　　　　　　　　　G. 防水 防震

8) various styles　　　　　　　　　　　　　　　H. 最新工艺

9) fashionable patterns　　　　　　　　　　　　I. 优质原料

10) with a longstanding reputation　　　　　　　J. 久享盛名

5.6.3　Translate the following ad into English.

"时代"浴室（STYLE BATHROOM）一流设备豪华气派

"时代"浴室专卖商为您提供各种类型的浴缸，洗手盆（washbasin），抽水马桶（toilet）及其他浴室洁具（bathroom facilities）。

联系我们，您马上可以少花二百元！我们提供：

20 多种款式、颜色供您挑选

型号齐全（有大、中、小各型号）

提供免费浴室设计服务

马上与我们联系吧，我们是全国最好的厂商，为您提供周到的服务！
我们将免费送货上门。
地址：广州白云区龙岗村中华路 41 号
电话：020-37737067，37737065
传真：020-37737091
邮箱：sales@ pietra-bianca. com
网站：www. pietra-bianca. com

5. 6. 4　Writing tasks.

Task 1: Write an ad with the information given below.

Situation: ABC trading company wants to place an ad for its Nike sports shoes to be sold at a reduced price of RMB100 Yuan. The regular price is 180 Yuan. There is a wide selection of style and colors. In order to promote the sale, they offer a bonus sale of a second pair at 50% of the regular price.

Task 2: Finish the BASA videophone brochure based on the following information:

Features:

- Small and elegant
- Easy to set up
- Easy to use
- Full-color motion video, adjustable picture settings, good audio quality
- Preview mode and privacy mode
- Ideal for the home, office or the trip

BASA Videophone

BASA videophone guarantee:

Appearance: _____

User-friendliness: _____

Special features: _____

Just as with any means of communication, it is worthwhile to have a set. It is really _____. Put yourself in the picture!

Module Five 模块五
Writings for Foreign Trade Correspondence
对外贸易函电

Module Briefing

In international trade, a good deal may be concluded after many rounds of negotiations. Most of these negotiations are made by correspondence. The main negotiating topics for foreign trade business include business relations establishment, inquiry, offer, counter-offer, acceptance, orders or contract, L/C or payment, packing, shipment, insurance, etc. In this module, you are going to be trained to negotiate with customers through writing for foreign trade business.

Objectives

Upon the accomplishment of this module, you should be able to establish good business relationship with your potential customers and negotiate with them on all topics relevant to your import and export business in written English.

Focuses and Difficult Points

1. To get familiar with useful expressions and sentences used in foreign trade correspondence
2. To acquire skills in writing or replying to letters relevant to foreign trade business

Section 1
Letters on Establishing Business Relations and Inquiries
建交、询盘函

1.1 Lead-In Introduction（导入介绍）

A: Letters on Establishing Business Relations

A successful business is always based on a fruitful relationship with partners and customers. No customer no business, no business no money. So establishing business relations is the first step for a foreign-trade firm to start a good deal. Having obtained the necessary information from a certain source, the importer or the exporter may start contacting the prospective customers by correspondence and establishing business relations with them by sending a letter.

For the sake of creating good will and leaving a good impression, any letter of this nature received must be answered in full, with courtesy and without the least delay.

B: Letters on Inquiries

An inquiry is a request for business information, such as price list, catalogs, samples, and details about the goods or trade terms. It is usually made by the importer, but sometime can also be made by the exporter. According to the contents of the letter, there may be general inquiries and specific inquiries. If the buyer wants to have a general idea of the products or commodities, which the seller is in a position to supply, he may ask the seller to send him a catalog, a price list, samples, etc. This is a general inquiry. If the buyer intends to purchase a certain product or commodity, he may ask the seller to make an offer or a quotation on this product. This is a specific inquiry. Inquiries should be brief, specific, courteous and reasonable.

On receiving an inquiry, it is a regular practice that the receiver should reply to it without delay. The answers to an inquiry should be prompt, courteous and helpful.

1.2 Guidelines for Writing (写作指南)

A: Letters on Establishing Business Relations

Shaping business relationship is a work of art. When writing a letter aiming at establishing business relations with potential clients, the writer is expected to maintain a sincere and earnest tone, and the language should adhere to the following main points:

- telling the prospective customers how their names and address are known
- self-introduction
- indicating your desire to enter into business relations and sometimes making general inquiries
- expressing your expectation of cooperation or an early reply

A letter replying to these letters generally includes the following contents:

- expressing thanks for the in-coming letter and the willingness to establish business relations
- making self-introduction and replying to the requirements in the incoming letter
- expressing hope for doing business together

B: Letters on Inquiries

When making an inquiry, you should better

- introduce yourself and tell the addressee where you have heard about his product or company.
- explain why you are writing.

- list the specific information you need in the form of detailed questions.
- close your letter with appreciation and a request for an early reply.

The replies to inquiries normally become offers. They would be discussed in the next section.

1.3　Sample Study（范例学习）

Sample 1: An Importer's Request for the Establishment of Business Relations

MacDonald & Evans Co., Ltd.
58 Lawton Street, New York, USA
Tel: 23456　Fax: 34567
E-mail: smith@mecl.com

September 20, 2020

Guangdong Light Industrial Products Import & Export Corporation
52 South Dezheng Road, 510002
Guangzhou, China

Dear Sirs,

Through the courtesy of[1] Mr. Freemen, we *are given to understand that*[2] you are one of the *leading*[3] exporters of Chinese light industrial products in your area and are now writing to you for the establishment of business relations.

We are very well connected with all the major dealers of sport shoes. We *need a regular supply of*[4] this *item*[5] and feel sure we can sell large quantities of Chinese products if we get your offers at *competitive prices*[6].

Please let us have all necessary information regarding your products for export.
We look forward to your early reply.

Yours sincerely,

John Smith
John Smith
Manager of Import Department

Notes

1. Through the courtesy of…相当于 obtain sth. from …，可译为"承蒙……的介绍/关照"。
2. We are given to understand that … 相当于 We learned that …。be given to understand 相当于 get to know。
3. leading 这里指"主要的""占主导地位的"，也可以表达为 major。如 major dealer 可译为"主要的经销商",而 large dealer 则译为"大的经销商"。
4. need a regular supply of...定期需要
5. item 这里指"某项商品"
6. competitive price 这里指"有竞争性的价格",即"优惠价"。也可以表达为:attractive price, best price, lowest price, bottom price 等。

Sample 2: The Exporter's Reply to Sample 1

Guangdong Light Industrial Products Import & Export Corporation
52 South Dezheng Road, 510002
Guangzhou, China
Tel: 12345678   Fax: 23456789
E-mail: panchj@glip.com.cn

September 25, 2020
John Smith
MacDonald & Evans Co., Ltd.
58 Lawton Street, New York, U.S.A.

Dear Mr. Smith,

Thank you for your letter of the 20th September, 2020 requesting the establishment of business relations. We are willing to *enter into business connection*[1] with your *firm*[2].

We are a *state-operated*[3] corporation, *handling*[4] for many years the export of sports shoes products. We have business relations with more than 80 countries in the world. *We are confident that*[5] our joint business efforts can be developed to our mutual benefits.

In compliance with[6] your request, a *catalogue*[7], a *latest price list*[8] together with a booklet including a general introduction, the *scope*[9] of business and other topics are *enclosed*[10] for your *reference*[11]. Should you require any further information, *please don't hesitate to let us know*[12].

We shall be glad to have your *specific inquiries*[13] and hope we can do business together in this *line*[14].

Yours sincerely,

Pan Changjiang
Pan Changjiang
Manager of Export Department

Notes

1. enter into business connection 建立业务联系，同 establish a business relation 或者 establish business relationship。

   其他同义表达还有：build up business relations，set up business relations。也可以用 establish 的名词形式 establishment。例如 establishment of business relations。

2. firms 指公司、商号。英语中表示"公司"的词很多，常用的有 firm，以及后面出现的 house 等。"股份有限公司"常用 Co. Ltd. 或 Corp. Inc. 表示，前者是 company limited 的缩写，后者是 corporation incorporate 的缩写。

3. state-operated corporation 指"国有公司"。也有表达为 state-run corporation 。

4. handle 指"从事、经营"。也可以表达为 specialize in、engage in、trade in、dealing in 或 be in the line of。

5. We are confident that… 意为"我们深信……"。

   to be confident that… （对……有信心/确信）

   e. g.：We are confident that we can push the sale of your products in this market. （我们确信能在此市场推销你方产品）

   注意该句型的搭配变化和用法。如：

   to be confident of (in) …；

   e. g.：We are confident of persuading our customer to place a trial order. （我们有把握说服客户试订。）

   to have confidence in…；

   e. g.：I'm sorry I don't have confidence in that financial institute. （对不起，我对那家金融机构信不过。）

   to have confidence that…；

6. in compliance with 相当于 according to 或者 in agreement with，意思为"按照、符合""与……相一致"。例如，The price is in compliance with the international market. （价格与国际市场行情一致）。

   该表达的动词形式为：comply（+ with）遵从，按照，根据，与……一致

   e. g.：We comply with your request and enclose a latest catalogue. （应贵方要求，我们随函附寄一份最新的目录表）。

7. catalog (catalogue)：a list, usually in the form of a book, of goods for sale with or without prices or pictures. （商品目录，产品目录）

   cf. brochure / pamphlet / leaflet /prospectus

   brochure：a small book consisting of a few pages in a paper cover, advertising material in this form. （小册子）

   pamphlet：an unbound, printed publication with no cover or a paper cover （一种未经装订、无须封面的简易宣传材料）

leaflet: a single sheet of printed paper, sometimes folded to form several pages, containing matter either advertising a product or giving directions on how to use it. It is usually handed out for free. (免费派发的活页宣传单)

prospectus: a leaflet, or a printed paper giving information about a product. It is usually a printed statement that is distributed to prospective buyers or investors. (产品说明书)

booklet: just a little book, or a pamphlet 小本子

8. latest price list 最新价目表。其他同类表达还有 latest catalogue （最新目录）
9. scope 范围、范畴。所以 falls within the scope of...指"属于...的经营范围"。
10. enclose 随函附寄

    enclose sth. 随函附上某物

    Enclosed please find … 随函附上……，请查收

    Enclosed are / is … 随函附上的是……

11. for your reference 供贵方参考
12. Note that you use "Please (don't hesitate to) …" when someone may want sth. from you. If you want someone to send you sth., do not use it but simply say "please" or "We would <u>appreciate it</u> / <u>be obliged</u> / <u>be grateful</u> if you would …"
13. specific inquiry 具体的询盘
14. line：相当于 range，指的是行业、范围。所以 line of business 或者 business line 有"经营范围，产品范围，业务范围"等意思。其他相关的表达还有：be in the line of …，意指"经营……"。

Sample 3: An Importer's General Inquiry for Toys

Wills Kenly Toy Ltd.
108 West Street
New York, U. S. A.

September 26, 2020

Huaxin Trading Co., Ltd.
14th Floor Kingstar Mansion
676 Jilin Road, 20000, Shanghai, China

Dear Sirs,

We are a toy store *specializing in*[1] baby toys. Seeing your advertisement in *China Trade Directory*, we have noticed that your baby toys are very popular, particularly the musical ones. We *are desirous to*[2] establish business relationship with you.

Please send us catalogs and price lists of your products, especially those of *stuffed animals*[3] and baby toys.

We would *appreciate*4 it if you reply as soon as possible as we hope to *promote*5 them during the Christmas season. We are looking forward to hearing from you soon.

Sincerely,

David Law

David Law

Purchasing Manager

Notes

1. specialize in 专门经销，专营

    e. g.：This shop specializes in car parts. 这家商店专售汽车零件。

2. be desirous to 意为 have a desire to，be eager to，be anxious to，可翻译为"热切盼望" "渴望"。通常用法为：be desirous to do sth. 或者 be desirous of doing sth.。

3. stuffed animals 填充动物玩具

4. appreciate v. 欣赏，感激，赏识。外贸函电中经常把该词用在 I would appreciate it if you could …这样的句式中，表达"如蒙……将不胜感激"的意思。同样意义的表达还有 I shall be obliged if you…，I shall be grateful if you …等。

5. promote v. 促销，促进，提升

    e. g.：Your job is to promote the new product. 你的工作是促销这一新产品。

Sample 4: An Importer's Specific Inquiry for Dishwashers

Dongfang Foreign Trading Co. Ltd.

32 Wuyi Road

Changsha，410000，Hunan，China

September 4，2020

Carrol Machinery Trade Co.

5983 Maplewood Cove

Memphis，TN 38117

Dear Sirs,

We *take the pleasure*1 of introducing to you our company which is one of the largest importers of light industrial products in this city. The New York Machines Co. Ltd. informed us that you are exporting *dishwashers*2.

Will you kindly send us your *quotation*3? We would require 100 sets. Please quote us your lowest price *CIF*4 Shanghai, stating the earliest date of *shipment*5.

Module Five >> Writings for Foreign Trade Correspondence
对外贸易函电

We are looking forward to your immediate reply.

Yours Faithfully,

Lu Yanfei

Lu Yanfei

Manager of Import Department

Notes

1. take / have (the) pleasure 很高兴，很荣幸。相当于 be delighted，be pleased。一般可以接 of doing sth，in doing sth. 以及 to do sth.。
2. dishwasher 洗碗机
3. quotation 报价，行情

    e. g.：With regard to our quotation, we will discuss it later.

    关于我们的报价，以后再讨论。
4. CIF 成本加运费保险费到目的港码头价

    交易的一种方式，英文全称为 cost, insurance and freight，成本、保险费加运费。

    e. g.：Is this your C. I. F. quotation? 你们的报价是目的港码头交货价吗？
5. shipment 装运、装船

    e. g.：Purchase is manageable at indication and shipment is arranged in June or July at seller's option.

    一切按指示洽购，但装船要在六、七月间，由卖方自行选定。

1.4　Useful Phrases and Expressions（常用短语和表达）

1) through the courtesy of…　承蒙……
2) be given to understand　得悉、获悉
3) leading / major dealer　主要的经销商
4) specialize in　专门经营
5) establish / enter into business relations / connection　建立业务关系
6) in compliance with　按照，与……相一致
7) latest price list　最新价目表
8) for your reference (only)　（仅）供贵方参考
9) be desirous to　热切盼望
10) fall within the scope of …　属于…的经营范围内

1.5　Typical Sentences（典型例句）

1) Through the courtesy of Mr. Freemen, we are given to understand that you are one of

the leading exporters of Chinese light industrial products in your area.

（承蒙弗里曼先生的介绍，我们得知贵公司是当地轻工产品的主要出口商之一。）

2) We are one of the major importers of light industrial products in Guangzhou. We are willing to establish business relations with your corporation.

（我们是广州轻工产品的主要进口商之一，愿与贵公司建立业务关系。）

3) We are a state-operated corporation, handling the export of light industrial products and we have business relations with more than 80 countries in the world.

（我们是国有公司，经营轻工产品出口业务。我们与世界80多个国家有业务关系。）

4) Specializing in the export of Chinese foodstuffs, we wish to express our desire to trade with you in this line.

（我们专营中国食品的出口业务，希望和贵公司做本行业的买卖。）

5) We specialize in the exportation of Chinese textile products. Our products are excellent in quality and reasonable in price.

（我们专营中国纺织品出口业务。我们的产品质量上乘，价格合理。）

6) As the items falls within the scope of our business activities, we shall be pleased to enter into direct business relations with you.

（由于这些商品正好属于我们的经营范围，我们会很高兴与贵公司建立直接的业务关系。）

7) We are now writing you for the establishment of business relations. We shall be obliged if you could send us quotations and sample books.

（特致函建立业务关系。如蒙惠寄报价单及样品本，将不胜感激。）

8) To give you a general idea of our business lines, we enclose a copy of our export list, showing the main items in stock, and we hope that you would contact us if any of the items is of interest to you.

（为让贵方对本公司的产品范围有一个大致的了解，我们随函附上出口商品清单一份，上有我方可现货供应的主要商品项目。如感兴趣，希望与我方联系。）

9) A booklet including a general introduction, the scope of business and other topics is enclosed for your reference.

（随函附上公司概况、业务范围和其他方面的小册子一本，供参考。）

10) Should you be interested in any of our products, please let us know.

（如对我方任何产品感兴趣，务请告知。）

11) Should you require any further information, please don't hesitate to let us know.

（如需详情，务请告知。）

12) Please let us have all necessary information regarding your products for export.

（请告知所有与贵公司出口产品相关的必要信息。）

13) We shall be glad to have your specific inquiries and hope we can do business

together.（我们会很乐意得到你方的具体询盘并能共同做生意。）

14）Thank you for your letter of the 20th September, 2020 requesting the establishment of business relations. We are willing to enter into business connection with your firm.

（感谢贵方2020年9月20日要求与我方建立业务关系的来函。我们愿与贵公司建立业务联系。）

15）We would appreciate it if you reply as soon as possible as we hope to promote them during the Christmas season.

（若贵方能尽快答复我方将不胜感激，因为我们希望能在圣诞节促销。）

1.6 Training and Practice（操练与实践）

1.6.1 Complete the following sentences with one of the given words. Change the forms if necessary.

latest	for one's reference	be given to understand
quote	competitive	place an order with sb. for sth.
appreciate	in compliance with	fall within the scope of
enclose	state-operated	enter into business relations

1) We are willing to _____ with you.

2) We have seen your advertisement in newspaper and should _____ it if you could send us your price list and details of your terms.

3) We are _____ two catalogues and a _____ price list giving you the details of our products.

4) Please let us have your _____ prices so that we can conclude the transaction.

5) As requested, we are airmailing to you a sample each of Art. No. 1025 and 1026 _____.

6) Please _____ us your best price by Internet stating payment terms and time of shipment.

7) The item you mentioned just _____ our business activities.

8) Through the courtesy of Fort & Co., Ltd., we _____ that you are one of the leading importers of ceramic products in America.

9) _____ your request, we are sending you our latest catalogue.

10) We are a _____ corporation, handling the export of textile products and we'd like to establish business relations with your corporation.

1.6.2 Supply the missing words in the blanks of the following letter. The first letters are given.

Dear Sirs,

We have come to know the name of your **f** ___(1)___ and take the **p** ___(2)___ of addressing this letter to you in the hope of **e** ___(3)___ business relations with you.

We **s** ___(4)___ in the exportation of Chinese light industrial products that have enjoyed great popularity in world markets.

We **e** ___(5)___ a copy of our **c** ___(6)___ for your **r** ___(7)___ and hope that you would contact us if any of the **i** ___(8)___ is of **i** ___(9)___ to you.

We look forward to **h** ___(10)___ your reply soon.

Yours faithfully,

1.6.3 Put the following English into Chinese or Chinese into English.

1）如蒙……，我们将不胜感激。

2）falls within the scope of our business activities

3）具体的询盘。

4）Should you be interested in any of our products, please don't hesitate to let us know.

5）Would you please send me a copy of your catalog with details of your prices and payment terms?

6）We are exporters of fresh water pearls（淡水珍珠）, and we have years of experience in this particular line of business.

7）Specializing in the export of Chinese bicycles, we wish to express our desire to trade with you in this line.

8）承蒙 ABC 公司的介绍，我们得知贵公司的名称和地址。

9）请详告价格、质量、可供数量及其他有关情况。

10）我们是美国陶瓷制品（ceramic product）的主要出口商之一，愿与贵公司建立业务关系。

1.6.4 Writing tasks.

Task 1: Write a letter for establishing business relations according to the following information.

Situation: Imagine yourself being a manager of Import Department of H. Simpson & Co. Ltd. in U.S. Recently you got some information about Guangdong Textiles Import & Export Corporation at Guangzhou Fair. You are very interested in their products, so you want to send them a letter in the hope of establishing business relations with them. Now compose a letter covering the message given below.

Message:

1）告诉对方你是从广州中国进出口商品交易会（**Guangzhou Fair**）上得悉其公司名称和地址的。

2）去函目的是希望与对方建立业务关系。

3）告诉对方你公司专门经营中国纺织品进口业务，是美国主要的中国纺织品经销商。

4）问对方索要最新的产品目录及价格表。

5）表达希望尽早收到对方答复并与之达成交易的迫切心情。

Task 2: Write a letter for making an inquiry according to the following information.

Situation: You are a manager of Import & Export Department of Guangming International Trading Co. Ltd. in P. R. CHINA. Your company plans to import vacuum cleaners from Messrs. Arthur Grey & Son Co. Ltd. So you want to send them a letter to inquire the detailed information about the products. Now compose a letter of inquiry covering the message given below.

Message:

1）告诉对方你是从中国对外贸易促进会得悉其公司名称和地址的。

2）去函目的是打算就 100 台真空吸尘器（**vacuum cleaner**）向对方询盘。

3）希望对方能够提供关于商品价格、支付条款、装运时间和包装条款等方面的详情。

4）向对方索要最新的带插图的产品目录。

5）表示希望尽早收到对方答复

Section 2
Letters on Offers and Counter-Offers
报盘、还盘函

2.1　Lead-In Introduction（导入介绍）

A: Letters on Offers

An offer is a promise to supply goods on the terms and condition stated. In an offer, the seller not only quotes the price of the goods he wishes to sell but also indicates all necessary terms of sales for the buyer's consideration and acceptance.

An offer may either be firm within a certain time limit（firm offer）or be made without engagement（non-firm offer）. In the latter case, it is subject to confirmation by the seller after being accepted by the buyer. When offering, this must be made clear to avoid possible disputes in future.

B: Letters on Counter-offers

In international trade, when the offeree accepts the terms and conditions stated in the offer, the transaction is concluded. However, in most cases, the offeree would reject part or totality of the terms and conditions in the offer and state his own terms and conditions by return. The rejection or partial rejection of the offeree to the offerer is called counter-offer.

A counter-offer is virtually a counter proposal initiated by the original offeree. Once the counter-offer is made, the original offer is no longer valid, and the offeree now becomes the offeror as the counteroffer becomes the new offer. Counter-offer constitutes the main part of business negotiations. So counter-offers are usually time consuming and may go many rounds before business is concluded or dropped.

2.2　Guidelines for Writing（写作指南）

A: Letters on Offers

A satisfactory offer will include the following:

- An expression of thanks for the inquiring, if any
- Name of the goods, quality or specifications, quantity, details of prices, discounts, terms of payment, time of shipment, and packing conditions so as to enable the buyer to make a decision
- The period for which the offer is valid if it is a firm offer, otherwise, a remark to the effect that the offer is made without engagement
- Favorable comments on the goods themselves
- A supplementary short paragraph to draw the customer's attention to other products likely to interest the buyer
- An expression of hopes for an order

B: Letters on Counter-offers

A typical letters of counter-offers will usually include the following main points:

- Thanking the offeror for his offer
- Expressing regret at inability to accept and state the reasons
- Making an appropriate counter-offer
- Expecting the acceptance or favourable reply

2.3　Sample Study（范例学习）

Sample 1: An Exporter's Firm Offer for Animal Toys

AAA Trading Co., Ltd.
×× th Floor Kingstar Mansion
××× Jilin Road, 200001, Shanghai, China
Tel: 7568××××; Fax: 7819××××; E-mail: ××××

Module Five >> Writings for Foreign Trade Correspondence
对外贸易函电

Re: Offer No. 334

October 1, 2020

BBB Toy Ltd.

×××West Street

New York NY ××××, U.S.A.

Dear Mr. Law,

In answer to your recent inquiry dated September 26, 2020, we are making the following offer for musical stuffed animal toys:

Item No.	Animal	Size	Colors	Unit Price ($)
23	bear	small	blue, brown, black	5.00
24	bear	large	blue, brown, black	8.00
32	pig	small	red, brown, white	5.00
34	pig	large	red, brown, white	8.00
43	dog	small	brown, black, white	5.00
44	dog	large	brown, black, white	8.00

Prices are on *FOB*[1] San Francisco basis. Our *terms of payment*[2] are by *a confirmed irrevocable letter of credit by draft at sight*[3]. *Discounts*[4] are 0.5% for orders of 100-200, 1% for 200-500, and 1.5% for 500-1,000.

Each item is *individually*[5] boxed with our company *logo*[6]. All cartons are waterproof and standard for overseas shipment. Delivery *is guaranteed to*[7] be within four weeks after receipt of L/C.

As you know, our musical toys are very popular and come with a guarantee for six months, we are sure that your customers will continue to be satisfied with our products. We look forward to receiving your order *promptly*[8] as the prices are *valid*[9] for only 10 days.

Sincerely,

Chen Wen

Chen Wen

Sales Manager

Notes

1. FOB 装运港船上交货价。FOB 的全文是 Free On Board

e.g.: Could you offer us FOB prices? (给我们报个装运港船上交货价吧好吗?)

e.g.: It's U.S. $400 per ton FOB Shanghai. (上海装运港船上交货价是每吨400美元。)

2. term of payment 支付条款

   e.g.: I am sorry to say the only term of payment we can accept is 100% irrevocable documentary letter of credit.
   (抱歉地说，我们能接受的付款条件只有100%不可撤销跟单信用证。)

   e.g.: If possible, we'd like to revise the term of payment.
   (如果可能的话，我们想修改一下付款条件。)

3. a confirmed irrevocable L/C by draft at sight 已保兑的、不可撤销的、凭即期汇票支付的信用证

   letter of credit （银行签发的）信用证，简写为 L/C。

   e.g.: Since you insist, I must amend the letter of credit.
   (既然你坚持，我就只好修改信用证。)

   confirm: *vt.* 证实；确定/认；支持；批准

   e.g.: Please confirm your order by fax. (请来传真确认你方订单。)

   e.g.: We are confirming your letter of Aug. 30. (兹确认你方八月三十日的来函。)

   confirmed L/C 确认的、保兑的信用证

   e.g.: I am sorry to say the only term of payment we can accept is a confirmed irrevocable letter of credit by draft at sight. (抱歉地说，我们能接受的付款条件只能是保兑的、不可撤销的、凭即期汇票支付的信用证。)

4. discount *n.* 折扣，贴现率

   v. 打折扣，贴现

   折扣（discount）是卖方按原价给予买方的价格减让。在国际贸易中，对价格的调整有时是通过折扣来实现的。

   e.g.: We give a 10 percent discount for cash. (现金付款，我们九折优惠。)

   e.g.: We would allow a discount of 2%. (我们允许有2%的折扣。)

5. individually *adv.* 个别地，单独地

   e.g.: You'll have to register individually. (你们必须分别登记。)

6. logo *n.* a design used by an organization on its letterhead, advertising material, and signs as an emblem by which the organization can easily be recognized 图形，商标，企业标志

   e.g.: A baseball cap with the Olympic logo. (带有奥运会标志的棒球帽)

7. be guaranteed to 保证

   e.g.: This novel is guaranteed to be a bestseller! (这本小说一定会成为畅销书的!)

8. promptly *adv.* 敏捷地，迅速地

   e.g.: Net cash 30 days unless specified otherwise. Advise promptly if incorrect.
   (除非另有说明，30日后全额付现，如有错误，请立即通知。)

9. valid *adj.* 有确实根据的，有效的，正当的

　　e. g.：Is it valid for two weeks?（有效期是两个星期吗？）

　　e. g.：The cheque is not valid if it is not signed by the finance director.
　　　　　（如果没有主管财务的董事签字，支票就无效。）

Sample 2: An Exporter's Non-firm Offer for Dishwashers

AAA Machinery Trade Co.
×××Maplewood Cove
Memphis, TN 38117
Tel: 0185-86-215××; Fax: 0185-86-214××; E-mail: ××××

September 10, 2020

BBB Foreign Trading Co. Ltd.
××Wuyi Road, 410000
Changsha, China

Dear Mr. Lu,

With reference to[1] your inquiry of September 6, we are pleased to quote without engagement as follows, **subject to**[2] our final confirmation:

Commodity: Dishwasher

Term of shipment: During September-November

Package: In cartons or in wooden cases, at buyer's option

Payment: By confirmed irrevocable L/C available by draft at sight

We are willing to allow 2% discount for all orders over 500 sets. We are awaiting your prompt reply.

Yours sincerely

Gillian Reeve

Gillian Reeve
Manager of Export Department

Notes

1. with reference to　关于（根据）；就……而言

　　e. g.：We would like to send you a sample with reference to the last shipment.
　　　　　（我们寄去有关上次交货的样品。）

2. be subject to　以……为条件，以……为准

　　e. g.：This offer is subject to our confirmation.（本报盘以我方确认为准。）

　　e. g.：offer subject to sample approval（以样品确定为准的报盘。）

e. g. : offer subject to our written acceptance（须经我方书面接受确认的报盘。）

Sample 3: An Importer's Counter-Offer on Price Reduction

AAA Foreign Trading Co. Ltd.
××Wuyi Road, 410000, Changsha, China
Tel: 7568×××; Fax: 7819×××; E-mail: ××××

October 20, 2020

BBB Machinery Trade Co.
×××Maplewood Cove
Memphis, TN 38117

Dear Gillian Reeve,

We thank you for your offer of October 10 for 300 sets of dishwashers.

In reply, we *regret*[1] to inform you that we cannot do the business *at your price*[2]. We have compared your offer carefully with that of a *regular supplier*[3] and found his price more *favorable*[4]. We don't deny that the quality of your products is slightly better, but the difference in price should, in no case, be as big as 10 percent. No doubt *the keen competition*[5] in the appliance business makes even lower prices most necessary.

The *alternative*[6] is for you to adjust your prices by reducing them by 10 percent, in which case we should be pleased to place our order for 300 units. We hope you will *take advantage of*[7] this chance so that you will benefit from the expanding market.

Please advise us as soon as possible if you agree to our proposal.

Yours sincerely,

Lu Yanfei
Lu Yanfei
Manager of Import Department

Notes

1. regret *vt.* 抱歉，遗憾

    e. g. : We regret having to report that we have not yet received the goods ordered on 3rd June. （很遗憾，6月3日所订货物尚未收到。）

    e. g. : We regret (to say) that we cannot accept your price.
    （很抱歉，我们不能接受你方价格。）

    e. g. : We are very regretful that we are not in a position to supply the items you need at present. （很抱歉你方所需商品目前无货可供。）

2. at your price   按你方价格；类似表达还有：at your price of …   按你方……的报价
3. regular supplier   正常供货的厂家；固定的供应商
4. favorable *adj.*   有利的，赞许的，良好的

   e. g.：They give us a favorable answer.（他们给了我们一个赞成的答复。）

   e. g.：Your favorable reply is anticipated with keen interest.（静候佳音。）

   e. g.：Our clients have a favorable impression on your products.
   （我方客户对你方产品的印象良好。）

5. the keen competition   激烈的竞争

   e. g.：We have to adjust the structure of our products so as to survive in the keen competition.
   （我们必须调整一下我们的产品结构以便在激烈的竞争中生存下来。）

6. alternative *adj.* 两者择一的 *n.* 替换物，取舍 *v.* 两者取一

   e. g.：Please find alternative means of transport.（请另外找一个运输方法。）

   e. g.：We have no alternative but to go on.（除了继续下去，我们没有选择的余地。）

7. take advantage of   占……的便宜，利用

   e. g.：I'm going to take advantage of this shoes sale.
   （我要好好地利用这一次的鞋子拍卖会。）

Sample 4: Exporter's Declination to the Importer's Counter-Offer

AAA Commercial Trade Company
××××^th Floor, ××××Building
×× Changchun Road, 519000
Zhuhai, China
Tel: 6253××××;   Fax: 6257××××;   E-mail: ××××

October 20, 2020

BBB Co., Ltd.
×× White Street
London ×××, England

Dear Mr. Smith,

Thank you for your letter dated October 15. Much as we would like to do business with you, we very much regret to say that there is no *possibility*[1] of our cutting the price to the *extent*[2] you *indicated*[3], i. e. 10%.

The price we have quoted is quite reasonable. We have received *substantial*[4] orders from other sources at our level.

If you could improve your offer, please let us know. Since the supplies of this product are limited at the moment, we would ask you to act quickly.

We assure you that all your inquiries will receive our prompt attention.

Yours sincerely,

Liu Bo

Liu Bo

Manager of Sales Department

Notes

1. possibility *n.* 可能性

    e. g.: We have little possibility to win. (我们取胜的可能性很小。)

    e. g.: Downsizing is now a strong possibility. (很可能会裁员。)

2. extent *n.* 广度，宽度，长度，大小，范围，程度

    e. g.: I was amazed at the extent of his knowledge. (我对他知识的渊博感到惊奇。)

    e. g.: To a large extent, I agree with you. (在很大程度上，我同意你的看法。)

    e. g.: To some extent, you're right. (在某种程度上你是正确的。)

    extend *v.* 延长期限，使展期；扩展；提供

    e. g.: We hope you will extend your offer for two weeks.

    （希望贵方能将报盘延长两星期。）

    extension *n.* 延长

3. indicate *v.* 显示，象征，指示；指明，表明

    e. g.: Please indicate your expected salary in your resume.

    （请您在简历中注明您所期望的薪水。）

    e. g.: Advice from abroad indicates that war is about to begin.

    （来自国外的消息表明战争即将开始。）

4. substantial *n.* 重要部分，本质   *adj.* 大量的，实质上的，有内容的

    e. g.: We are in substantial agreement. (我们实际上意见一致。)

    e. g.: Attending our speech club has substantial advantages.

    （参加我们演讲社团的好处很多。）

2.4 Useful Phrases and Expressions（常用短语和表达）

1) to make an offer   报盘，发盘
2) firm offer   实盘
3) non-firm offer   虚盘
4) without engagement   不受约束，无约束力

5）quote the price of...　报……的价
6）counter-offer　还盘，还价
7）with reference to　关于；就……而言
8）be subject to　以……为条件，以……为准
9）FOB　Free On Board 的缩写，译为"装运港船上交货价"
10）terms of payment　支付条款

2.5　Typical Sentences（典型例句）

1）Prices are on FOB San Francisco basis.（价格为旧金山码头船上交货价。）
2）Our terms of payment are by a confirmed irrevocable letter of credit by draft at sight.（我们的支付方式是在保兑的、不可撤销的信用证条件下，凭即期汇票支付。）
3）In answer to your recent inquiry dated ..., we are making the following offer for ...（关于您×月×日的询价，我方就……报价如下。）
4）With reference to your inquiry of September 6, we are pleased to quote without engagement as follows:（关于您9月6日的询价，我们很高兴为您做如下无约束力的报价：）
5）We are awaiting your prompt reply.（企盼您早日答复。）
6）The price we have quoted is quite reasonable.（我们的报价相当合理。）
7）Since the supplies of this product are limited at the moment, we would ask you to act quickly.（鉴于目前该产品供应不足，恳请您尽快行动。）
8）We assure you that all your inquiries will receive our prompt attention.（我们保证将迅速答复你方所有的询价。）
9）In reply, we regret to inform you that we cannot do the business at your price.（我们很遗憾地通知您，以贵方的报价我们无法达成交易。）
10）If you could improve your offer, please let us know.（如果贵方能够提高您的还价，请通知我方。）

2.6　Training and Practice（操练与实践）

2.6.1　Complete the following sentences with the correct expressions of the given words. Change the forms if necessary.

offer	quote	withdraw	conclude
expire	valid	advantage	be subject to
submit	counter-offer	reduction	competition

1）This offer _____ on August 20. Your immediate reply by E-mail will be appreciated.
2）Our offer is a firm and remains _____ until July 20, 2020, Beijing time.
3）It's a pleasure for us to _____ you the goods as follows:

4) To have this business _____, you need to lower your price at least by 10%, I believe.

5) We regret being unable to _____ on FOB basis, as it is our general practice to do business with all our clients on CIF terms.

6) This is our rock-bottom price, we can't make further _____.

7) As requested, we are offering you the following _____ our final confirmation.

8) This offer must be _____ if not accepted within six days.

9) It is in view of our long-standing relationship that we make you such a _____.

10) We hope you will take _____ of this chance and accept our counter-offer.

2.6.2 Read the following letter and fill in the blanks with one of the given prepositions.

to	at	of	with	in	during	for	without	by

Dear Sirs,

　　We thank you __(1)__ your letter __(2)__ January 20, in which you express your interest __(3)__ our T-shirt.

　　__(4)__ reply, we are making you, subject __(5)__ your reply reaching us __(6)__ February 5, Beijing Time, the following offer: 1,000 pieces of T-shirt, __(7)__ $5 per piece CIF C 2% Shanghai, __(8)__ shipment during March-April, 2020. Other terms and conditions the same as usual.

　　It is very likely that the market price will rise. It would be __(9)__ your advantage to place orders __(10)__ delay.

　　We are anticipating your early reply.

　　Yours sincerely

2.6.3 Put the following English into Chinese or Chinese into English.

1) without engagement

2) regular supplier

3) discount and commission

4) 支付条件

5) 由买方选择

6) 不断扩大的市场

7) We look forward to receiving your order promptly as the prices are valid for only 10 days.

8) We are willing to allow a 5% discount for all orders over 1000 sets.

9) 我们不否认你方产品质量较好，但无论如何价格差距不应该超过10%。

10) 我方遗憾地通知您，我方所报价格很合理，以你方的报价我们无法达成交易。

Module Five >> Writings for Foreign Trade Correspondence
对外贸易函电

2.6.4 Supply the missing words in the blanks of the following letter. The first letters are given.

May 3, 2020

Re: Prices of Sheet Sets

Dear Sirs,

    I was so **p_____(1)** to receive your offer of April 29. We have considered your offer carefully and are pleased with most of the **t_____(2)**.

    We find the **q_____(3)** you offer to be on the small side. It is our **c_____(4)** to order at least 30 at a time, especially as this is the time that we prepare for our annual bedding sale. So, we would request that you be able to **p_____(5)** at least 30 of each item at a time.

    We are most happy with your products and would not like to go to another **s_____(6)** to fill our needs. So we hope that you will be able to **i_____(7)** the amount of each shipment to 30 each.

    Please **a_____(8)** within this week if this is **a_____(9)** so that we can draw up the **c_____(10)** as soon as possible and meet our timetable for the sale.

    Sincerely

2.6.5 Writing tasks.

Task 1: Write a letter for making an offer according to the following information.

Situation: You are a manager of Export Department of AAA Import & Export Company in P. R. China. You received an inquiry letter from BBB Corporation in Hong Kong on March 23, 2020. Now make an offer according to the given information and message.

Information:

Sender's Name: AAA Import & Export Company

Sender's Address: ××Beijing Road, Shanghai 210401, China

Tel: 86-21-6211××××   Fax: 86-21-6211××××   E-mail: ×××i@126.com

Receiver's Name: BBB Corporation

Receiver's Address: ××××Royal Road, Hong Kong

Tel: 00852-2323××××   Fax: 00852-2324××××   E-mail: ××××@yahoo.com

Message:

1) 告诉对方已收到其2020年3月23日发出的询价信。

2) 现提供所询商品的实盘报价，具体如下：

    品名：远足牌男式休闲鞋

    规格：棕色橡胶底、黑色棉布鞋面

尺寸：大码50，中码30

包装：每件塑料袋内装一双男式休闲鞋，每一加固板箱内装两打

数量：200打

价格：每打120美元，目的港（纽约）码头交货价

发货：2020年5-6月

支付：保兑的不可撤销的即期信用证

3）表达希望尽早收到对方订单并与之达成交易的心情。

Task 2: Write a letter in reply to the letter in Task 1 for making a counter-offer according to the following message.

Message:

1. 感谢您3月25日给予我方200打远足牌男式休闲鞋纽约目的港码头交货价每打120美元的报价。

2. 每打120美元太贵。因为同等品质的鞋子，本地的百货公司零售价格低很多。

3. 提出的条件：将价格降低20%，如果能实现，可能会订购300打。

Section 3

Letters on Acceptance/ Confirmation and Orders/ Contracts
接受、确认函与订单、合同函

3.1　Lead-In Introduction（导入介绍）

A: Letters on Acceptance and Confirmation

An acceptance or a confirmation is in fact an unreserved assent of the buyers or the sellers, who after mutual negotiations are willing to enter into a contract in accordance with the terms and conditions agreed upon. A deal is concluded when a firm offer or a counter-offer containing all necessary terms and conditions is accepted or an acceptance to a non-firm offer is confirmed.

Generally, it is only after the exchange of a number of letters, E-mails or faxes that the two parties come entirely to terms. In such a case, the buyers, when finally placing a formal order, would confirm the terms and conditions agreed upon. After that, a contract or an S/C, the short form of Sales Contract or Sales Confirmation, would be made out.

B: Letters on Orders and Contracts Sending

An order is a request for the supply of a specific quantity of goods. It may result from the buyers' acceptance or confirmation of a firm offer made by the sellers, or result from the sellers' acceptance or confirmation of a counter-offer made by the buyers.

Once a transaction is concluded, the order will be written in the contract, and the two parties are bound by the contract, which is generally a formal written document and is signed by both sides.

After the contract is signed by one of the parties, the party will send it to the other party to ask for their counter-signature.

3.2 Guidelines for Writing (写作指南)

A: Letters on Acceptance and Confirmation

Points to be considered while writing a letter of acceptance or confirmation:

• Express thanks for the offer, counter-offer or acceptance (if it is a confirmation to acceptance).

• Declare to accept the offer or counter-offer or confirm the acceptance.

• Assure all terms and condition (all main clauses should be mentioned again in the letter).

• Advise the opening of a L/C and ask for early shipment OR promise an early shipment. (if any)

• Expect a successful and pleasant cooperation and further orders.

B. Letters on Orders and Contracts Sending

Letters concerning an order are usually divided into two kinds: buyers' placing an order and sellers' confirming an order. They are actually letters on acceptance and confirmation (see Guidelines A).

Letters concerning contract sending usually have the following main points:

• confirming the business
• stating the sending of a S/C
• asking for counter-signature and other requirements
• expectation of early reply

Letters replying to the above letters generally include the following:

• confirming the receiving of the S/C
• stating the returning of the S/C with counter-signature
• stating the opening of a L/C and the arrangement of shipment (if any)
• expectation of successful fulfillment of the contract

3.3 Sample Study（范例学习）

Sample 1: Accepting A Counter-offer and Placing An Order

AAA Import and Export Trade Corp.

××Youth Street Shenhe District,

Toronto××××, Canada

Tel: 01-086-7563××××　Fax: 01-086-7567×××

October 15, 2020

BBB Trading Co., Ltd.

××th Floor××× Mansion,××× Jinlin Road, 200000

Shanghai, China

Dear Mr. Liu Huaxin,

We are pleased to confirm the letters exchanged between us. From your last letter we found the quality *is up to*[1] the standard and the price you quote is satisfactory. In order to promote our business relations and our friendship, we accept your 5% discount, we therefore airmail you our Order No. 43 as follows:

Order No. 43

Commodity	Article No.	Quantity（piece）	Unit Price（$）	Total
Ladies' sweaters	1123	500	20	$10,000.00
Children's sweaters	1124	300	15	$45,000.00
Sum:				$55,000.00

The L/C will be opened by the Bank of China in 15 days *in favor of*[2] your company. Please note that the *sales season*[3] is drawing near and the goods are *urgently*[4] needed in our market. We shall appreciate it if you can *dispatch the goods as soon as possible*[5].

Looking forward to your early reply.

Yours sincerely,

JOHN BROWN

JOHN BROWN

Manager

Notes

1. be up to　达到，符合。也可表达为：measure up to 或 come up to

   e.g.：The quality of the goods must be up to our requirements.

   （你方产品质量必须达到我们的要求。）

e. g. : After reinspection we found that the quality of the goods did not come up to our standard. （复检后发现所交货物的质量未达到我们的标准。）

e. g. : All the goods covered by our order must measure up to the sample in both quality and style. （我方订单的所有商品在品质与款式上必须与样品相符。）

up to now 直到现在

up to mark 达到标准

up to specification 符合规格

2. in favor of　赞成……；支持……；有利于……。此处用作"以……为受益人"。也可以表达为：

in one's favor 以……为受益人，以……为抬头。

e. g. : We open an irrevocable L/C No. 123 in favor of CITIC Trading Co. Ltd. （兹开立第 123 号不可撤销信用证，受益人为中国国际信托投资总公司贸易公司。）

3. sales season 销售旺季

4. urgent *adj.* 紧迫的，紧急的

an urgent cable/telegram　加急电报

in (urgent) need of...　（急）需要……

urgent dispatch　急件

5. dispatch the goods as soon as possible　尽快装运

dispatch 发运

e. g. : Please advise us of the dispatch of the goods. （货物发出请通知我们.)

e. g. : A messenger was dispatched to take the news to the soldiers at the front. （一名通讯员被派去给前线士兵送消息。）

Sample 2: Accepting and Confirming the Order of Sample 1

BBB Trading Co. , Ltd.

××th Floor ×××Mansion，×××Jinlin Road，200000

Shanghai，China

Tel: 086-03-5633 ××××　Fax: 086-03-5635 ××××

October 18，2020

AAA Import and Export Trade Corp.

×× Youth Street Shenhe District，

Toronto，Canada

Dear Mr. John Brown，

We acknowledge the receipt of your letter of 15th October, and thank you for the order No. 43 for Ladies' and Children's sweaters. We now accept your order and confirm the supply of the above-mentioned goods at the prices stated in your letter as follows:

Order No. 43

Commodity	Article No.	Quantity (piece)	Unit Price ($)	Total
Ladies' sweaters	1123	500	20	$10,000.00
Children's sweaters	1124	300	15	$45,000.00
Sum:				$55,000.00

We are glad to tell you that all the above items are *in stock*[1]. We believe that you will be satisfied with the quality of our products.

Your method of payment, *a draft at sight under L/C*[2], is quite acceptable to us. Upon receiving your credit from the bank, we will prepare your order, and *effect the shipment*[3] as soon as possible.

We sincerely hope this order will lead to further business between us and *mark the beginning of our happy trade relationship*[4].

Yours sincerely,

Liu Huaxin

Liu Huaxin

Manager

Notes

1. in stock 有现货 这里 stock 指"存货"。
   out of stock / no stock 无货
   a stock of … 一批……货
   e.g.: Sewing machine is out of stock now.（缝纫机现在没有货。）
   or: We're out of stock of sewing machines.
   e.g.: We can supply these goods from stock.（我们可以现货供应这些商品。）
2. a draft at sight under L/C 信用证项下凭即期汇票付款
3. effect the shipment 实施装运，进行装运
4. mark the beginning of our happy trade relationship 标志着我们之间愉快贸易关系的开始。

Sample 3: Sending a Contract for Ladies' and Children's Sweaters

AAA Trading Co., Ltd.

×××Jinlin Road, 200000, Shanghai, China

Tel: 086-03-5633 ×××× Fax: 086-03-5635 ×××

October 23, 2020

BBB Import and Export Trade Corp.

×× Youth Street Shenhe District, Toronto ××××, Canada

Dear Mr. John Brown,

Thank you for your order No. 295 dated October 21, 2009 for the Ladies' and Children's Sweaters. We are pleased to confirm having *concluded*[1] with you the *transaction*[2] of 400 pieces of Ladies' sweaters and 200 pieces of Children's sweaters. We have made out our *S/C*[3] No. 322 *in duplicate*[4] in which please *counter-sign*[5] and return one copy to us *for our file*[6]. We trust you will open the relative L/C at an early date.

As the sales season is approaching, if you place *repeat orders*[7], please act as soon as possible.

We look forward to your early reply.

Yours sincerely,

Liu Huaxin

Liu Huaxin

Manager

Notes

1. conclude 达成，得出，实现

   conclude the business 达成交易，也可以表达为 conclude a transaction。

   e.g.: If you could reduce the price to our level, there is a possibility to conclude the business. （如你方将价格降至我方水平，我们有可能达成交易。）

   e.g.: Usually, we conclude business on CIF terms with our customers.
   （通常我们以 CIF 的价格和我们的顾客成交。）

2. transaction *n.* 交易，成交，处理，办理

   e.g.: The transaction afforded him a good profit. （这笔买卖使他赚了一大笔。）

   conclude a transaction / deal with sb. 与某人达成交易

   the conclusion of a transaction 交易的达成

   e.g.: The conclusion of this transaction will mark the beginning of our long friendly relations.（这次交易的达成标志着我们长期友好关系的开始。）

transact *v.* 做生意，成交

transact a business with sb. in sth.

transact sth. with sb.

3. S/C 销售合同，销售确认书。

   S/C 是 Sales Confirmation（销售确认书）或是 Sales Contract（销售合同）的简称。其实两者并无本质差别，都是买卖双方签订的书面销售协议。若其中对双方的某些商务行为都做了法律后果界定的话，就都可以作为日后用于循法律途径解决争议和纠纷的依据之一。

4. in duplicate　一式两份，也可以表达为：in two copies, in two originals

   e.g.：Please send the duplicate of the contract countersigned to us.

   （请将已会签的合同一份寄给我方。）

   其他表示"一式……份"的单词有：

   in triplicate　一式三份

   in quadruplicate　一式四份

   in quintuplicate　一式五份

   in sextuplicate　一式六份

   in septuplicate　一式七份

   in octuplicate　一式八份

   in nonuplicate　一式九份

   in decuplicate　一式十份

5. counter-sign *v.* 副署，会签

   e.g.：Enclosed is our contract No. 345 in duplicate, of which please countersign and return one copy to us for our file.

   （随函附上我方第 345 号合同一式两份，请会签并回寄一份供我们存档。）

6. for our file　供我方存档

   e.g.：These documents will be arranged for our file in order to be consulted.

   （这些文件将被整理好供我方存档，以备查阅。）

7. repeat orders　续订单

Sample 4: The Reply to Sample 3

BBB Import and Export Trade Corp.

× × Youth Street Shenhe District,

Toronto × × ×，Canada

Tel: 01-086-7563 × × ×　Fax: 01-086-7567 × × ×

October 28, 2020

AAA Trading Co., Ltd.

××th Floor XXXX Mansion

×××Jinlin Road, 200001, Shanghai, China

Dear Mr. Liu Huaxin,

We have received your S/C No. 322 for 400 pieces of Ladies' sweaters and 200 pieces of Children's sweaters. We have counter-signed it and now enclose the duplicate for your file.

The relevant L/C is being opened[1]. We will inform you by telephone once it is opened so that you may *arrange shipment duly*[2].

We look forward to an effective and successful fulfillment of the contract.

Yours faithfully,

JOHN BROWN

JOHN BROWN

Manager

Notes

1. The relevant L/C is being opened. （相关信用证正在开立。）
   "开立"信用证可用动词 open、establish、issue 等。

2. arrange shipment duly　适时安排装运
   duly　及时。相当于 in due course, in time。
   e.g.：A bill was received and duly paid. （账单收到并及时支付了。）

3.4　Useful Phrases and Expressions（常用短语和表达）

1) concludes a transaction / deal　达成交易

2) for one's file　供某人存档

3) in duplicate　一式两份

4) Sales Contract　销售合同

5) enclose sth. together with …　随……附上某物

6) be up to the standard　达到标准，符合标准

7) sales season　销售旺季

8) in (urgent) need of…　（急）需要……

9) in stock　有现货

10) effect shipment　实施装运，进行装运

11) repeat order　续订单

12) in favor of　有利于……; 以……为受益人

3.5 Typical Sentences（典型例句）

1) We confirm the supply of the above-mentioned goods at the prices stated in your letter and will arrange shipment in the next week.
   （我们确认按你方信中所提的价格供货，并且于下周安排发货事宜。）

2) In order to promote our business relations and our friendship, we accept your 5% discount, we therefore airmail you our Order No. 520. （为促进我们的贸易关系和友谊，我方接受贵公司百分之五的折扣，因此我方空邮了我们的第520号订单。）

3) We confirm having purchased from you shirts, for which a confirmation of order is enclosed for your reference.
   （我方确认向你方订购衬衫，随函附上订购确认书一份，供参考。）

4) Enclosed is our Sales Contract No. 221 in duplicate in which please countersign and return one copy to us for our file.
   （随函附上221号订购合同一式二份，请签字并退回我方一份，以便归档。）

5) We sincerely hope this order will lead to further business between us and mark the beginning of our happy trade relationship.
   （希望这份订单会给我们之间带来更多的业务并成为我们之间愉快贸易关系的开始。）

6) We acknowledge the receipt of your letter of the 10th July, and thank you for the order you have given us.
   （贵公司7月10日函收悉，对此次订货，我公司表示感谢。）

7) We are glad to confirm that all items are in stock. We believe that you will be satisfied with the quality of our products.
   （我方很高兴地确认所订货物均有现货，我方相信贵方会对我们产品质量满意的。）

8) Upon receiving your credit, we will prepare your order, and effect the shipment as soon as possible.
   （一收到贵方的信用证，我方就会备货，尽快办理装运。）

9) Your method of payment, confirmed irrevocable L/C, is quite acceptable to us.
   （你方保兑的、不可撤销信用证的付款方式，我们是可以接受的。）

10) We are pleased to confirm having concluded with you the transaction of Ladies' sweaters. （很高兴与你方就女式毛衣达成交易。）

11) We enclose our S/C No. Q12 in duplicate of which please counter sign and return one copy to us for our file.
    （兹随附我方购货合同Q12号一式两份，请会签后退还一份以供存档。）

12) As the sales season is approaching, if you would place repeat orders, please act as soon as possible. （由于销售旺季来临，如贵方要续订，请尽快办理。）

13) We have duly received your Sales Contract No. 666 in duplicate for 100 sets of sofas.
    （我们已如期收到你方关于100套沙发的购货合同666号一式两份。）

14) As requested, we have counter-signed it and now enclose the duplicate for your file.

(按照要求，我们已会签并随附一份副本以便你方存档。)

15) The relevant L/C is being opened. We will inform you by telephone once it is opened so that you may arrange shipment duly.

(相关信用证已在开立中，一旦开立我们将电话通知贵方，以便你方及时安排装运。)

3.6 Training and Practice（操练与实践）

3.6.1 Complete the following sentences with one of the given words. Change the forms if necessary.

extend	in stock	confirm	in favor of
accept	be up to	conclude	in duplicate
repeat order	for your file	countersign	transaction

1) We are glad to _____ your offer and _____ the above mentioned terms.
2) We are pleased to inform you that the item you requested can be supplied _____ _____.
3) Enclosed we are sending you Contract No. HC354 _____, one of which please sign and return to us by airmail.
4) The quality of the goods must _____ the standard of the international market.
5) We trust this trial order may lead to more important _____.
6) The relevant L/C should be established _____ the seller.
7) You need to sign first when you buy a traveler's check and _____ it when you are going to use it.
8) Once the price had been agreed, a deal was quickly _____.
9) Thank you for your _____ which, as usual, is receiving our immediate attention. As requested, we will effect the shipment well in time.
10) We have received your S/C No. 222 in triplicate for 5,000 cases of tea. We have counter signed them and now return one copy to you _____.

3.6.2 Read the following letter and fill in the blanks with one of the given prepositions.

| to | at | of | with | in | on | for | from | onto | into |

Dear Ms Liu Ying,

____(1)____ reference __(2)__ the e-mails exchanged between us, we are pleased __(3)__ confirm having concluded __(4)__ you a transaction __(5)__ 30 metric tons of groundnut kernels. Enclosed you will find our Sales Contract No. 354 __(6)__ duplicate of which please countersign and return one copy __(7)__ us __(8)__ our file.

Please open the relative L/C __(9)__ an early date, so that we can arrange the shipment earlier.

Looking forward __(10)__ your immediate reply.

Yours sincerely,

3.6.3 Put the following English into Chinese or Chinese into English.

1) sales season
2) in triplicate
3) arrange shipment
4) 销售合同
5) 开立信用证
6) We acknowledge with pleasure the receipt of your order No. BTS-001 of 16th April for cotton shirts and welcome you as one of our customers.
7) We are pleased to confirm having concluded with you a transaction of 300 units of electric mowers and enclose our sales confirmation No. 850 in duplicate.
8) 按照要求，我们已会签并随附副本一份以供你方存档。务请注意货物须于10月底之前装运以赶上圣诞的旺销季节。
9) 贵方7月10日函收悉，感谢此次订货。我们保证你方收到货物后一定会非常满意。
10) 希望首笔交易能够带来我们之间更多的业务往来，并标志着友好贸易关系的开始。

3.6.4 Supply the missing words in the blanks of the following letter. The first letters are given.

> Dear Sirs,
>
> Thanks for your Sales **C** ___(1)___ No. 111 for 2,000 sets of electric heaters. We have **c** ___(2)___ and returned one **c** ___(3)___ completed to you for your **f** ___(4)___.
>
> An **r** ___(5)___ L/C has been **e** ___(6)___ with the Bank of China and sent to you. We hope it will reach you in due course.
>
> As our clients are in **u** ___(7)___ need of the goods, your prompt **s** ___(8)___ will be much appreciated. Please advise us of the **n** ___(9)___ of the steamer and **d** ___(10)___ of sailing as soon as possible.
>
> Yours faithfully,

3.6.5 Writing Tasks.

Task 1: Write a letter for acceptance or confirmation.

Situation: You are a manager of Sales Department of AAA International Trading Company in P.R. CHINA. You received an order from BBB International Trading Co., Ltd. in U.S.A. You are writing to confirm the order. Now compose the letter according to the information and message.

Information:

Sender's Name: AAA International Trading Company Limited
Sender's Address: Room ××××, ××Yudao Road, 210000, Nanjing, CHINA
Tel: 86-25-6711×××× Fax: 86-25-6711×××× E-mail: ××××@163.com

Receiver's Name: BBB International Trading Co., Ltd.

Receiver's Address: ×××West Street, New York NY ××××, U.S.A.

Tel:001-212-541×××× Fax:001-212-541×××× E-mail:××××@yahoo.com

Message:

1) 告诉对方很高兴收到其12月6日棉质长裤的订单。

2) 现确认按对方信函中所开列的价格供应棉质长裤,并安排于两周后装运。

3) 相信对方收到货物后,定会感到完全满意。

4) 相信首次交易将会增加双方日后更多更重要的贸易往来。

Task 2: Write a letter for sending a contract and asking for counter-sign.

Situation: Recently, AAA Native Produce Import. & Export. Corp received an order for Laoshan Green Tea from BBB Trading Co. Ltd.. You are the assistant of the sales manager of this corporation. Now please write a business letter according to the given information and message.

Information:

Sender's Name: AAA Native Produce Imp. & Exp. Corp

Sender's Address: ××Hong Kong Road, Qingdao, China

Tel:0532-8675×××× Fax:0532-8675××××

Receiver's Name: BBB Trading Co. Ltd.

Receiver's Address: ××Coast Road, New York, USA

Message:

a. 确认崂山绿茶的订单(No. 432)。

b. 发送合同S/C No. A-54,请求会签。

c. 希望尽快开立相关信用证。

d. 确保及时装运。

e. 希望再次合作。

Section 4
Letters on Trade Terms Negotiations
主要交易条款磋商函

4.1 Lead-In Introduction(导入介绍)

Before the conclusion of a transaction, the two parties must negotiate the trade terms by sending letters. These terms mainly include terms of payment, packing, shipment and insurance.

A: Terms of Payment

Payment is very complicated in international trade. Before placing an order, the method of payment for the transaction is to be agreed upon between two trading parties. There are three major modes of payment in international trade: Remittance, Collection and Letter of Credit. The most often adopted one is Letter of Credit (L/C), which is safer and more reliable, facilitating trade with unknown customers and giving protections to both sellers and buyers.

Usually, after a sales contract is signed, the buyers should issue a L/C at least one month before the day of delivery according to sellers' request. The L/C must be in complete conformity with the contract. Otherwise the sellers will ask the buyers for an amendment to the L/C.

B: Terms of Packing

Packing is of great importance in foreign trade. There are two types of packing, the packing for sale (inner packing) and the transportation packing (outer packing). The packing in the context of international trade in this section refers mainly to the latter type, the transportation packing, which provides protection for goods transported for long distance, mostly by sea. It provides easy marks for operation staff at the docks to distinguish the goods they handle and for consignees to identify their goods when receiving them at the destination ports.

A packing clause is an integral part of a sales contract or a letter of credit.

C: Terms of Shipment

Shipment is one of the essential links in the chain of international trade. Goods can be transported by road, rail or air, but in most cases of international trade, by sea. The shipment discussed in this section focuses on the most common conveyance method—ocean transportation.

In a sales contract, sales confirmation or letter of credit, terms of shipment are indispensable. Terms of shipment are the requirements of shipment, such as the latest shipment time, ports of loading and unloading, shipment documents needed and stipulation of partial shipment and transshipment, agreed by both the seller and the buyer who enter into the sales contract. In addition to these requirements, more instructions about shipment are given to the seller by the buyer in a written document called the "shipping instructions", which states, other than what have been regulated in the sales contract or the letter of credit, the packing requirements and shipping marks of the cargo.

D: Terms of Insurance

Insurance is very closely related to foreign trade. It aims to protect the trader against losses caused by dangers on the delivering trip over long distance. It is provided to cover almost any kind of occurrence that may result in loss. But, as a large percentage of international trade goes by ships and risks are generally great for ocean freight, what mainly concerns us here is the marine insurance.

Almost every international transaction by sea gets involved in insurance because the risks in the sea voyage are unexpected and varied. Therefore it now has become common sense that insurance should be bought in an international transaction, either by the exporter or the importer.

4.2 Guidelines for Writing (写作指南)

A: Letters on Terms of Payment

The letter on terms of payment usually includes the following main points:

- referring to the relative order or contract
- putting forward the payment term you prefer to use and stating the reasons
- expecting acceptance or an early reply

A letter replying to these letters generally includes two kinds, agreement or disagreement:

- extending thanks for the in-coming letter
- accepting the requirements in the in-coming letter or, in case of disagreement, expressing the regret for the inability to accept, stating the reasons and suggesting a new term of payment or insisting the previous one
- expressing the hope for doing business smoothly or, in case of disagreement, expecting acceptance

B: Letters on Terms of Packing

As a buyer, when writing letters concerning packing, the writer may

- mention the relevant letter or order or contract.
- raise or propose the specific packing or marking requirements and explain the purpose or reason.
- give shipping instructions and ask for advice after shipment (if any).
- expect a favourable reply.

As a seller, when replying letters concerning packing, the writer may

- acknowledge the receipt of correspondence.
- inform the completeness of packing.
- inform the specific marking.
- notify the shipment (if any).

C: Letters on Terms of Shipment

As a buyer, when writing letters concerning shipment, the writer may

- ask for shipment and give shipping instructions before shipment.

- ask for shipping advice.
- occasionally, ask for advance shipment for some urgent reasons and apologize for this change.
- wish a reply.

As a seller, when replying letters concerning shipment, the writer may

- acknowledge the receipt of correspondence.
- give shipping advice and state the name of ship, dates of departure and arrival, etc.
- notify the enclosed shipping documents (if any).
- express the assurance of shipment.

D: Letters on Terms of Insurance

When writing letters concerning insurance, the writer may

- mention the number of the order or S/C or L/C and the goods insured.
- raise requirements or requests about the insurance, or, reply to the requirements in the incoming letter.
- state clearly the name of the insurer, risks covered, the total value covered and the amount of premium.
- express one's expectation of an early reply or cooperation.

4.3 Sample Study (范例学习)

Sample 1: Suggesting *Paying*[1] by L/C

AAA Co., Ltd.

×× Lawton Street, New York NY ××××, USA

Tel: 00-1-1212- 345××××   Fax: 00-1-1212-463××××   E-mail: ××××

September 20, 2020

Steve Stewart

BBB & Co., Ltd

×× Regent Street

London ×××, UK

Dear Mr. Stewart,

We would like to confirm and accept your order for 500 Irina 262 electric typewriters *at your price of*[2] USD 300 each, CIF Lagos, for shipment during July/August.

We would like you to pay for this order by an L/C at sight. Since this is a big order involving US $ 150,000 and we have only *moderate*[3] cash reserves, funds *tied up*[4] for three or four months would cause problems for us.

Module Five >> Writings for Foreign Trade Correspondence
对外贸易函电

We much appreciate the support you have given us in the past and would be most grateful if you could ***extend***[5] this favour to us. If you agree, please establish the relevant L/C as soon as possible.

Yours sincerely,

Tony Smith
Tony Smith
Chief Seller

Notes

1. pay　付（款项，费用等）
   pay in advance　预付
   pay by installments　分期付款
   pay on delivery　货到付款
   payment　支付，支付的款项
   terms of payment　支付条款。也可以表达为：payment terms
   make payment　付款

2. at your price of ...　按你方……的报价

3. moderate 有节制的，稳健的；温和的；中庸的；中等的；适度的；普通的

4. tie up　原意是"捆绑"，这里用作资金的"占用"，指冻结资金，占用而积压资金。
   e. g.：It's unwise to tie up all your money in shares.
   （把所有的钱全困在股票上是不明智的。）

5. extend　给予（欢迎，帮助等），寄予（同情等）
   e. g.：extend financial help to sb（给予某人资助）

Sample 2: The Reply to Sample 1

BBB & Co., Ltd
× × Regent Street
London × × ×, UK
Tel: 00-44171-1245 × × ×　Fax: 00-44171-1246 × × ×　E-mail: × × × ×

September 25, 2020

Tony Smith
AAA Co., Ltd.
× × Lawton Street, New York NY × × × ×, USA

177

Dear Mr. Smith,

Thank you for your accepting our order for 500 Irina 262 electric typewriters.

We have considered your proposal to pay by a letter of credit at sight. We do not usually accept this term of payment. However, *in view of*[1] our long and mutually *beneficial relationship*[2], *we are willing to*[3] *make an exception*[4] this time.

I must stress that[5] this departure from our usual practice relates to this transaction only. We cannot *regard it as*[6] setting a *precedent*[7] for future transactions.

I enclose our sales contract No. 83 covering the order. I would be grateful if you would follow the usual *procedure*[8].

Yours faithfully,

Steve Stewart

Steve Stewart

Manager of Import Department

Notes

1. in view of　鉴于，考虑到

   c f. with the view of...　以……为目的，为了……

   e. g.：with a / the view of saving trouble　为了省去麻烦

2. mutually beneficial relationship　互利的关系

   mutual benefit　互惠互利

3. we are willing to...　我们愿意……

4. make an exception　例外

   e. g.：We will make an exception in this particular case.

   （我们将把这个例子当作例外。）

5. I must stress that...　我必须强调……

6. regard...as　把……当作是

7. precedent　先例，前例

8. procedure　过程，步骤；程序，手续

Sample 3: A Buyer's Requirement for *Packing*[1] and *Shipping Instructions*[2]

AAA Imports & Export Co., Ltd.

×××Leach St, Victoria, Australia

Tel: 61-4555-××××   Fax: 61-7896-××××

5th December, 2020

Zhang Liang

BBB Industrial Import & Export Corporation

×××Jingtian Road, 333000

Jingdezhen, Jiangxi, China

Dear Mr. Zhang Liang,

We have received your letter dated December 3, but we find that the packing clause in it is not clear enough. In order to *eliminate*[3] possible future trouble, we would like to make clear beforehand our packing requirements as follows.

The ordered wine glasses (Order No. MEC1201) need to be *wrapped up*[4] by *corrugated paper*[5] and packed in wooden cases with *foam*[6]. Please *limit the weight of each wooden case to*[7] 100 kg. *All cases need to be tied in stacks of three*[8].

With reference to *marking*[9], we would like to give some instructions as follows: The marking should includ our *company initials*[10], port of destination, order number, an "M" label and *handling instructions*[11] should be listed as below:

　　MEC
　　Victoria, Australia
　　MEC1201
　　"M"

Glassware Don't Throw[12]

Since the purchase is made on FOB basis, please arrange shipment of the goods ordered by us on *S. S*[13] "Prince" without delay. We would appreciate it if you could advice us by fax when the shipment arrangement is complete.

We believe the above requirements and instructions are clear to you and await your shipping advice. If you have any doubts about the above information, please contact me directly.

Yours sincerely,

Eric Swath

Eric Swath

Manager of Import Department

Notes

1. packing *n.* 包装
   pack *v.* 包装
   packing clause 包装条款
   关于包装的常用词组有：
   packing charges 包装费用
   packing list 装箱单
   outer packing 外包装
   inner packing 内包装
   neutral packing 中性包装
2. shipping instruction 装运须知、装运指南
   c f. shipping advice 装船通知
   在国际贸易中，shipping instructions 是"装运须知"，是进口商（买主）发给出口商（卖主）的。然而 shipping advice 则是"装运通知"，是由出口商（卖主）发给进口商（买主）的。其他与 shipping 有关的名词词组还有 shipping agent（装运代理），shipping marks（唛头），shipping space（舱位）等等。
3. eliminate 消除，避免
4. wrap up 包装，相当于 pack
5. corrugated paper 瓦通纸
   部分常用的出口包装容器名称：
   bag 袋包
   gunny bag 麻袋
   ploy bag 塑料袋
   bale 大包，大捆
   barrel 琵琶桶
   box 盒，箱
   bundle 捆
   cardboard carton 纸箱板
   case 箱
   wooden case 木箱
   cask 木桶
   keg 小圆桶
   drum 铁皮圆桶
   pallet 托盘，小货盘
6. foam 发泡塑料，一种包装填充料。包装时常用的填塞物料还有 hessian cloth（粗麻布）等。

7. limit the weight of each wooden case to 把每个木箱的重量限制在……范围内
8. All cases need to be tied in stacks of three. 木箱三个为一组捆起来。stack 作名词意思为"堆、叠物"，作动词则为"堆放，把……堆起来"之意。
9. mark　唛头 又叫 shipping mark（运输标记）
   在货物的外包装上用易于辨认的文字、符号等作为标记，以表明卸货港、货主及数量等信息。这些标记俗称"唛头"。通常由港口标记（port mark）、目的港（port of destination）、数量（quantity）和注意标记（care mark）等组成。
10. company initials 公司名字的首字母缩写
11. handling instructions　包装（搬运）警示语（指令）
    常用的包装标识警示语有：
    危险 dangerous
    易燃物 inflammable
    易碎 fragile
    易腐物品 perishable goods
    保持干燥 keep dry
    保持冷藏 keep cool/ keep in cool place
    此面朝上 this side up
    请勿用勾 no hooks
    请勿堆放 don't stack
    小心搬运 handle with care
    避免日光直射 keep out of the sunlight
12. Glassware Don't Throw　玻璃器皿请勿乱掷（这也是包装/搬运警示语中的一个）
13. S. S 也写成 s. s，是轮船 steamship 的缩写。所以 S. S "Prince" 可译为 "'王子号'轮"

Sample 4: The Seller's Reply for Sample 3

BBB Industrial Import & Export Corporation
×××Jingtian Road，333000
Jingdezhen，Jiangxi，China
Tel：0798-24635-××××　Fax：0798-2476-××××

15th December, 2020

Eric Swath
AAA Imports & Export Co., Ltd.
×××Leach St, Victoria ××××, Australia

Dear Mr. Swath,

Thank you for your letters of December 5 and 6, 2020. We are pleased to inform you that the 1,000 wine glasses you ordered *have been packed as requested*[1].

The wooden cases were *stenciled*[2] with your company initials, port of destination, order number, mark "M" and handling instructions. The packing charge was covered by the *freight*[3].

The goods were shipped on December 14 by Vessel "Prince", which *is due to*[4] arrive at New York on January 15.

We have mailed to you by air on December 13 the following documents as required in the contract: Invoice No. 2354 in duplicate; Packing List No. 679; Non-negotiable *Bill of Lading*[5] No. 390; *Insurance Policy*[6] No. 876

We trust that the goods will reach you *in good condition*[7] and give you complete satisfaction.

Yours sincerely,

Zhang Liang

Zhang Liang,
Manager of Export Department

Notes

1. have been packed as requested ……已经按要求包装妥当
2. stencil 印上模板图案或字样
3. freight *n.* （运输的）货物；货运；运费
   freight forward (or: collect)　运费到付
   freight paid (or: prepaid)　运费付讫，运费已付
   freight rate 运费率
   freight space 舱位
   e.g.: This freight must be carefully handled when loading.
   （这种货物装载时须小心搬运。）
   e.g.: Ocean freight is the most widely used form of transportation in international trade.（海洋运输是国际贸易中使用最广泛的运输形式。）
4. due *adj.*
   1) 预定的、预期的、应到的。常用于 be due to do sth 结构，此处 to 是动词不定式，后面跟动词原形。
   e.g.: When is the steamer due (to be here)?（这船预定何时到？）

e.g.: We are due to leave tomorrow.（我们定于明天动身。）

e.g.: The express for New York is due to leave at 5 o'clock.
（开往纽约的快车定于 5 点离站。）

2）因为，由于……。常用于 due to 结构，相当于 because of 和 owing to。在这种用法中，to 是介词，后面要跟名词、代词或动名词。

5. Bill of Lading 提单

   常用的提单有：

   Non-negotiable Bill of Lading 不可转让提单

   Clean（on board）Bill of Lading （已装船）清洁提单

6. Insurance Policy 保险单

7. in good condition 状况良好。此用法中还可以把 good 换成 sound.

   in perfect condition 完好无损

   in poor condition 状况不佳（尤指货物在送抵目的地时被损坏，或有所损伤的状况）

Sample 5: A Buyer's Request for Advance Shipment

AAA Commercial Company

××Cambridge Road, New York NY ××××, USA

Tel:（852）4567×××　Fax:（852）4565×××

E-mail: ××××@yahoo.com

December 5, 2020

Wu Zijing

BBB Motorcycle Export Company

××××Nanping Road, 400000, Chongqing, China

Dear Mr. Wu,

For the Order No. 1345, we would like to ask for changing *the scheduled date of delivery*[1] from December 15 to December 10, due to an urgent request from our client.

We realize that the change in delivery date may cause you inconvenience, but hope you understand that we would not ask for *earlier shipment*[2] if we are not in an urgent need. Please try to arrange the shipment as early as possible if the suggested delivery date cannot be met.

We *apologize for*[3] any inconvenience caused due to early shipment, and look forward to your reply to our request soon.

Yours sincerely,

David Lynne

David Lynne

Manager of the Import Department

Notes

1. the scheduled date of delivery 规定交货日期
2. earlier shipment 提前装运，相当于 advance shipment
3. apologize for... 为……而道歉，后面接道歉的原因 sth，若要表明向谁道歉，应用 apologize to sb for sth

Sample 6: A Buyer's Enquiry of Insurance

AAA Co., Ltd.

××Paradise St, Bangkok, Thailand

Tel.：+66（0）2633×××× Fax：+66（0）2633××××

E-mail：××××@tisco.co.th

Re. Order No. 345

December 15, 2020

Kenneth Beare

BBB International Trade Corporation

××Zhongshan Road, 510000

Guangzhou, China

Dear Mr. Beare,

With regard to[1] our order of 200 porcelains, we have issued an irrevocable L/C at sight which takes your company as the beneficiary.

You will be advised by the Shanghai Branch of the Bank of China very soon. So you can prepare for production and shipment **without any concern**[2].

There is another request we want to make here. As we know, the price that has been stipulated in both the S/C and L/C is based on CFR term and hence *insurance lies within our* **responsibilities**[3]. For the sake of convenience we wonder whether you could have the goods insured, **on behalf of us**[4], against **All Risks**[5], **Breakage**[6], and War Risk for 110% of the invoice value at your end. The premium charge is, of course, *for our account*[7].

Hope this request will meet with your approval.

Yours faithfully,

Zhao Kunshan

Zhao Kunshan

Manager of AAA Co., Ltd.

Notes

1. with regard to 指"关于"。表达该意思的词或短语很多，常用的有：regarding, referring to, as to, about, with reference to, in regard to 等。
2. without any concern 意为"不用担心"。之所以这样讲，是因为信用证已开，有了银行的付款保证，只要出口人在有效期内交齐信用证要求的单证，并确保所交单证填写无误，就一定能收到货款。若信用证没开，就没有第三方（银行）的信用保证，出口方则存在收款风险。
3. insurance lies within our responsibilities 保险由我方负责办理。这是外贸函电较正式的说法，也可以说"We (The buyer) should have the goods insured."。
4. on behalf of us 代表我方。这是整个句子的状语，可以放在句末。在这里把它像插入语般地放在这个位置是行文的自然节奏。说话人讲到这里时想强调这一点，他就先讲了。英语母语人士在讲话或撰文时往往如此表现。
5. All Risks 一切险（综合险）
6. Breakage 破损险
7. for sb's account 即"paid by sb."

    e.g.: According to the prevailing practice, the extra premium of the additional insured value and insured coverage should be for the buyer's account. （按照目前的惯例，对额外的保险金额及保险险种所收的保险费应由买方支付。）

Sample 7: The Reply to Sample 6

BBB International Trade Corporation

×× Zhongshan Road, 510000

Guangzhou, China

Tel.: 86-020-8966××× Fax: 86-020-8966×××

E-mail: ××××@tom.com, http://www.××××

December 20, 2020

Zhao Kunshan

AAA Co., Ltd.

×× Paradise St, Bangkok, Thailand

Dear Mr. Zhao,

Sub: Order No. 345

This is to acknowledge the receipt of your letter informing the opening of the L/C and requesting us to *cover insurance*[1] for the *captioned goods*[2] on your behalf.

We are willing to accept your request. Before completing the shipment we will *insure the consignment with*[3] the local branch of the PICC *as per*[4] the risks *coverage*[5] and insured value you mentioned. Then we will send you the insurance policy together with *a debit note*[6] for the *premium fee*[7].

We hope we could *serve your company to your satisfaction*[8].

Yours faithfully,

Kenneth Beare

Kenneth Beare

Manager of BBB International Trade Corporation

Notes

1. cover insurance   v. 投保，办理保险
   cover the goods against   将货物投保……险别
   cover the insurance with   向……投保
   cover against   投保……险
   投保还可以用 insure 表达。
2. captioned goods 指"标题中提到的货"，即 345 号订单项下的货物
3. insure the consignment with... 向……为货物投保
   insure vt. 为…保险；给…以保险；为……投保（后接货物或险别）
   insure vi.，投保……险（后多接介词 against 然后再加险别）
   insure against
   常用的表达方式：
   insure... (货物) for... (金额) with... (保险公司) against... (险别)
   e.g.: We generally insure our export shipment for 130% of its invoice value with the PICC against all risks. （我们通常对出口货物按发票金额的 130% 向中国人民保险公司投保一切险。）
   e.g.: We've covered insurance with People's Insurance Company of China on the 100 metric ton of wools for 110% of the invoice value against all risks at the rate of

3%。(我们已与中国人民保险公司将100吨羊毛按发票金额的110%投保一切险,保险费率为3%。)

the insurer 保险人

the insured 被保险人

4. as per 按照

   e. g.：quality as per buyer's sample（凭买方样品质量交货）

   e. g.：quality as per seller's sample（凭卖方样品质量交货）

   e. g.：as per order（按照订单）

5. coverage *n.*　保险范围,承保险别。有时也称 insurance coverage。

   e. g.：Regarding insurance, the coverage is for 120% of the invoice value up to the port of destination only.（关于保险,是按发票金额的120%投保至目的港。）

6. a debit note 借记账单,还款通知

7. premium fee *n.* 保险费

   premium rebate　保险费回扣

   premium rate　保险费率

8. serve your company to your satisfaction　为贵公司提供令你们满意的服务。

   to one's satisfaction　令……满意

   e. g.：We can process the supply material to your satisfaction.（我们可以进行来料加工并保证让您满意。）

4.4　Useful Phrases and Expressions（常用短语和表达）

1. at your price of …　按你方……的报价
2. tie up　冻结资金,占用而积压资金
3. in view of　鉴于,考虑到
4. mutually beneficial relationship　互利的关系
5. make an exception　破例
6. terms of payment　支付条款
7. to be packed as requested　按要求包装
8. to be stenciled (or printed or marked) with…　被印（或刷或标）上……
9. be due to do sth　预计要做某事
10. Bill of Lading　提单
11. in good condition　状况良好
12. shipping instruction　装运须知、装运指南
13. shipping advice　装船通知
14. as stipulated in the contract　按照合同的规定
15. cover insurance　投保,办理保险
16. premium fee　保险费

17. captioned goods　标题中提到的货物
18. insurance coverage　保险范围
19. on behalf of sb.　代表某人
20. insure the consignment with…　向……为货物投保

4.5　Typical Sentences（典型例句）

1. Since we have only moderate cash reserves, funds tied up for three or four months would cause problems for us.
（由于本公司只储备适量现金，占用资金三四个月将给我方造成很多麻烦。）

2. We much appreciate the support you have given us in the past and would be most grateful if you could extend this favour to us.
（承蒙贵公司一向照顾，若能继续给予优惠，本公司感激不忘。）

3. We do not usually accept this term of payment. However, in view of our long and mutually beneficial relationship, we are willing to make an exception this time.
（我们一般不接受这样的支付条款，但鉴于贵我双方长期互惠关系，我们这次乐意破一个例。）

4. I must stress that this departure from our usual practice relates to this transaction only. We cannot regard it as setting a precedent for future transactions.
（我必须强调此次非同寻常的做法，仅适用于本次交易，下不为例。）

5. In order to eliminate possible future trouble, we would like to make clear beforehand our packing requirements as follows.
（为避免将来可能的麻烦，我方欲提前说清楚如下包装要求。）

6. Please limit the weight of each wooden case to 100 kg.（请把每个木箱的重量限制在100公斤以内。）

7. The marking including our company initials, port of destination, order number, an "M" label and handling instructions should be listed as below.（唛头包括本公司的首字母缩写、目的港、订单编号、"M"字图案及小心处理的字句，书写格式如下。）

8. Please arrange shipment of the goods ordered by us on S/S "Prince" without delay.
（请立即安排将我们预定的货物装上"王子"号货轮。）

9. The goods were shipped on December 14 by Vessel "Prince", which is due to arrive at New York on January 15. We trust that the goods will reach you in good condition and give you complete satisfaction.（货物已经于12月14日装上"王子"号轮，预计将在一月15日抵达纽约。相信货物将安然抵达贵公司，并令您完全满意。）

10. For the Order No. 1345, we would like to ask for changing the scheduled date of delivery from December 15 to December 10, due to an urgent request from our client.
（关于1345号订单项下的货物，由于顾客的急迫需求，我们希望可以把原定的交货期从12月15日提前到12月10日。）

11. The price that has been stipulated in both the S/C and L/C is based on CFR term and

hence insurance lies within our responsibilities. (按照销售合同和信用证中规定的价格条款是CFR，因此保险由我方负责。)

12. For the sake of convenience we wonder whether you could have the goods insured, on behalf of us, against All Risks, Breakage and War Risk for 110% of the invoice value at your end. (为了方便起见，贵方是否可以代表我们在你们当地对货物按发票金额110%投一切险、破损险及战争险呢?)

13. The extra premium will be for our account. (额外保险费由我方负担。)

14. Before completing the shipment we will insure the consignment with the local branch of the PICC as per the risks coverage and insured value you mentioned. (在货物运输之前，我们将在中国人民保险公司本地分公司按贵方所提到的险种和金额投保。)

15. We will send you the insurance policy together with a debit note for the premium fee. (保险单及有关保险费的还款通知将一同邮出。)

4.6 Training and Practice（操练与实践）

4.6.1 Complete the following sentences with one of the given words or expressions. Change the forms if necessary.

payment	exception	consignment	package charge
to cover	advance	tie up	stencil
eliminate	have insured	wrap	in good condition

1) Our _____ terms are by a confirmed, irrevocable L/C payable by draft at sight.
2) Could you make an _____ and accept D/A or D/P?
3) The _____ of fund for 3 or 4 months in the bank is particularly taxing, owing to the tight money conditions.
4) As regards shipping marks outside the wooden case, the wording "Made in China" is _____.
5) The ordered goods have been packed as requested and the _____ was covered by the freight.
6) In order to _____ the future trouble, we would like to give the following packing requirements.
7) According to the contract, vases should be _____ up in wooden cases with foam.
8) The goods have arrived in Shanghai _____.
9) Would you please _____ the shipment from July 20 to July 10?
10) As requested, we _____ the shipment with the PICC against all risks for $4,500.

11) Generally, we _____ the porcelain ware for 110% of the invoice value against WPA and All Risks in the absence of definite instructions from our clients.

12. We have insured the _____ with the local branch of the PICC for the amount of USD 20,000.

4.6.2 Read the following letters and fill in the blanks with one of the given propositions.

by	below	in	under	above	as		within	up	between	to
for	about	on	till	with	of		against	from	without	at

Letter A:

Dear Sirs:

We are pleased that the businesses __(1)__ us have proved to be very smooth and successful. Our past purchase of Bed Covers from you has been paid __(2)__ a rule __(3)__ confirmed, irrevocable letter of credit.

__(4)__ this basis, it has indeed cost us a great deal. From the moment we open the credit __(5)__ the time our buyers pay us, our funds are tied __(6)__ for about four months. __(7)__ the present circumstances, this question is particularly taxing due __(8)__ the tight money conditions and the unprecedented high bank interest. If you would kindly grant easier payment terms, we are sure that such an accommodation would be conducive to encouraging more business. We propose payment either __(9)__ CAD (Cash against Documents on arrival of goods, 货到后凭单付现) or Drawing on us at three months sight (开出三个月期的汇票向我方收款).

Your kindness in giving priority to the consideration __(10)__ the above request and giving us an early favorable reply will be highly appreciated.

Yours sincerely

Letter B:

Dear Sirs,

Thank you for your letter dated December 3 inquiring __(1)__ the packing and the shipping marks __(2)__ the goods __(3)__ contract NO. 1122.

All tea is packed __(4)__ tins, the lids of which are sealed __(5)__ tape. Ten tins are packed in a wooden case which is nailed.

Please mark the bales __(6)__ our initials MAA __(7)__ a diamond, __(8)__ which comes the destination Bremen with order number 2020 again.

We look forward __(9)__ receiving your shipping advice and thank you __(10)__ advance.

Yours faithfully

Letter C:

Dear Sirs,
　　This is to acknowledge the receipt ___(1)___ your letter asking us to cover the leather shoes ___(2)___ Guangzhou ___(3)___ Antwerp ___(4)___ behalf of you.
　　We are willing to accept your request. We have gone through all the insurance procedures ___(5)___ the PICC Guangzhou Branch. The premium is ___(6)___ the rate of 0.8% of the declared value ___(7)___ the risks you demanded.
　　The insurer is preparing the policy and will send to you ___(8)___ one day or two. And they have confirmed that the consignment is held covered ___(9)___ from today.
　　We hope we could serve your company ___(10)___ your satisfaction
　　Yours faithfully

4.6.3　Match the following English expressions with their Chinese equivalents.

1. mutual benefit		A. 订购（下订单）	
2. place an order		B. 互惠，互利	
3. shipping advice		C. 装运通知	
4. Handle with care		D. 支付条款	
5. packing list		E. 装箱单	
6. Don't stack		F. 请勿堆放	
7. keep cool		G. 保持冷藏	
8. terms of payment		H. 小心搬运	
9. keep dry		I. 保险险别	
10. Insurance Policy		J. 尽早装运	
11. bill of lading		K. 提单	
12. All Risks		L. 投保	
13. earlier shipment		M. 保险单	
14. cover insurance		N. 一切险	
15. insurance coverage		O. 保持干燥	

4.6.4　Put the following English into Chinese or Chinese into English.

1）我们的付款条件是保兑的不可撤销的信用证，这是国际贸易中的惯例，我们不能接受其他的付款条件。

2）所有盒子的重量以 50 公斤为限。

3）The company initials should be marked clearly on every container.

4）As our users are in urgent need of the goods, please get the goods dispatched within the stipulated time.

5) We are pleased to inform you that the goods have been shipped on board S/S "Shanghai".

6) 我们对因提前装运而带来的不便表示歉意。

7) 请立即安排装船，我方等待着你方的装船通知。

8) If coverage against additional risks is required, the extra premium involved would be for the buyer's account.

9) 请按发票金额的110%为货物投保一切险。

10) As per your confirmation we will send you the insurance policy together with a debit note for the premium fee.

4.6.5　Writing tasks.

Task 1: Write a letter on terms of payment.

Situation: You are a manager of AAA Import and Export Corp. You have received a letter from BBB & Co. Ltd. in U.S. asking for payment by D/P. Now you are going to compose a replying letter on the terms of payment. The basic information is shown as follows.

Information:

Sender's Name: AAA Import and Export Corp.

Sender's Address: ××Beijing Road, 510000, Guangzhou, China

Tel：86-020-8675××××　Fax：86-020-8673××××

Receiver's Name: BBB & Co. Ltd.

Receiver's Address: ××Port Angeles, W. A××××, USA

Tel: 1-781-769××××　Fax: 1-781-769××××

Date: November 10th, 2020

Message:

1) 感谢对方6月10日来函提议关于试购陶瓷品付款方式一事；

2) 很遗憾经研究不能接受承兑交单付款方式；

3) 告诉对方我方通常要求以保兑的、不可撤销的信用证为付款方式；

4) 考虑到我们双方的友好关系，我们准备破例接受即期付款交单的方式付款；

5) 希望对方能接受并速复。

Task 2: Write a letter on packing.

Situation: You are purchasing 20,000 raincoats from Mr. Thompson in China. In order to make the packing clause clear, you send a letter to him to give the packing and marking instructions. Now compose the letter according to the given information and message.

Information:

Sender's Name: AAA Clothes Co. Ltd.

Sender's Address: ×××Lexiton Street, London ×××, UK.

Module Five >> Writings for Foreign Trade Correspondence
对外贸易函电

Tel: +44 (0) 222111 ×××× Fax: +44 (0) 222111 ××××
E-mail: ××××@hotmail.com
Receiver's Name: BBB Clothes Factory
Receiver's Address: ××South Road, Economic Developing District, Chongqing, China
Tel: 86-23-8903 ×××× Fax: 86-23-8903 ×××× E-mail: ××××@sina.com

Message:
1) 雨衣每件装在纸盒内，十件装一纸箱；
2) 外包装上刷上一个三角形，内刷我公司首字字母 SAR, 其下应刷目的港及我订单号；
3) 另外，还要表明"保持干燥"的警示性标志；
4) 期待收到对方装船通知。

Task 3: Write a letter on shipment.

Situation: Suppose you are the manger of Import Department of AAA Import & Export Company. You send a letter to Mr. Jiang from Export Department of BBB Industrial Company to request him to advance the shipment of the electronic fans you ordered on February 20. Now compose the letter according to the information and message below.

Information:
Sender's Name: Luis Bacon from AAA Import & Export Company
Sender's Address: ×××Bill St., Chicago, USA
Tel: +000190 ×××× Fax: +000190 ×××× E-mail: ××××@hotmail.com
Receiver's Name: Jiang Jianjun from BBB Industrial Company
Receiver's Address: ××××Yishan Road, Xuhui District, Shanghai
Tel: 86-21-8703 ×××× Fax: 86-21-8703 ××××
E-mail: ××××@alibaba.com

Message:
1. 关于5,000台电风扇订单的装运事宜，提出提早装运的要求；
2. 由于我方顾客的迫切需要，请求将装运期从3月20日提早到3月10日；
3. 强调提出这样的要求实属无奈，请求并希望对方谅解；
4. 期待尽早收到装船通知。

Task 4: Write a letter on Insurance.

Situation: You are the manager of AAA Textiles I/E Corp. Now you are going to compose a letter on insurance concerning one of your transactions. The basic information and message are shown as follows.

Information:
Recipient's Name: BBB & Co. Ltd.
Recipient's Address: XXX Arlington Street, Boston, Massachusetts, the US.

Sender's Name: AAA Textiles I/E Corp.

Sender's Address: XX Zhongshan Road，Shanghai, P. R. China.

Message:

1）告知已收到要求你方对标题货物代办保险的来函；

2）告知你方愿意代表对方在中国人民保险公司上海分公司为标题货物（订单项下的5000件毛衣）投保综合险，保险金额为发票金额的110%；

3）可望一两周内将保险单和保险费的借记通知寄发对方；

4）祝双方合作成功，同时表现出必要的商务礼仪和进一步扩大商业合作的愿望。

Module Six 模块六 International Event Documents and Business Contracts 国际会展文案及商务合同文书

Module Briefing

With the rapid development of the global economy and the dramatic increase of international interactive activities, business events and international trade are currently becoming powerful engines for local economics. International business events include business trade shows, exhibitions, conferences, meetings, etc., and they are making increasing contribution to international trades and business communications.

The dramatic development of economics depends on the success of every single business event and commodity transaction, while the event documents and business contracts play important roles in achieving the success. Moreover, the writing of event documents and business contracts is also one of the basic skills for foreign trade and its participants.

Generally, event documents vary in forms for different event purposes while a business contract is an agreement, enforceable by law and specifies the nature of the business in question.

In this module, 4 common event documents and a frequently used sales contract will be introduced and you are going to be trained to write for all these business activities.

Objectives

Upon the accomplishment of this module, you should be able to

1. choose and use the proper form of event documents to describe and convey your message to the receivers so as to reach specific event purposes.

2. read, draft and alter the frequently used sales contracts.

Focuses and Difficult Points

1. To be fully aware of the distinct significance and effect of each kind of event document

2. To be able to apply key skills in writing different event documents under different event contexts

3. To get familiar with the format and layout of business contracts

4. To get familiar with the contents of a sales contract and a sales confirmation

5. To understand the meaning of legal terms used in business contracts

Section 1
Invitation Letters to Exhibition and Conference
展会邀请函

1.1 Lead-In Introduction（导入介绍）

The success of any international exhibition and conference begins with successful advance publicity, while invitation is one of the most crucial marketing documents to any international fairs or meetings. Event organizers attract targeted participants largely through invitations, which are usually printed as brochures, pamphlets or even leaflets with important conference information. Invitations are also the main source for event participants to acquire preliminary information. Hence, writing an invitation is a prerequisite task for the successful operation of exhibition and conference.

Even though invitations to exhibition and conference have much in common, they are distinct from each other somehow since they are written for two different kinds of events. Moreover, according to the receivers, usually there are two types of invitation to exhibition, one for exhibitors and the other for audiences, especially professional audiences (also known as "professional visitors" or "buyers"). Generally speaking, most invitation letters for audiences are written by exhibitors to invite their clients to attend some specific fairs as visitors or buyers. Different types of invitation letters will be introduced in later parts.

1.2 Guidelines for Writing（写作指南）

Whenever you are holding an event, it is very essential to let people know about it. The invitation letter to attend the event is the best way to invite targeted people. The contents of the letter should be formal and informative on the upcoming event so that the reader will be encouraged to make a quick and positive decision about attending the event.

- There should be a title before writing any invitation letters.
- There are three forms for salutation:

1) letters to organizations: using the full name rather than abbreviation for the sake of respect;

2) letters to an exact person: using honorifics such as dear, honorable, distinguished, etc. before the name;

3) letters to the public: omitting the salutation, or using "to whom it may concern".

- Illustrate the backgrounds and objectives of hosting the event.
- Provide all the essential information regarding the event, including date, time, duration, venue and so forth.

- Indicate and highlight the attractive elements, such as event themes or topics, number of attendants, VIP or distinguished members' presence, intriguing on site activities, etc.

- Remind the readers that the date by which they should confirm their attendance or reply if necessary.

- Express hope for their attendance.

- Inscribe the invitation letter with the inviter's full name. A stamp or signature of the inviter will make it decent;

- Enclose the invitation letter with other documents such as registration forms, reply forms, contracts, etc.

1.3 Sample Study (范例学习)

Sample 1: An invitation letter to an exhibition for exhibitors

An Invitation to Exhibitors

Water Environment Association *Conference*[1]

August 18, 2020.

Dear *Vendor and Exhibitor*[2],

You're cordially invited to join more than 300 people involved in the water quality field in California at the 2020 Water Environment Association Conference. Attendees are *vocational specialists*[3] responsible for the operation and maintenance of wastewater facilities. In addition, most *have direct influence on*[4] the purchasing of equipment and supplies for their agencies.

Exhibiting your products/ services is one of the most *cost-effective*[5] marketing tools available because it puts you in contact with your potential customers, reduces your outside sales calls, and helps you build new business and *cement customer relationships*[6].

Event Schedule:
- Tuesday, September 8, 2020:
    1:00 p.m. — 7:00 p.m.: Set-up in Hotel Ballroom
    6:30 p.m. — 8:30 p.m.: Ice-Breaker Reception at Doubletree Hotel
- Wednesday, September 9, 2020:
    8:00 a.m. — 8:30 a.m.: Set-up, Finishing touches in Ballroom
    9:00 a.m. — 5:00 p.m.: Exhibits Open
    12:00 p.m. — 1:30 p.m.: Exhibitor Hosted Lunch

4:30 p.m. — 5:00 p.m.: Exhibitor Hosted Refreshments and Door Prizes

5:00 p.m. — 10:00 p.m.: Breakdown

Our goal is to provide exhibitors at our conference with the best possible *exposure*[7] and consequently build a long term working relationship with a set of industry exhibition partners. So join us at the 2020 Water Environment Association Conference, where wastewater industry leaders will *be exposed to*[8] your products, services, and information needed by them. We will work hard to *make your time at the conference beneficial*[9].

Please review the enclosed materials carefully and send in your registration material before August 25, 2020. We assign *booths*[10] as applications and payments are received. Historically, this conference has been a lot of fun, was *informative*[11], and *well attended*[12] by many agencies. Booth space is limited so don't miss this opportunity to showcase your business.

We look forward to having you join us in Sacramento to help make this a memorable event for everyone who attends!

Sincerely,

Steven Cline

Steven Cline

Exhibit Chair

Notes

1. 虽然是个会议，但大型会议往往附设展览。这篇范文就是针对展览参展商发出的邀请函。

2. vendor and exhibitor 意思是"卖家和参展商"，在展览中，卖家即参展商，与他们相对应的是买家和观众，即 buyer and audience/visitor。

3. vocational specialist 这里指"行业专家"，vocational 意为"职业的，行业的"。也可以表达为：industry expert, industry specialist 等。

4. have direct influence on 意思是"有直接影响力"。也可以表达为：is directly influential to

5. cost-effective 这里指"划算的、性价比高的"。类似的表达有：cost-efficient。

6. cement customer relationship 意思是"巩固/加强客户关系"。类似的表达还有：enhance/strengthen/solidify/ customer relationship。

7. exposure 意思是"曝光"。

8. be exposed to 意思是"曝光于……，接触到……"。原文意思为"……废水行业领导者们将接触到你的产品、服务及信息……"。

9. make your time at the conference beneficial 意思是"让你在大会期间受惠"。

make someone beneficial 是指"让某人受惠/让某人获得好处",也可以表达为: make benefit for someone, make benefit to someone 等。

10. booth 原意指"货摊,公用电话亭",这里指"展位、展台"。在展会中,展位同样可以表达为 stand。

11. Informative 告知性的,教育性的,有益的,情报的,信息量大的。这里指展会内容丰富。

12. be well attended 意思是"受欢迎,参加人数众多"。be well attended by someone 是指"受到某人欢迎/某人踊跃参与"。

Sample 2: An invitation Letter from an Exhibitor to Audience

**INVITATION FROM PRECISION MASTECH
OF THE ELECTRONICA FAIR 2020**

November 3, 2020

Dear Valued Customers,

Precision Mastech would like to thank you for the great support for all these years in advance.

We are of great pleasure[1] to invite you to the 2020 Electronica which will take place soon, starting from 2020/11/14 and ending on 2020/11/17. As one of the *major*[2] European Electronic fairs. The Electronica Fair is the World's leading electronics trade fair event. As many crucial and *cutting-edge*[3] electronics products are included in the exhibition, Munich Electronica Fair attracts thousands of companies from the electronics industry with good credibility and sound financial capabilities to participate.

The detail of the exhibition is shown as below:

Date: November 14 — 17, 2020 (Tue – Fri)
Time: 08:00 am — 18:00 pm
Venue: Hall A1
Booth: NO. A1.175/ 4

The booth of Precision Mastech will be *located at*[4] number A1.175/4. *Up-to-date*[5] products will be presented and the Mastech sales team is willing to provide the most appropriate service in the exhibition. You are welcome to contact the sales team if you would like to arrange an appointment with the Mastech management at the booth. In order to prepare the necessary information for the meeting, advance agenda is *highly appreciated*[6].

Meanwhile, excuse us for the inconvenience that we might bring to you by the late reply of E-mails during the time. Feel free to contact us earlier with any of your inquiries, and we will reply you as soon as possible. Thank you for the kind consideration.

We are looking forward to meeting you there.

Best regards,
Sales Team of Precision Mastech

Notes

1. be of great pleasure   意思是"非常高兴"。通常用法是 be of great pleasure to do sth.，类似于 be glad to do sth 和 be happy to do sth. 等。
2. major   *n.* 主要的，重要的；较多的。与 leading electronics trade fair event 中 leading 表达的同样的意思。
3. cutting-edge   意为尖端的，先进的，前沿的。
4. locate at   意思是"位于……"。类似的表达还有 locate in, locate on 等。
5. up-to-date   最新的，最近的，新式的。类似于 new 或者 newest 的用法。
6. be highly appreciated   非常感激，不胜感激。

Sample 3: An invitation Letter to A Conference

Invitation to the Tech Conference

August 13, 2020.

Dear Mr. Williams

On behalf of the Tech Conference, I am pleased to invite you to our *inaugural*[1] technology conference that will be held on August 30, 2020

This conference is the *brainchild*[2] of the 5 top Technology firms in the country, and it aims to bring together the best of brains to some round-table discussions on the direction and flow of technology for the nation and the world in the next decade. The Tech Conference 2020 is expected to be the largest Tech Conference with approximately more than 2,000 participants.

We would be delighted to[3] have you present at this conference to hear what the technology gurus and researchers have to share about the technology advancements and their impact on our businesses and daily lives. We would also love to hear your thoughts and opinions on such matters.

Kindly respond to this invitation before July 1, 2020 *to secure a place*[4] before *attendance*[5] is open to the public by July 2, 2020.

Your attention to this letter would be highly appreciated, and we look forward to your *confirmed presence*[6] at the Tech Conference.

Respectfully Yours,

Cecilia Dobson

Cecilia Dobson

Conference Chairperson

Tech Conference

Notes

1. inaugural *adj.* 创始的，开始的，最早的；就职的，就任的。在此篇例文中表示"首届大会"的意思，类似于 the first technology conference。
2. brainchild *n.* 脑力劳动的产物。
3. we would be delighted to 意思是"我们会很高兴……"。是比 we would be glad/happy to 更正式的一种表达方式。
4. to secure a place 指"获得参会名额"。
5. attendance *n.* 原意是"出席、到场"，这里指参会资格。
6. confirmed presence 在这里意思是"确认出席"。

1.4 Useful Phrases and Expressions（常用短语和表达）

1) vocational specialist 行业专家
2) cement customer relationship 巩固客户关系
3) make something beneficial 让某事有利益可享
4) be well attended 受欢迎的，参加人数众多的
5) locate in/on 坐落于/位于
6) exhibition package 参展套餐
7) on behalf of 代表……；以……的名义
8) up-to-date 最新的/最近的
9) exhibition breakdown 展会闭幕
10) secure a place (of) 保证/确保……的资格
11) be exposed to 曝光于……；接触到……
12) bring together 集合；使……团结在一起；聚在一起
13) take place 发生，举办
14) be expected to 预计
15) be highly appreciated 不胜感激，非常感激

1.5　Typical Sentences（典型例句）

1) The conference aims to bring together young start-up entrepreneurs and seasoned veterans, as well as government officials, bankers and other vocational specialists. （这次会议的目的是把年轻的初期创业者、有经验的企业家、政府官员、银行家以及其他行业专家聚集在一起。）

2) The international audience of over 5,000 will be exposed to your products and services for four days during our exhibition.
（超过5,000名国际观众将在四天展会期间接触到贵方的产品与服务。）

3) The International Car Parts Fair will take place soon in Guangzhou, China, November 8 to 12 of 2020.
（国际汽车零配件交易会很快将于2020年11月8日到12日在广州举办。）

4) The conference organizers are pleased to invite your enterprise or company to join the on-site exhibition. （大会主办方高兴地邀请贵司到现场参展。）

5) Last year, our exhibition was well attended by industry colleagues both domestic and abroad. （去年，海内外的行业同仁踊跃参与了我们的展览。）

6) Being located in Pazhou, Guangzhou, the Canton Fair attracts more than 24,000 of China's best foreign trade companies with good credibility and sound financial capabilities, and 500 overseas companies to participate. （广交会坐落于广州琶洲，吸引了24,000多家资信良好、实力雄厚的国内企业及500多家国外企业参展。）

7) Booth space is limited so don't miss this opportunity to showcase your business.
（展位有限，商机难得。）

8) Up-to-date products will be presented and our sales team is willing to provide the most appropriate service in the exhibition. （我们将展出最新式的产品，我们的销售团队也乐意在展览现场提供最合适的服务。）

9) Our goal is to provide exhibitors at our conference with the best possible exposure and consequently build a long term working relationship with a set of industry exhibition partners. （我们的目标是向大会参展商提供最高的曝光度，从而与一批行业参展伙伴建立长期合作关系。）

10) We will work hard to make your time at the conference beneficial.
（我们将努力让您在大会期间获益匪浅。）

11) Your attention to this letter would be highly appreciated, and we look forward to your confirmed presence at the conference.
（感谢您对此信函的关注，我们期待您确认参与此次大会。）

12) Your attention to this letter would be highly appreciated, and we look forward to your participation and to meeting you in Shanghai, October 2020.
（感谢您对此信函的关注，我们期待您的参与并在2020年10月于上海与您相见。）

13) Please review the enclosed materials carefully and send in your registration material before August 25, 2020.

(请仔细查看附件并在2020年8月25日前发送您的登记材料。)

14) Exhibiting your products/ services is one of the most cost-effective marketing tools available because it puts you in contact with your potential customers, reduces your outside sales calls, helps you build new business and cement customer relationships.

(在展览上展出你的产品/服务是最划算的营销方式，因为在展览上能和你的潜在客户接触，减少外部销售电话，建立新的业务，并且巩固客户关系。)

15) Kindly respond to this invitation to secure a place before attendance is open to the public by July 2, 2020.

(请在2020年7月2日对公众开放前回复此邀请函以确保获得参会名额。)

1.6 Training and Practice（操练与实践）

1.6.1 Complete the following sentences with one of the given words. Change the forms if necessary.

take place	vocational specialist	be highly appreciated
up-to-date	be exposed to	participation and support
well attended	make it beneficial	be expected to
on behalf of		

1) I am writing to you _____ the conference organizers to invite you to our fascinating event.

2) We look forward to your _____.

3) The 118th Canton Fair _____ Guangzhou, from 1st to 18th, October 2020.

4) We will do our best to _____ during your time in our Expo.

5) Over 30,000 overseas buyers _____ attend the 2020 trade fair.

6) Over 10,000 domestic and overseas visitors _____ your company and products during the 11th Pearl River Expo.

7) More than 900 domestic companies with their _____ products will exhibit on the upcoming trade shows.

8) Your attendance and participation _____.

9) The conference was _____ by overseas industry colleagues last year.

10) Approximately 200 company owners, _____ and professionals confirmed their presences for the next session of congress.

1.6.2 Put the following English into Chinese or Chinese into English.

1) 此次展会将在广州举办。

2) 接近500名海外专家预计会出席今年的大会。

3）非常感激您的参与，我们期待与您相会于此。

4）去年的会议吸引了超过3,000名与会者。

5）我们诚挚邀请您的企业在我们大会上参展。

6）For further information about the exhibition, please refer to the attachment below.

7）The conference will bring together enterprise owners, renowned experts and industry researchers.

8）We will strive to（努力、致力于）provide exhibitors with the best possible exposure.

9）To register or book exhibition booths please contact our staff.

10）The car show will be open to the public after June 15th.

1.6.3 Writing tasks

Task: Write an invitation letter to exhibition for exhibitor according to the following information.

Situation: Imagine yourself being a member of the organizers of Guangzhou International Automobile Exhibition. You are responsible for the marketing tasks of the exhibition. And now you are going to send your invitation to targeted exhibitors. Please compose an invitation letter covering the message given below.

Message:

1）代表广州市政府（Guangzhou Municipal Government）诚挚邀请汽车生产企业参加广州国际车展。

2）此次车展将于2020年11月20日至29日在广州中国进出口商品交易会展馆（China Import and Export Fair Complex）举行。

3）展会将聚集企业高管、行业专家、媒体及普通消费者。在这里可以与行业同仁进行深入的交流，同时获取最新的市场信息，并向10万观众展示最新产品。

4）去年车展吸引了超过60万人次（person-times）的观众，100多家参展企业。预计今年有将近63万人次的观众参与展会。

5）我们将会努力使参展商得到最大程度的宣传曝光。

6）提醒对方查看附件以获取更详尽信息。

7）表达希望尽早收到对方答复并期待对方参与。

Section 2
Post-Exhibition Reports
展会报告

2.1 Lead-In Introduction（导入介绍）

The post-exhibition report is one of the most widely applied event documents. The purpose of a post-exhibition report is to assess the effectiveness of an exhibition, trade show or fair and identify the reasons for its success or failure. The report helps organizers measure the return on their event-related expenditures and provides a basis for planning improvements or changes for future events. The readers of a post-exhibition report include sponsors of the event, teams organizing the event and exhibitors, visitors and other participants.

2.2 Guidelines for Writing（写作指南）

You need to write a post-exhibition report to determine whether an exhibition was successful by comparing its results against its objectives or results of past exhibitions. It's an important means through which exhibition stakeholders can determine whether they should make changes. There are ways you can ensure your report is more successful:

◆ Start the report with an executive summary, which is a concise version of the more detailed full report, including statistics that would be relevant to the readers. Such statistics could be:

- total attendees,
- number of visitors and exhibitors,
- number of sales leads generated,
- and so forth.

◆ Indicate the changes or discrepancies of outcomes comparing with exhibition objectives or previous exhibitions.

◆ Use bullet point to illustrate if it helps the reader to read or understand.

◆ Describe any operational problems that necessarily affected the outcome of the event.

◆ Finish the report with a brief conclusion, and make a series of recommendations if possible.

2.3 Sample Study（范例学习）

Sample: The RIUF Post-Exhibition Report

Romanian International University Fair 2nd Edition
Post Exhibition Report

The 2nd edition of RIUF-Romanian International University Fair *took place*[1] on April 1-2. RIUF was organized by Romanian College Union, *in cooperation with*[2] 5 other European higher education organizations. Over 4,500 visitors from Romania and Moldova *were present*[3] at the fair and received information and advice from the fair's 74 exhibitors from 18 countries.

This year RIUF's *thematic focus*[4] was on 'International Study Programs', *shining the spotlight on*[5] programs that provide Romanian students with more options for international study. More than 1,500 visitors also attended a wide range of mini courses, workshops and presentations, covering multiple topics.

Promotional Activities & Media Coverage

RIUF was covered extensively by a wide range of local and national media thanks to the promotional campaign.

The promotional campaign *deployed*[6] with the help of our media partners consisted of:

- 14 large ads in the main national newspaper,
- 1,100,000 + *online banners*[7] on several of the main Romanian general and business websites,
- News and banners inserts in several online newsletters.

In addition, we also used:

- 5 Press releases,
- Several announcements and promotional messages on 18 online community groups,
- *Direct promotion*[8] to about 1,500 students from the best Romanian high-schools,
- 2,000 posters and 30,000 flyers,
- Direct mail to more than 5,000 targeted audience,
- More than 200 sets of *media-kit*[9] that was sent to relevant journalists.

And the campaign results are:

- 20 news reports, editorials and interviews on the main national newspapers and magazines,
- 11 news reports and interviews with the organizers and shows where they were guests, on all the main TV channels,
- 11 news reports and interviews with the organizers on the main radio stations,
- Hundreds of news reports and articles on tens of different websites and blogs,
- And of course… 4,500 visitors at the fair.

Exhibitors

Of the 74 exhibitors *present at*[10] RIUF, 54 were universities & other academic institutions, 8 were non-governmental organizations and representatives of other educational systems such as the British Council, DAAD etc., and 12 were other types of participants, including educational agents, HR companies, media partners, sponsors and so on. Exhibitors from 18 countries showcased their products, programs and services in the fields of undergraduate education, postgraduate education, international exchange, etc. on this session.

Visitors

More than 4,500 visitors attended RIUF. *Compared with last session, the number of visitors increased by* 29.11%. Visitors from Northern Romania account for more than half of all visitors that came to RIUF this year. They are interested in gathering information on studying abroad, meeting and *interacting with*[11] the representatives of international academic institutions and learning from the experiences of other young Romanians that are already students or graduates of *prestigious*[12] institutions all over the world.

Conclusion

The 2nd Edition of RIUF recorded an increase in the overall quality of the event, meeting most of the expectations of the exhibitors, visitors and organizers and thus starting to grow its own tradition. The extraordinary support attracted by the event creates the premises or continuous future developments and commands greater efficiency in meeting every stakeholder's objectives: exhibitors, visitors, partners of the event and organizers.

Notes

1. take place 这里指是"举办",也有"发生"的意思。
2. in cooperation with 相当于 in collaboration with 或 in concert with,意思是"与……合作"。
3. be present 相当于 attend,意思是"出席,参加"。
4. thematic focus 相当于 theme,这里指"主题,主要焦点"。
5. shine the spotlight on 原意指"把光照向……",这里特指"聚焦于……/把焦点集中在……",相当于 focus on。
6. deploy 这里指"活动开展"。原意是"部署、展开"。
7. online banner 相当于 website banner,指网页上的横幅广告。
8. direct promotion 意思是"直接推销"。promotion 有"推销,促销"之意。
9. media-kit 特指"宣传资料,媒体资料包,媒体宣传袋"。
10. present at 相当于 exhibit at,指"在……展示,展出"。
11. interact with 相当于 communicate with,这里指"交流,互动"。同时也有"与……相互作用"的意思。
12. prestigious 指"有声望的,有名望的"。

2.4 Useful Phrases and Expressions（常用短语和表达）

1) take place 举行,发生
2) be present 出席,参加
3) present at 在……展示
4) interact with 互动,交流
5) compare with 与……相比
6) increase/up by 增长了……

7) decrease/down by 减少了……

8) account for 占（比例）

9) rise/grow to 增长至……

10) reduce/decrease to 减少至……

11) in cooperation with 与……合作

12) thematic focus 焦点，主题

13) shine the spotlight on 聚焦于……/把焦点集中于……

14) be covered extensively by 被……广泛报道

15) in the field of 在……领域

2.5　Typical Sentences（典型例句）

1) The 2nd edition of RIUF-Romanian International University Fair took place on April 1-2.（第二届罗马尼亚国际大学展于4月1日至2日举行。）

2) Over 4,500 visitors from Romania and Moldova were present at the fair and received information and advice from the fair's 74 exhibitors from 18 countries.
（超过4,500名来自罗马尼亚和摩尔多瓦的观众出席了本次展览，从来自18个国家的74个参展商处获取信息与建议。）

3) Compared with last session, the number of visitors increased by 29.11%.
（与上一届展会相比，观众人数增加了29.11%。）

4) Visitors from Northern Romania account for more than half of all visitors that came to RIUF this year.（来自北部罗马尼亚的观众占了所有参加今年RIUF观众的一半以上。）

5) The Guangdong Food Festival was organized by Guangzhou Provincial Government, in cooperation with China Food Association.
（广东美食节是由广东省政府联合中国美食协会共同举办的。）

6) This year RIUF's thematic focus was on 'International Study Programs', shining the spotlight on programs that provide Romanian students with more options for international study.（此次RIUF是以"国际深造项目"为主题举行的，聚焦于为罗马尼亚学生提供更多国际深造的选择。）

7) More than 1,500 visitors also attended a wide range of mini courses, workshops and presentations, covering multiple topics.
（超过1,500名观众参与了多种多样的迷你课程、研讨会和说明展示，涵盖了多个主题。）

8) Exhibitors from 18 countries showcased their products, programs and services in the fields of undergraduate education, postgraduate education, international exchange, etc. on this session.（来自18个国家的参展商在这届展会上展示了他们在本科教育、研究生教育及国际交流等领域的产品、项目和服务。）

9) Thanks to the promotional campaign, RIUF was covered extensively by a wide range of

local and national media.

(多亏了此次推广活动，RIUF被多家地方与全国媒体广泛报道。)

10) They are interested in gathering information on studies abroad, meeting and interacting with the representatives of international academic institutions.

(他们的兴趣在于收集国外留学的信息，与国际学术机构代表会面并交流互动。)

11) The annual Education Fair is the leading international exhibition for education industry in Southern China, encompassing all aspects of the education-related business. (一年一度的教育展是华南地区首屈一指的国际教育行业展览，包括了教育关联产业的方方面面。)

12) Among regular buyers, 51,479 attended the Fair for over 10 times, up by 3.55% over last year, which indicates that regular buyers are showing a higher degree of loyalty.

(在定期参加展会的买家中，有51,479名参加了超过10届展会，比去年增加了3.55%，这表明定期买家们表现出更高的忠诚度。)

2.6　Training and Practice（操练与实践）

2.6.1 Complete the following sentences with one of the given words. Change the forms if necessary.

increase to	take place	a wide range of	interact with
down by	in cooperation with	cover	compare with
annual	account for		

1) The 27th International Fair for Coffee, _____ from November 23—28, 2020, at the "Pazhou Complex" in Guangzhou.

2) Female audience _____ over 60% of the all visitors in Beauty Expo.

3) The conference will provide _____ on-site services to facilitate audience from abroad.

4) _____ last year, the exhibition suffers a slight decrease in the number of overseas visitors.

5) Since domestic enterprises are becoming more interested in communicating with foreign partners, the number of domestic exhibitors _____ 532 during this session.

6) _____ influential local firms, the Temple Fair was successfully held by the municipal government.

7) The _____ event will be held around the same dates next year.

8) The amazing event was _____ massively by over 300 media both online and offline, from domestic to overseas.

9) Altogether 1,457 international chain companies attended the Fair, _____ 3.57% compared with last session.

10) Approximately 200 overseas students came to the summer camp to _____ local educational institutions.

2.6.2 Put the following English into Chinese or Chinese into English.

1）在3,000名参与此次大会的人中，大学生观众占了约40%。

2）今年，超过500个来自全国的参展商在展会期间展示了他们在各个领域的产品和服务。

3）与去年相比，来自江苏的参展商增加了24%，来自上海的增加了8%。

4) 2020 Guangzhou Temple Fair was covered extensively by over 200 local and national media, including television stations, newspapers, magazines, websites as well as radio stations.

5) The fair was launched under the theme of "Global Cooperation", which is focusing on providing participants with more communication opportunities.

6) About 2,000 buyers from 12 countries in Europe were present at the event to interact with 67 local enterprises.

2.6.3 Writing tasks.

Task 1: Write a post-exhibition report according to the following information.

Situation: Imagine yourself being a staff from International Languages and Cultures Exhibtion. You are required to write a post-exhibition report after holding the event. Now compose a report covering the message given below.

Message:

1）国际语言文化展（International Fair for Languages and Cultures），于2020年6月21-25日在广州琶洲展馆（Pazhou Complex）举办。

2）吸引了19,742名观众到场与多种文化和超过50种语言进行了交流互动。

3）来自29个国家的165个参展商在这届展会上展示了他们在语言学习与教育领域的产品、项目和服务。

4）该展会也提供了多种多样的微型语言课程，研讨会和说明展示，涵盖了语言学习旅游（language study travels）、语言测试及国际交流项目等主题。

5）该展会是亚洲中文地区首屈一指的国际语言与文化展览，包括了语言教育市场的方方面面。

6）2020年国际语言文化展被300多家当地、全国及海外媒体广泛报道，包括电视台、报纸、杂志、网站及电台。

7）同时，该展览还受到了包括中国日报、轻松调频（Easy FM）等媒体的支持。

Section 3
Conference and Exhibition Agendas
展会日程表

3.1 Lead-In Introduction（导入介绍）

An agenda is a list of items and/ or issues that has to be discussed and/ or arranged during a business event. One key to a successful business event is agenda planning. The difference between business events with and without agendas can be the difference between chaos and very good accomplishments. An agenda communicates to attendees that the event will be conducted in an orderly fashion. Businesses hold conferences and exhibitions to share information, make trades and exchanges, communicate with business partners, develop plans, provide clarity and make decisions. An event agenda can ensure that the event stays on track and that those special projects and routine operations proceed as intended. An agenda can as well help a group of staff function as an effective team.

3.2 Guidelines for Writing（写作指南）

Business employees are expected to produce an agenda for the conferences or exhibitions they organize. Writing an agenda for a program — especially a multi-day program — is sometimes challenging because the agenda needs to be brief, but provide comprehensive information. After all, most guests and attendees want to be familiar with the event, but they don't want to carry around an extensive document to know where they should be and when.

An agenda should provide the following pieces of information:

◆ Name, date and location of the conference or exhibition should be provicled.
◆ Specific time and days for activities should be specified.
◆ Items should be brief and easy to follow.
◆ Every activity must have a time and place.
◆ The event schedule should be full.
◆ Attendees should know where they can find more information.

3.3　Sample Study（范例学习）

Sample 1: The Exhibition Agenda

The International Fair of Investment & Trade (IFIT)

Sept 8-11, 2020
Xiamen, China

Time	Item	Place
8:30-17:00, Sept. 4th-6th	• Exhibitors check-in, to get *Exhibitor Passes*[1] and the *Booth Setup & Dismantling*[2] Passes, and to set up booths. • Documents required for check-in: a copy of booth rental payment proof and booth confirmation letter.	"Exhibitor Check-in Counter" located at the Guest Registration Center on the West-wing *Foyer*[3] of Hall L, Building II, Xiamen International Conference & Exhibition Center (IFIT venue)
12:00, Sept. 7th	• Booth setup completed, security check starts	IFIT venue
9:00, Sept. 8th	• The *Opening Ceremony*[4] of the fair	Foyer, Building I, CIFIT venue
Sept. 8th-11th	Exhibition and negotiation	IFIT venue
16:00, Sept. 11th	Booth dismantling starts	IFIT venue

Note:

1. After 12:00, Sept. 6th, all the Booth Setup & Dismantling Pass holders shall enter and exit the Venue from the back doors of the exhibition halls.

2. During IFIT, the exhibition opens from 9:00 to 17:00. Exhibitor Pass holders have to *access*[5] the venue from the back doors and get booths prepared 30 minutes before the opening of the exhibition, and exit the venue within 30 minutes after its closing.

Notes

1) Exhibitor Passes　这里指"参展商通行证"，可译为"参展证"。
2) Booth Setup & Dismantling　这里指"装展与撤展"，意思是"展位的搭建与拆除"。
3) Foyer　这里指"大堂、大厅"；同时也有"门厅、休息室"之意。
4) Opening Ceremony　意为"开幕式，开幕典礼"
5) access　这里指"进入"，同时也有"使用""接近"等意思。

Sample 2: A Conference Agenda Overview

2020 Global Leadership Conference Agenda Overview

Space permitting[1], all events are open to all conference participants, *unless otherwise indicated*[2] as a *ticketed event*[3].

Tuesday-October 10

14:00-17:00	Check-in & Help Desk	Entrance Hall
14:00-17:00	Onsite Staff & Volunteer Office	VIP Room
20:00-22:00	*Spanish Tapas Reception*[4] & *Networking Event*[5] (Ticketed Event-no onsite tickets available)	Meetings 23, C/Sant-Joaquim 23

Wednesday-October 11

…	…	…
8:00-18:00	*Pre-Conference*[6] Workshops (See attachment for Details)	Various Locations
18:15-20:00	Welcome to Barcelona! & Opening Reception	Banquet Hall
18:30-20:00	Exhibit Hall Open	Banquet Hall
18:30-20:00	Leadership Bookstore Open	Banquet Hall

Thursday-October 12

…	…	…
9:00-10:30	Plenary	Rooms 111 & 112
10:45-12:00	*Concurrent*[7] Session One	See attachment for details
12:15-13:15	Concurrent Session Two	See attachment for details
13:30-14:45	Conference Colleagues Networking *Luncheon*[8] (Ticketed Event)	Banquet Hall
15:00-16:30	Concurrent Session Three	See attachment for details
16:45	Afternoon Coffee & Tea in Exhibit Area	Banquet Hall

17:00-18:25	***Interactive Roundtable Discussions*[9]** (See attachment for details)	Banquet Hall
18:30-20:00	Leadership Education	Room 118
18:30-19:15	Leadership Development Member Interest Group Meeting	Room 116
20:30-22:30	Deans, Directors and Chairs Networking Dinner (Ticketed Event)	El Cangrejo Loco Restaurant
20:30-22:30	Public Leadership Networking Dinner (Ticketed Event)	La Fitora Restaurant
...	...	...

Saturday- October 14

7:30-12:00	Check-in & Help Desk	Entrance Hall
7:30-12:00	Onsite Staff & Volunteer Office	VIP Room
8:00-8:45	Annual Membership Meeting	Room 122
9:00-10:30	Concurrent Session Nine	See attachment for details
10:45-11:45	Concurrent Session Ten	See attachment for details
12:00-13:30	Closing Plenary	Rooms 111 & 112
12:45-19:00	Post-Conference Workshops (See attachment for details)	***Various Locations*[10]**

✻ Notes

1) space permitting 这里指"如果空间/场地允许",类似用法还有 room/time permitting,指"如果空间/时间允许"。

2) unless otherwise indicated 意思是"除非另有说明",类似的表达还有 unless otherwise noted/ specified/ stipulated/ stated 等。

e. g. : Unless otherwise indicated, all transportation and catering fees are included in the conference package. 除非另有说明,所有的交通与餐饮费用都包含在大会套餐内。

3) ticketed event　这里专指"需要购买门票的活动"。同时，ticketed participant/ audience/ passenger 还可以指"持票参与者/观众/乘客"。

4) Spanish tapas reception　可理解为"点心招待会"。Spanish tapas 原指"西班牙餐前点心"；reception 则指"招待会、接待会"。

5) Networking Event　指"交流活动、社交活动"。类似用法还有下文中的 Networking Dinner，指"交流晚宴"。

6) Pre-Conference　指"大会前的，会前的"，pre-conference events 指"会前活动"；下文中的 Post-Conference 则指"大会后的、会后的"。

7) concurrent　指"同时发生的"，会议日程表中常用 concurrent session 表示同期会议，类似的表达还有下文中的 parallel session。

8) luncheon　指"午宴、正式午餐"。

9) Interactive Roundtable Discussions　指"互动圆桌讨论"。

10) Various Locations　指"多个地点"。

3.4　Useful Phrases and Expressions（常用短语和表达）

1) opening ceremony　开幕式、开幕典礼
2) unless otherwise indicated　除非另有说明
3) space/room permitting　如果空间/场地允许
4) ticketed event　须购买门票的活动
5) ticketed participant　持票参与者、持票与会者
6) networking event　交流活动
7) pre-conference　大会前的、会前的
8) post-conference　大会后的、会后的
10) group session　小组讨论
11) keynote speech　专题演讲、主题演讲
12) concurrent/parallel sessions　同时进行的会议/平行会议/同期会议

3.5　Typical Sentences（典型例句）

1) All conference staffs and volunteers will be onsite before the opening ceremony.
（所有大会工作人员及志愿者会在开幕式之前就位。）

2) Unless otherwise indicated, all concurrent sessions during the conference will be free of charge.（除非另有说明，所有大会期间的同期会议都将是免费的。）

4) Both pre- and post-conference events are ticketed events, and tickets are available on the conference official websites only.
（会前与会后活动均须购票，门票仅在大会官网出售。）

5) All caterings, including tea breaks, are open to ticketed participants.
（所有餐饮项目，包括茶歇，均向持票与会者开放。）

3.6 Training and Practice（操练与实践）

3.6.1 Match the following English expressions with their Chinese equivalents.

1) opening ceremony   A) 参展证
2) Spanish tapas reception   B) 交流活动
3) group session   C) 须购买门票的活动
4) ticketed event   D) 大堂、大厅
5) keynote speech   E) 点心招待会
6) concurrent/parallel sessions F) 持票参会者
7) ticketed participant   G) 专题演讲/主题演讲
8) networking event   H) 开幕式、开幕典礼
9) Exhibitor Passes   I) 平行会议/同期会议
10) Foyer   J) 小组讨论

3.6.2 Writing tasks.

Translating a conference agenda into an English version.

Situation: Imagine yourself being a staff of the 2020 Annual Conference, you are required to make a conference agenda. Now translate the agenda into an English version with message given below.

Message:

2020 年年会

中国●武汉

2020 年 6 月 17-19 日

会议日程

6月17日		
9:00-19:00	注册与签到	武汉会议中心入口大厅
14:00-22:00	注册与签到	弘毅酒店、茶港商务酒店
18:30-20:30	招待会	老门茶馆
6月18日		
7:50-17:50	注册与签到	武汉会议中心入口大厅
9:00-9:30	开幕式（由武汉市长致欢迎辞）	武汉会议中心长江厅
9:45-10:00	茶歇	武汉会议中心3层门厅
10:00-12:00	主题演讲 （发言嘉宾：Robert Cervero, Niraj Verma, Chris Webster, 张廷伟, 吴志玲）	武汉会议中心长江厅

（续）

12:15-13:15	午餐	武汉会议中心宴会厅
13:30-17:30	平行会议（具体安排见附件）	武汉会议中心长江厅、黄鹤厅、月湖厅、江岸厅、盘龙厅、琴台厅
15:10-15:40	茶歇	武汉会议中心3层门厅
18:00-19:30	晚餐	明珠园餐厅
19:30	乘车返回酒店	
6月19日		
8:30-12:00	平行会议（具体安排见附件）	武汉会议中心长江厅、黄鹤厅、月湖厅、江岸厅、盘龙厅、琴台厅
10:00-10:30	茶歇	武汉会议中心3层门厅
12:30-13:30	午餐	武汉会议中心宴会厅
13:30-16:45	平行会议（具体安排见附件）	武汉会议中心长江厅、黄鹤厅、月湖厅、江岸厅、盘龙厅、琴台厅
17:00-18:00	全体会议	武汉会议中心长江厅
18:30-21:00	闭幕式及闭幕晚宴	武汉会议中心宴会厅

Section 4
Registration, Application and Booth Reservation Forms
会展注册、申请与展位预订表

4.1 Lead-In Introduction（导入介绍）

How could we know about the probable number of participants, the exact area of venue needed and services required by participants before an event takes place? One of the most practical and efficient ways is to send out registration, application or booth reservation forms. Generally, these forms are always attached to event invitation letters. By sending and collecting registration, application or booth reservation forms, event organizers can estimate and calculate the number of event participants, the needed area to host events, and thus they can prepare accordingly in advance. Furthermore, collecting these forms help to gather the participants' basic information and requirements toward the event, with which event organizers can provide necessary and specific services to them.

4.2 Guidelines for Writing（写作指南）

When creating a registration or reservation form for any business events, including both exhibitions and conferences, it is highly recommended to consider capturing all factors that will help event organizers service participants (including exhibitors, visitors, audience and so forth) in the most efficient manner. The information gathered from these forms will provide a foundation for servicing customer needs.

◆ Write down the categories of information that you want to obtain from potential participants, including:
- customer demographics (name, age, nation, firm, position, etc.),
- customers' service requirements.

◆ Determine the question and answer format for each category included on the form. Formats to consider include:
- short questions,
- yes or no,
- multiple choices,
- open-ended questions.

◆ Show relevant rates or fares clearly.

◆ Also, try to find out how they have learned about your company as a way to measure marketing effort.

◆ Inform the potential participants how to complete the form.

◆ Don't forget to give them an incentive to register or apply, such as:
- having certain privileges by early registration or application,
- staying informed of latest event news or promotion,
- receiving better event services.

4.3 Sample Study (范例学习)

Sample 1: The Annual Conference Registration Form

The Annual Conference and Exhibit Show

March 15-17, 2020   Los Angeles, California, USA

Registration Form

Registrant[1] Information—Only one registrant per form. Please type or print clearly.

Name (Mr./Ms./Mrs./Dr.)	Member ID (*If known*[2])
Job Title (Required)	Organization
Mailing Address	
City	State/Province
Post Code	Country
Office Phone	Home Phone
Fax	E-mail Address

Module Six >> International Event Documents and Business Contracts
国际会展文案及商务合同文书

Conference Options

	Early Bird[3]	Regular	On-Site
Member	$259	$359	$399
Non-member	$325	$425	$465
Presenter	$179	$179	$179
Student/Senior	$129	$139	$149

Conference Registration Information

Payment Must Accompany Registration Form

- Online: You can pay online (www.ascd.org/annualconference) with a MasterCard, VISA, American Express, or Discover Card.
- By Phone: You can pay by phone (1-800-933-2723 or 1-703-578-9600, then press 1) with a MasterCard, VISA, American Express, or Discover Card.
- By Fax: You can pay by fax (1-703-575-5414) with a purchase order.
- By Mail: You can pay by mail with a MasterCard, VISA, American Express, Discover Card, money order, purchase order, or check.

Save When You Register Early

Registering by January 30, 2020, saves 20% of total payment on booth and increases your chances of obtaining a better booth placement.

Save When You Send A Team

Every fifth person who registers from your school or district may attend Annual Conference for FREE. All team members must register at the same time and for the same choice of events. All registration forms must be sent together and faxed to 1-703-575-5414.

Transportation Specials

The conference website, www.ascd.org/annual conference, will list specials from airlines and Amtrak. Make your reservations early for the best selection and prices.

Save On Hotels

Securing your reservation with Travel Planners, the official housing company of the Annual Conference and Exhibit Show, is the only way to get access to the special room rates. Visit www.ascd.org/annualconference for details.

Cancelation

If you are unable to attend an event you have registered for, contact us by E-mail or regular mail no later than 14 days *prior to*[4] the start of the event to request a gift certificate, which can be used for products or events, or a refund. After the 14-day timeframe, you are *ineligible*[5] for a gift certificate or refund, but you may send a nonregistered person *in your place*[6], with registration confirmation or *written authorization*[7] from you. For all cancellations, there is a $50 processing fee. E-mail: cancel@ascd.org

Notes

1. registrant　意思为"登记者、注册者"。
2. if known　意为"如果知道、如果知道的话、如果已知"。
3. early bird　意为"提前注册、提早注册",指提前注册所享受的优惠,常用于活动门票销售。也可直译为"早鸟票、早鸟价",取自典故 the early bird gets the worm "早起的鸟儿有虫吃"。
4. prior to　意思是"在……之前",相当于 before。
5. ineligible　意思是"无资格的",相当于 unqualified。eligible 意为"合格的,符合条件的,有资格的"。
6. in your place　这里指"替代你,取代你"。
7. written authorization　意思是"书面授权"。

Sample 2: The Hosted Buyer Application Form

International Tourism Expo 2020

International Conference & Exhibition Center

29-31 August 2020

Hosted Buyer[1] **Application Form**

All participants interested in becoming the International Tourism Expo 2020 Hosted Buyer must complete and return this form before 30th June 2020 via E-mail at cgite. hbuyer @ cems. com. sg for *validation*[2] purposes. Please complete all questions below accurately and only completed forms will be processed. All information will be treated as *confidential*[3]. Submission of the application form is not a *confirmation of acceptance*[4] and the organizers *reserve the rights to*[5] approve or decline any buyer's application. Only successful applicants will *be notified*[6] via E-mail. Exhibitors and co-exhibitors of last year are not eligible for participation.

Hosted Buyer's Information

Name (Mr. /Ms. /Mdm.):　　　　　　　Company:
Address:　　　　　　　　　　　　　　*Designation*[7]:
Country:　　　　　　　　　　　　　　Telephone:
Mobile:　　　　　　　　　　　　　　　Fax:
Email:　　　　　　　　　　　　　　　Website:

Module Six >> International Event Documents and Business Contracts
国际会展文案及商务合同文书

Buyer's Profile (Please check where applicable)

1. What is your organization's *nature of business*[8]?
   - ( ) Conference/ Meeting & Incentive Planners
   - ( ) Destination Management Company
   - ( ) Inbound Travel   ( ) *Trade Associations*[9]
   - ( ) Outbound Travel   ( ) Trade Publication/ Media
   - ( ) Leisure/ Attraction   ( ) Others, please specify: _____

2. What are your major products and/or areas you would like to *source for*[10]?
   - ( ) Airlines/ Cruise lines   ( ) Health Resorts & Spas
   - ( ) Convention & Visitors Bureau   ( ) Hotel/ Accommodation Providers
   - ( ) Inbound Tour Operator   ( ) Magazine/ Media Publishers
   - ( ) Outbound Travel   ( ) Online Travel Agent
   - ( ) Retail Travel   ( ) Others, please specify: _____

3. Which geographical areas are you interested in?

ASEAN	Asia	Australia & Oceania	Rest of the World
( ) Brunei	( ) China	( ) Australia	( ) Africa
( ) Cambodia	( ) India	( ) Maldives	( ) Europe
( ) Indonesia	( ) Japan	( ) Mauritius	( ) South America
( ) Malaysia	( ) Pakistan	( ) New Zealand	( ) Middle East
( ) Myanmar	( ) Sri Lanka		( ) North America
( ) The Philippines			( ) Others: _____
( ) Singapore			
( ) Thailand			
( ) Vietnam			

4. How many tours/ groups did your company organized in 2019 to China?
   - ( ) Less than 10   ( ) 11-30   ( ) 31-50
   - ( ) 51-70   ( ) 71-90   ( ) 91 and above

5. What is your purpose/ objective in attending the exhibition?
   - ( ) Evaluate for future participation   ( ) Purchase / Place Order
   - ( ) Visit business associates   ( ) Gather information
   - ( ) Source for new products/ services   ( ) Others, please specify: _____

6. How did you come to know about the exhibition?
   - ( ) Direct Mail (from organizers)   ( ) Direct Mail (from exhibitors)
   - ( ) E-mail invitation   ( ) Industry Associates
   - ( ) Internet websites   ( ) Newspaper advertisements

( ) Trade Associations ( ) Others, please specify: _____

7. Have you been invited as Hosted Buyer to any other of the travel/ tourism trade shows?

( ) Yes, please specify: _____ ( ) No

Please complete this form and submit to: Conference & Exhibition Management Services PTE LTD, Tel: +65 6278 8666, E-mail: cgtie. hbuyers@ cems. com. sg

Notes

1. hosted buyer　这里指"特邀买家"。
2. validation　这里指"验证、确认",类似表达还有 confirmation, verification 等。
3. confidential　指"机密的、保密的"。
4. confirmation of acceptance　指"申请资格确认、同意申请、接受申请"。
5. reserve the rights to　意思是"保留……的权利"。

e. g. : Booth assignment is on a first come first serve basis. Trade show office reserve the rights to adjust a few number of booths. (展位安排以"先申请、先安排"为原则,展会办公室对少量展位的调整持保留权。)

6. be notified　相当于 be informed,意思为"被通知、被告知"。
7. designation　这里指"职位、职务",类似于 position。designation 原指"指定;称号;定名"之意。
8. nature of business　指"公司性质、业务性质、经营范围"。
9. Trade Associations　指"行业协会、商业团体"。类似的,下文中的 Trade Publication/ Media 则指"行业出版物、行业媒体"。
10. source for　这里指"寻找供应商"。

Sample 3: The AEGPL Booth Reservation Form

AEGPL Congress

Genoa, Italy 14-15, May

Booth Reservation Form

Please complete this form and return it by E-mail or fax to:

Email: rpecilunas@ worldlpgas. com and exhibition@ aegpl2014. com

Fax: +33 (0) 1 53 85 82 83

Company

Company name: _____

Contact person: _____ Position: _____

Address: _____
City: _____ Postal Code: _____ Country: _____
Tel: _____ Fax: _____
Email: _____
Company name to indicate on the website and publications:
_____

AEGPL MEMBER (please tick the appropriate option): ◆Yes   ◆No

List of Presented Products
_____
_____

Booth Choice and Rates
We wish to rent: _____ square meters at: _____
Euros (€) per booth module.
Please tick the appropriate option: ◆*Shell Scheme*[1] ◆*Space Only*[2]
(Please see detailed descriptions of these options on Booth Specifications)

This reservation is a binding commitment[3] and subject to[4] all cancellation conditions.

Booth No. Choice:
1st choice: _____ 2nd choice: _____ 3rd choice: _____

Booth Rates (Euros□) —*VAT*[5] Excluded

	6 sqm (2m * 3m)	9 sqm (3m * 3m)
Space Only	€2,625	€3,675
Shell Scheme	€3,465	€4,935

1) AEGPL Members get a 20% discount on booth prices as a member benefit.

2) Value Added Tax (VAT): According to the European Tax Legislation, organizers of international exhibition and service companies have to *invoice*[6] all services with 21% Italian Value Tax. Foreign companies (EU or non-EU) are, under certain conditions, *entitled*[7] to a refund of VAT paid. Please contact the organizing *secretariat*[8] at exhibition @aegpl2014.com for more details.

Booth Specifications
Exhibitors can rent either a Space Only or a Shell Scheme booth.

Space Only: Nothing will be provided but the exact floor measurements of the booth.

Shell Scheme: Booth package consists of a *modular*[9] construction with:

- Booth structure 2.50 meters,
- 1 booth sign,
- Spotlights,
- 2 Stools & 1 Counter,
- 1 Waste Paper Bin,
- Carpet (color will be confirmed in the technical manual),
- Standard electricity power supply.

Payment

Payment of the 50% must be made immediately by either:

♦ **Check**: to the order of AEGPL CONGRESS 2020/MCI in EUROS (　) and sent to: AEGPL CONGRESS 2020/MCI - 24 rue Chauchat — 75009 Paris — France

♦ **Credit card**: VISA/MASTER/EUROCARD (no other cards accepted)

I authorize the Organizing Secretariat to debit my card for the amount indicated here above.

Card Number: _____

Card verification code: _____

Expiry date: _____ (please do not forget)

Cardholder Name and Signature: _____

♦ **Bank transfer**: to the order of AEGPL CONGRESS 2017/MCI

Agency: CREDIT LYONNAIS — Direction Enterprise — 19 boulevard des Italians — 75002 Paris

Bank code: 30002 — Sort Code: 05666 – Account number: 000 006 XXXX S

____ (please tick if agree) "We are aware that this is a binding contract and agree to the financial and administrative conditions as specified below."

Date: _____ Name: _____ Signature: _____
Company Stamp: _____

To secure your booth please send this form to Rita Pecilunas at rpecilunas@worldlpgas.com / exhibition@aegpl2014.com or fax it back to +33 (0) 1 53 85 82 83

Reservations are taken *based on time of receipt*[10]. It is important to note three choices to facilitate placement of your company. AEGPL members get one week prior to the other companies to make their booth reservations on all available floors.

CANCELLATION CONDITIONS

NOTE: This booth reservation form is a *contractual agreement*[11]. Signature indicates a binding contract subject to cancellation terms noted below:

- 25% of the agreed amount *due*[12] if the cancellation is made before 15th November 2020;
- 50% of the agreed amount due if the cancellation is made between 15th November 2020 and 1st December 2020;
- 100% of the agreed amount due if the cancellation is made after 1st December 2020.

After exhibition space has been confirmed, a reduction in space or any other kind of *modification*[13] is considered as a cancellation and will *be governed by*[14] the above cancellation policy. Reduction in space can result in *relocation*[15] of exhibit space *at the discretion*[16] of the organizers.

Notes

1. Shell Scheme　意为 standard booth，可翻译为"标准展位"。
2. Space Only　也可以用 raw floor 表达，意思是"光地"，指在展览中不提供其他任何设备设施，只按实际面积提供展位。
3. binding commitment　意思是"约束性承诺，具有约束力的承诺"。
4. subject to　意思是"受……限制、管制；以……为条件"。联系全句 This reservation is a binding commitment and is subject to all cancellation conditions. 可以理解为"该预订是一约束性承诺且适用于所有的取消条件。"
5. VAT　即 Value Added Tax，指增值税。下文的 Italian Value Tax 则专指"意大利增值税"。
6. invoice　vt. 意思是"开发票；开清单"。作名词时有"发票，清单，发货单"之意。
7. entitle　vt. 意为"称作……；授权给……"。文中 be entitled to a refund 专指"拥有退税的权利"。
8. secretariat　n. 秘书处，书记处。
9. modular　n. 意思是"模块化的，标准化的"。文中也可以用 standard 表示。modular construction 意为"标准化结构"，也可以用 modular package 表示，意思是"标准化套餐"。
10. based on time of receipt　意思是"以收到收据时间为准"，全句意思是"展位预订的确认以收到收据为准"。e.g.：based on time of purchase，以最终购买价为准。
11. contractual agreement　指"合约协议，合同"。
12. due　这里指"应付的"，25% of the agreed amount due 指"应支付协议数额的25%"。同时还有"应得的，到期的，预期的"等意思。e.g.：total amount due，意思是"合计应得/应付款"
13. modification　n. 意为"调整，修正，改变"。类似的表达还有 alteration, changing 等。
14. be governed by　这里指"按照……管理、处理"。govern 有"管理；支配；统治；

控制"之意。

15. relocation　　n. 重新安置；再布置。
16. at discretion　这里指"由……酌情决定"。

4.4　Useful Phrases and Expressions（常用短语和表达）

1）early bird　提前注册；早鸟票、早鸟价
2）prior to　在……之前，优先于……
3）hosted buyer　受邀买家
4）confirmation of acceptance　申请资格确认、同意申请、接受申请
5）reserve the rights to　保留……的权利
6）be notified/ informed　被告知，被通知；收到通知，收到消息
7）nature of business　业务范围、经验范围、公司性质
8）trade association　行业协会、商业团体
9）shell scheme/ standard booth　标准展位
10）space only/ raw floor　光地
11）binding commitment　具有约束力的承诺，约束性承诺
12）cancellation conditions　取消条件
13）modular construction　（展位的）标准化结构、标准化设备
14）based on time of　以……时候为准，以……为准
15）here above　上述部分，上述的

4.5　Typical Sentences（典型例句）

1）Registering by January 30, 2020, saves 20% of total payment on booth and increases your chances of obtaining a better booth placement.（在2020年1月30日前申请，将节省20%的展位费用并增加获得更好展位安排的机会。）

2）All registration or cancellation should be made two weeks prior to the start of move-in.（所有的注册或取消都应该在布展两周前完成。）

3）If you are unable to attend an event you have registered for, contact us by E-mail or regular mail no later than 14 days prior to the start of the event.（若您无法参加您所登记的活动，请在活动开始前14天以电子邮件或平信方式与我们联系。）

4）All participants interested in becoming the China Guilin International Tourism Expo (CGITE) Hosted Buyer must complete and return this form before 30th June via E-mail.（所有有意成为中国桂林国际旅游博览会特邀买家的参与者须在6月30日前完成申请表并通过电子邮件寄回。）

5）Please complete the registration form accurately and only completed forms will be further processed.（请正确填写申请表，只有完整填写的表格才会被进一步受理。）

6）Submission of the application form is not a confirmation of acceptance and the organizers reserve the rights to approve or decline any buyer's application.

（提交申请表并不代表申请通过，主办方保留同意或谢绝任何买家申请的权利。）

7) Registration forms will not be processed without a copy or a scanning copy of business card, and successful registration will be notified by E-mail or fax.

（没有企业名片复印件或扫描件的注册表不会被受理，成功注册后将会收到电子邮件或传真通知。）

8) Registrations must be postmarked or received by E-mail or fax by midnight, March 16, 2020, Beijing Time, in order to receive the Early Bird and Standard registration rates.

（注册表必须在北京时间2020年3月16日零点前通过邮件、电邮或传真发出，以获得早鸟注册价或标准注册价。）

9) Applications are confirmed based on time of receipt.

（申请的确认以收到收据时间为准。）

10) After exhibition space has been confirmed, a reduction in space or any other kind of modification is considered as a cancellation and will be governed by the above cancellation policy. （在确认展位后，任何减少展位或调整展位的行为都将被认为是取消展位，并将按照上述展位取消条款处理。）

11) Every fifth person who registers from your school or district may attend Annual Conference for FREE. （同一学校或地区每满五人注册可免费参加年度大会。）

12) Make your reservations early for the best selection and prices.

（尽早预订，省心省钱。）

13) Only successful applicants will be notified via E-mail.

（只有成功申请才会收到邮件通知。）

14) Members get one week prior to the other companies to make their booth reservations on all available floors.

（会员可比其他参展企业早一星期预订所有楼层可预订的展位。）

4.6　Training and Practice（操练与实践）

4.6.1　Complete the following sentences with one of the given words. Change the forms if necessary.

shell scheme	confirmation of acceptance	prior to
be notified	based on time of	will be processed

1) If you want to cancel your reservation, please contact us 7 days _____ the opening of the exhibition.

2) Exhibitors can rent either a Space Only or a _____.

3) You will receive _____ after submitting a complete form.

4) Only registration forms with a copy or a scanning copy of business card _____.

5) Registrations will be confirmed _____ receipt.

6) You will _____ as soon as you have successfully registered.

4.6.2　Match the following English expressions with their Chinese equivalents.

1) VAT   A) 行业协会、商业团体
2) space only   B) 登记者、注册者
3) nature of business   C) 秘书处，书记处
4) Hosted Buyers   D) 约束性承诺
5) trade association   E) 业务范围、公司性质
6) shell scheme   F) 特邀买家
7) secretariat   G) 早鸟价
8) binding commitment   H) 标准展位
9) early bird   I) 增值税
10) registrant   J) 光地

4.6.3　Put the following English into Chinese or Chinese into English.

1) 在确认展位后，任何减少展位或调整展位的行为都将被认为是取消展位，并将按照展位取消条款处理。

2) 主办方保留同意或谢绝任何公司或个人申请的权利。

3) 若您无法参加展览，请在开展前14天以电子邮件或致电的方式与我们联系。

4) 在2020年5月30日前申请，将为您节省费用并增加获得最佳住宿条件的机会。

5) Make your reservations early for the best location and prices.

6) Please complete the registration form and only accurately completed forms will be further processed.

7) Every third person who registers from a same company may attend Cocktail Reception（鸡尾酒会）for FREE.

8) All companies interested in participating the International Sport Industry Expo should complete and return the application form before 30th June via E-mail or fax.

4.6.4　Writing tasks.

Task: Write a registration form for an exhibition.

Situation: Imagine yourself being a manager of the International Furniture Fair. The organizers have decided to attract more overseas exhibitors this year, and you are required to make a Booth Reservation Form to facilitate foreign exhibitors. Now compose a Booth Reservation Form covering the message given below.

Message:

1) 展会名称是"国际家具展"，将于2020年12月3日-5日在广州国际会展中心举行。

2) 所有展位申请都应准确且完整填写后，在2020年11月3日前发送至电子邮箱：

gziff2020@ gziff. com，或是传真：+86 20-XXXXXXXX。

3）表格中应有海外参展商公司名称、业务范围、地址及邮编、所在城市及国家，以及联系方式等基本信息；同时还应有联系人的姓名及职位等信息。

4）展位有光地和标准展位两种选择。其中光地价格为每平方米 1,000 元；而标准展位 (3m * 3m) 则是 20,000 元，同时展位套餐包括: 一个展位结构、地毯、一张桌子、4 张椅子、一个废纸篓、射灯及标准电力供应。

5）展位预订的确认以到账时间为准（time of receipt），先到先得。并保留拒绝任何企业参展的权利。

6）可通过支票、信用卡及转账方式进行费用缴纳，且其中 30% 的费用必须在申请时付清。预订的成功以收到收据时为准。

7）若需要取消展位，则在 2020 年 11 月 13 日之前申请的，都将获得 60% 的退款。在其之后申请的，将不获得任何退款。

Section 5
Sales Contracts and Sales Confirmation
销售合同与销售确认书

5.1 Lead-In Introduction（导入介绍）

A sales contract is a legal document whereby the seller agrees to transfer the property goods to the buyer in return for a monetary consideration, namely, a certain amount of money the buyer has to pay for the property goods.

The language used in a sales contract (also called sales agreement) is usually formal and the sentences are usually extremely long and complicated, while a sales confirmation is usually short, concise and less formal.

5.2 Guidelines for Writing（写作指南）

The composition of a formal business contract usually consists of four parts: contract title, preamble, body and witness clause. A sales contract is no exception. The contents involved in a sales contract can be summed up as follows:

Parts	Contents
Title	contract title
Preamble	contract No.
	date of signing
	detailed information of both parties

(续)

Parts	Contents
Body	Commodity & Specifications
	Quantity
	Unit Price
	Total Amount
	Time of Shipment
	Port of Shipment and Destination
	Insurance
	Packing
	Shipping Mark
	Terms of Payment
	Shipping Documents
	Terms of Shipment
	Shipping Advice
	Guarantee of Quality
	Inspection and Claims
	Settlement of Claims
	Force Majeure
	Late Delivery and Penalty
	Arbitration
	Governing Law
	Effectiveness of The Contract
Witness Clause	Signature
	Seal of Both Parties

5.3　Sample Study（范例学习）

Sample: A Sales Contract

Sales Contract

Contract No.: CE129　　　　　　　　Date: November 5, 2020

Signed at Shanghai

Sellers: China National Light Industrial Products Import and Export Corporation Shanghai Branch

Address: 128 HuqiuRoad, Shanghai, China

Tel: Fax: E-mail:

Buyers: J. B. Lawson & Company

Address: 854 California Street, San Francisco, California 94104

Tel: Fax: E-mail:

This Contract is made by and between the Buyer and the Seller whereby the Buyer agrees to buy and the Seller agrees to sell *the under-mentioned commodity*[1] according to the terms and conditions stipulated below:

1. Commodity & Specifications: *Canvas Folding Chairs with Wooden Frame*[2]
2. **Quantity:** 5,000 **pcs**
3. *Unit Price*[3]: USD 12.00 Per Piece CFR San Francisco
4. Total Amount: USD 60,000
5. Time of Shipment: During July 2020
6. Port of Shipment: China Ports
7. Port of Destination: San Francisco
8. Insurance: To be covered by the Seller for 110% of invoice value against *War Risk*[4] and *All Risks*[5]
9. Packing: The goods should be packed with new strong cartons suitable for long distance ocean transportation and well protected against dampness, moisture, shock, rust and rough handling. The Seller shall *be liable for*[6] any damage to the goods *on account of*[7] improper packing and for any rust damage attributable to inadequate or improper protective measures taken by the Seller and in such a case or cases any and all losses and/or expenses incurred in consequence thereof shall *be borne by*[8] the Seller.
10. *Shipping Mark*[9]: *At the Sellers' option*[10]
11. Terms of Payment: The payment should be made by sight draft drawn under a confirmed irrevocable letter of credit payable against shipping documents. The Buyer shall open with a bank acceptable to the Sellers *an Irrevocable Sight Letter of Credit*[11] to reach the Seller 30 days before the month of shipment, *valid for negotiation*[12] in China until the 15th day after the month of shipment.
12. Shipping Documents:

    1) A full set of *Negotiable Clean On Board Ocean Bills of Lading*[13] marked "*Freight Prepaid*"[14] and made out *to order*[15], *endorsed in blank*[16] and notifying the Buyer;

    2) *Signed commercial invoice*[17] *in 5 originals*[18] indicating contract number, L/C number and shipping mark;

    3) *Packing list*[19] in 5 originals indicating quantity, measurement, and gross weight

of each package of the Contract Goods;

4) Certificate of Quality and Quantity and Test Report each in 5 originals issued by the manufacturer;

5) *Certificate of origin*[20] in one original and two copies issued by the local *Chamber of Commerce*[21];

6) *Insurance Policy*[22] or Certificate, covering War Risk and All Risks for 110% of CIF invoice value;

7) A copy of fax advising the Buyer of shipment within 48 hours after completion of the shipment of the contract goods as specified in Clause 14 of the Contract.

Immediately after the shipment is effected, the Seller shall express to the Buyer one set of the copy of the above mentioned documents with the exception of *shipping advice*[23].

13. Terms of Shipment:

The Seller shall ship the contract goods within the time of shipment from the port of shipment to the port of destination. *Transshipment*[24] is not allowed and *partial shipments*[25] are not allowed without the Buyer's prior consent. The vessel carrying the contract goods shall be seaworthy and cargo-worthy and the age of which shall not exceed 15 years without the Buyer's prior written consent. The Buyer is justified in not accepting the vessel that is not a member of *P&I Club*[26].

14. Shipping Advice:

The Seller shall, within 48 hours after the completion of the shipment of the contract goods, advise by fax the Buyer of the contract number, name of commodity, invoice value, quantity, packages, gross weight, net weight, name of carrying vessel, the date of shipment and *ETA*[27]. In case the contract goods are not insured in time owing to the Seller having failed to give timely advice, any and all consequent losses shall be borne by the Seller.

15. Guarantee of Quality:

The Seller guarantees that the contract goods hereof is made of the best materials with first class workmanship, brand new, unused and complies in all respects with quality, specification and performance stipulated in the Contract. The warranty period shall be 12 months counting from the date on which the Buyer, the end-user and the Seller sign *the Certificate of Final Acceptance*[28] of the contract goods.

16. Inspection and Claims:

1) After arrival of the Contract Goods at the port of destination, the Buyer shall apply to the *China Entry-Exit Inspection and Quarantine Bureau*[29] (hereinafter called the Bureau) for a preliminary inspection of the Contract Goods in respect of

their quality, specifications and quantity. If any discrepancies are found by the Bureau regarding the specifications or quality or quantity, except those for which either the insurance company or the shipping company is responsible, the Buyer shall, within 120 days after discharge of the contract goods at the port of destination, have the right either to reject the contract goods or to claim against the Seller *on the strength of*[30] the inspection certificate issued by the Bureau.

2) Within the warranty period stipulated in Clause 15 hereof, should the quality and/or specification of the contract goods be found not in conformity with the contracted stipulations, or should the contract goods prove defective for any reasons attributive to the Seller, including *latent defect*[31] or the use of unsuitable materials, the Buyer shall have the right to claim against the Seller on the strength of the inspection certificate issued by the Bureau.

3) Any and all claims shall be regarded as accepted if the Seller fails to reply within 30 days after receipt of the Buyer's claim.

17. Settlement of Claims:

In case the Seller is liable for the discrepancies and a claim is made by the Buyer within the period of claim or warranty period as stipulated in Clauses 15 and 16 of this contract, the Seller shall settle the claim upon the agreement of the Buyer in the following ways:

1) Agree to the rejection of the contract goods and refund to the Buyer the value of the contract goods so rejected in the same currency as contracted herein, and to bear all direct losses and expenses in connection therewith including interest accrued, banking charges, freight, insurance premium, inspection charges, storage and all other necessary expenses required for the *custody*[32] and protection of the rejected contract goods.

2) Devaluate the contract goods according to the degree of inferiority, extent of damage and amount of losses suffered by the Buyer.

3) Replace the defective contract goods with new ones, which conform to the specifications, quality and performance as stipulated in this Contract, and bear all expenses incurred to and direct losses sustained by the Buyer. The Seller shall guarantee the quality of the replacement of the contract goods for a further period of 12 months as specified in Clause 16 hereof.

18. Force Majeure:

The Seller shall not be held responsible for delay in shipment or non-delivery of the contract goods due to Force Majeure such as war, serious fire, flood, typhoon, earthquake or other cases which are agreed upon by both parties as the events of Force Majeure. However, the Seller shall advise the Buyer immediately of such occurrence and within 14 days thereafter, the Seller shall send by airmail to the Buyer for their acceptance a certificate of the accident issued by the competent government authorities at the place where the accident occurs as evidence thereof. Under such circumstances, the Seller, however, is still under the obligation to take all necessary measures to hasten the delivery of the contract goods. In case the accident lasts for more than 10 weeks, the Buyer shall have the right to cancel the Contract.

19. Late Delivery and Penalty:

In case of delayed delivery, except for Force Majeure events, the Seller shall pay to the Buyer for every week of delay a penalty amounting to 0.5% of the total value of the contract goods whose delivery has been delayed. Any *fractional*[33] part of a week is to be considered a full week. The total amount of penalty shall not, however, exceed 5% of the total value of the contract goods involved in late delivery and *is to be deducted from*[34] the amount due to the Seller by the paying bank at the time of negotiation. In case the period of delay exceeds 5 weeks after the stipulated delivery date, the Buyer shall have the right to *terminate this Contract*[35] but the Seller shall not thereby be exempted from the payment of penalty.

20. Arbitration:

All disputes in connection with this Contract or the execution thereof shall be settled friendly through negotiation. In case no settlement can be reached, the case under dispute may then be submitted for arbitration to the *China International Economic and Trade Arbitration Commission*[36] with the rules of the said commission. The arbitration shall take place in Shanghai, China. The decision rendered by the said commission shall *be final and binding upon*[37] both parties. Neither party shall *recourse to*[38] a law or other authorities for revising the decision. The arbitration fee shall be borne by the losing party, unless otherwise awarded by the Arbitration Commission.

21. Governing Law: This Contract shall be governed by *the United Nations Convention on Contracts for the International Sale of Goods*[39].

22. Effectiveness of this Contract:

This Contract shall come into force upon the signing of this Contract by the authorized representative of each following party. This contract is made out in both the Chinese and English languages, each in two originals and one original of each is to be held by Party A and Party B. Both versions are equally effective.

The Sellers   The Buyers

Notes

1. the under-mentioned commodity　下列商品
2. Canvas Folding Chairs with Wooden Frame　帆布木框折椅
3. Unit Price　单价
4. War Risk　战争险
5. All Risks　一切险
6. be liable for　对……承担责任
7. on account of　由于
8. be borne by　（费用）由……承担
9. Shipping Mark　唛头，装运标记
10. At the Sellers' option　由卖方选择
11. an Irrevocable Sight Letter of Credit　不可撤销即期信用证
12. valid for negotiation　议付有效
13. Negotiable Clean On Board Ocean Bills of Lading　可转让清洁已装船提单
14. Freight Prepaid　运费已付
15. to order　凭指示
16. endorsed in blank　空白背书
17. Signed commercial invoice　签章的商业发票
18. in 5 originals　5 份正本
19. Packing list　装箱单
20. Certificate of origin　原产地证明
21. Chamber of Commerce　商会
22. Insurance Policy　保单
23. shipping advice　装船通知
24. Transshipment　转运
25. partial shipments　分批装运
26. P&I Club:（Protection and indemnity club）　保证与赔偿协会，简称保赔协会。这是由各船舶公司组成的若干协会，它们对一般海运保险不予承保的那些风险提供保障。
27. ETA　Estimated Time of Arrival: 估计到达时间
28. the Certificate of Final Acceptance　最终验收证书
29. China Entry-Exit Inspection and Quarantine Bureau　中国出入境检验检疫局
30. on the strength of　依赖……，凭借
31. latent defect　隐蔽事故
32. custody　照管，监管
33. fractional　部分的

34. is to be deducted from 将从……中扣除
35. terminate this Contract 终止本合同
36. China International Economic and Trade Arbitration Commission 中国国际经贸仲裁委员会
37. be final and binding upon （仲裁结果等）是终局性的并且对……有约束力
38. recourse to 求助于
39. the United Nations Convention on Contracts for the International Sale of Goods 《联合国国际货物销售合同公约》

5.4 Useful Phrases and Expressions（常用短语和表达）

1) according to the terms and conditions stipulated below 根据下列条款
2) to be covered by 将由……投保
3) (certificates etc.) issued by…… 由某机构签发的（证书等）
4) effect shipment/payment/insurance 进行装船/付款/保险
5) shipping advice 装运通知
6) be borne by… （费用等）由……承担
7) in all respects… 在各方面
8) not in conformity with 与……不一致
9) claim against 向……提出索赔
10) come into force 开始生效

5.5 Typical Sentences（典型例句）

1) Payment is to be made by sight draft drawn under a conformed irrevocable letter of credit payable against shipping documents.
（货款在保兑的、不可撤销的跟单信用证条件下凭即期汇票支付。）

2) The insurance is to be covered by the Seller for 110% of invoice value against War Risk and All Risks （货物将由卖方按发票金额的110%投保战争险和一切险。）

3) The goods should be packed with new strong cartons suitable for long distance ocean transportation and well protected against dampness, moisture, shock, rust and rough handling. （货物要选用适合长途海洋运输且足够结实的新纸板箱包装，并且还必须能很好地防水、防潮、防震和防粗暴装运。）

4) Immediately after the shipment is effected, the Seller shall express to the Buyer one set of the copy of the above mentioned documents with the exception of shipping advice.
（发货完成之后，卖方必须立即把除了发货通知以外的整套运输单据副本快递至买方。）

5) The Seller shall ship the contract goods within the time of shipment from the port of shipment to the port of destination. Transshipment is not allowed and partial shipments are not allowed without the Buyer's prior consent.

(卖方必须在规定的装运时间内把合同项下的货物从装运港运至目的港。不准转船并且也不准不经买方同意分批装运。)

6) After arrival of the contract goods at the port of destination, the Buyer shall apply to the China Entry-Exit Inspection and Quarantine Bureau (hereinafter called the Bureau) for a preliminary inspection of the contract goods in respect of their quality, specifications and quantity. (货物抵达目的港之后,买方须向中国出入境检验检疫局(以下简称检验局)对合同项下的货物的质量,规格和数量进行初步检验。)

7) Any and all claims shall be regarded as accepted if the Seller fails to reply within 30 days after receipt of the Buyer's claim. (对于买方提出的任何索赔,如果卖方没能在收到后的30天内做出答复,则被视作接受。)

8) The Seller shall not be held responsible for delay in shipment or non-delivery of the contract goods due to Force Majeure such as war, serious fire, flood, typhoon, earthquake or other cases which are agreed upon by both parties as the events of Force Majeure.
(由于诸如战争,严重的火灾、洪灾、台风,地震或者双方认可的其他不可抗力因素造成的发货延迟或者无法交货,卖方无须承担责任。)

9) All disputes in connection with this Contract or the execution thereof shall be settled friendly through negotiation rather than submit it to arbitration or take legal proceedings.
(在出口贸易发生争议时,我们宁愿友好协商解决,而不是交付仲裁或提起诉讼。)

10) This Contract shall be governed by the United Nations Convention on Contracts for the International Sale of Goods. This Contract shall come into force upon the signing of this Contract by the authorized representative of each following party.
(本合同适用于《联合国国际货物销售合同公约》,以下双方授权代表签字后即生效。)

5.6　Training and Practice (操练与实践)

5.6.1　Fill in the blanks with appropriate prepositions.

Payment: The Buyers upon receipt (1) _____ the Sellers (2) _____ the delivery advice specified in Article 14 hereof, shall, in 15-20 days prior (3) _____ the date of delivery, open an irrevocable Letter of Credit with the Bank of China, (4) _____ favor (5) _____ the Sellers, (6) _____ an amount equivalent (7) _____ the total value of the shipment. The Credit shall be payable (8) _____ presentation of draft drawn (9) _____ the opening bank and the shipping documents specified (10) _____ Article 13 hereof. The Letter of Credit shall be valid until the 15th day after the shipment is effected.

Penalty: If the Sellers fail to effect the delivery at the contracted time (11) _____ delivery, the Buyers shall have the option to cancel this Contract and demand (12) _____ all losses resulted therefrom, or alternatively, the Sellers may postpone delivery (13) _____ the Buyer's consent, (14) _____ condition that the Sellers pay to the Buyers a penalty (15) _____ 1.5% (16) _____ the goods value (17) _____ a delay within 30 days and further 0.5% (18) _____ every 15 days thereafter. The penalty shall be deducted (19) _____ the paying bank during the negotiation (20) _____ payment.

5.6.2 Translate the following into Chinese.

1) The Buyer shall open with a bank acceptable to the Sellers an Irrevocable Sight Letter of Credit to reach the Seller 30 days before the month of shipment, valid for negotiation in China until the 15th day after the month of shipment.

2) The Seller shall, within 48 hours after the completion of the shipment of the contract goods, advise by fax the buyer of the contract number, name of commodity, invoice value, quantity, packages, gross weight, net weight, name of carrying vessel, the date of shipment and ETA.

3) In case of delayed delivery, except for Force Majeure events, the Seller shall pay to the Buyer for every week of delay a penalty amounting to 0.5% of the total value of the contract goods whose delivery has been delayed.

4) This contract is made out in both the Chinese and English languages, each in two originals and one original of each is to be held by Party A and Party B. Both versions are equally effective.

5.6.3 Writing tasks.

Complete the sales contract below by filling in the blanks with an appropriate title of the clause.

Sales Confirmation

Confirmation No.: PT152   Date: March 1, 2020

Signed at: Guangzhou

Buyers: China National Native Produce & Animal By-Products Import & Export
          Corporation, Guangdong Native Produce Branch

Address: No. 486, "623" Road, Guangzhou, China

Tel: Fax: E-mail:

Sellers: Datung Trading Co., Ltd.

Address: No. 165, Censa Road, Rangoon

Tel: Fax: E-mail:

The undersigned Buyers and Sellers have agreed to close the following transaction according to the terms and conditions stipulated hereunder:

1. _____: Burmese Tobacco Leaves

2. _____: First grade, moisture 11% minimum and 12% maximum
3. _____: 100 metric tons
4. _____: USD 1,890.00 per metric ton CFR Huangpu
5. _____: USD 189,000.00
6. _____: In bales of 100 kgs net each
7. Shipping Mark: At the Sellers' option.
8. _____: During May, 2020
9. _____: From Rangoon to Huangpu
10. Insurance: To be covered by the Buyers
11. _____: The payment should be made by Irrevocable Letter of Credit for 90% of the total invoice value of the goods to be shipped, in favor of the Seller, payable at the issuing bank against the Seller's draft at sight accompanied by the shipping documents stipulated in the Credit. The balance of 10% of the proceeds is to be paid only after the goods have been inspected and approved at the port of destination.
12. Delivery Terms: Certificates of Quality, Quantity, Weight and Origin are required. The Buyer has the right to have the goods re-inspected by the Guangzhou Entry-Exit Inspection and Quarantine Bureau of the People's Republic of China at the port of discharge. The relevant Inspection Certificates may serve as the basis of any claim to be lodged by the Buyer against the Seller.
13. _____: The Buyer has the right to lodge claims for all losses sustained within 60 days after discharge of the goods at the port of destination.
14. _____: All disputes in connection with this Confirmation or arising in the execution thereof shall first be settled amicably by negotiation. In case no settlement can be reached, the case under dispute may then be submitted for arbitration. The arbitration shall take place in the plaintiff's or defendant's country. The fees for arbitration shall be borne by the losing party unless otherwise awarded.
15. _____: This Confirmation shall be governed by the laws of the People's Republic of China.
16. Others:

References

参考文献

[1] 胡英坤,车丽娟. 商务英语写作 [M]. 北京:外语教学与研究出版社,2013.

[2] 邹渝刚. 商务英语写作 [M]. 北京:外语教学与研究出版社,2007.

[3] 郑卫,汪文格. 商务英语写作 [M]. 北京:对外经济贸易大学出版社,2010.

[4] 杨晓斌. 商务英语写作 [M]. 2版. 北京:对外经济贸易大学出版社,2017.

[5] 黄瑛瑛. 世纪英语——应用英语写作 [M]. 大连:大连理工大学出版社,2008.

[6] 陈丽红,何葆青. 高职应用文写作与翻译 [M]. 大连:大连理工大学出版社,2011.

[7] 中国国际贸易学会商务专业培训考试办公室. 国际商务英语写作(二级)[M]. 北京:中国商务出版社,2009.

[8] 虞苏美. 商务英语写作 [M]. 北京:高等教育出版社,2008.

[9] 吕晔,郭明静. 商贸英语写作教程 [M]. 上海:复旦大学出版社,2008.

[10] 谈芳,吴云. 高等学校英语应用文写作 [M]. 上海:学林出版社,2004.

[11] 谭红翔,季永青. 会展文案写作实务 [M]. 大连:东北财经大学出版社,2010.

[12] 胡秋华,吴思乐. 世纪商务英语外贸函电 [M]. 4版. 大连:大连理工大学出版社,2019.

[13] 吴敏,吴明忠. 国际经贸英语合同写作 [M]. 3版. 广州:暨南大学出版社,2005.